SUSTAINABLE CAPITALISM

SUSTAINABLE CAPITALISM

A MATTER OF COMMON SENSE

John E. Ikerd

Kumarian
Press, Inc.

Sustainable Capitalism: A Matter of Common Sense

Published in 2005 in the United States of America by Kumarian Press, Inc., 1294 Blue Hills Avenue, Bloomfield, CT 06002 USA

The text of this book is set in Palatino and Palatino Light

Design, production, and editorial services were provided by Publication Services, Champaign, Illinois.

Printed in the United States of America by McNaughton & Gunn. Text printed with vegetable oil-based ink.

∞ The paper used in this publication meets the minimum requirements of the American National Standard for Information Sciences—Permanence of Paper for printed Library Materials, ANSI Z39.48-1984

Library of Congress Cataloging-in-Publication Data

Ikerd, John E.
    Sustainable capitalism : a matter of common sense / John E. Ikerd.
        p. cm.
    Summary: "Provides a discussion on achieving and maintaining a new economics of sustainabililty, including how social and ethical values must be reintegrated into capitalist economics" —Provided by publisher.
    Includes index.
    ISBN 1-56549-206-4 (pbk. : alk. paper)
    1. Capitalism. 2. Sustainable development. 3. Environmental policy.
4. Social justice. 5. Social responsibility of business. I. Title.
HB501.I54 2006
330.12'2—dc22
                          2005011698

13 12 11 10 09 08 07   10 9 8 7 6 5 4 3 2

CONTENTS

FOREWORD

What makes you think you can write a book challenging neoclassical economics? This question, mostly unspoken, has plagued me since I began this task nearly a decade ago. My most honest answer is that someone had to do it and no one else seemed willing. Many other economists have greater professional credibility, more prestigious degrees, and greater intellectual capacity. But after giving the question some thought, I concluded I was probably as well qualified as any.

First, I am an agricultural economist. Questions of sustainability are seen most clearly by those most closely connected with the earth, as are farmers. Agriculture also is about relationships among people, within families on farms and in rural communities. Agriculture also is about economics, about making a living. The lack of sustainability of any society can be seen perhaps most clearly in its agriculture. In addition, agriculture is one of the last remaining sectors of the economy that fits the model of competitive capitalism, although this is becoming less so. The case of American agriculture makes clear the inherent lack of sustainability in the neoclassical economic paradigm. Perhaps I have had an opportunity to see this flaw more clearly than most.

Looking back, I can see that my life has prepared me for this task. I grew up on a farm, but I also worked in industry for a time. I did my graduate work in an agricultural economics department with a leaning toward institutional economics with a Harvard Business School flavor. My first faculty position was in a general economics department with a distinct Chicago School of Economics leaning. I had been a Goldwater Republican and had always found laissez-faire economics to my liking. In fact, I did not begin to question neoclassical economic thinking until I began to see it as the underlying cause of the farm financial crisis of the 1980s.

I soon began to see that the lack of economic sustainability in agriculture was integrally related to a lack of ecological and social sustainability. Then I began to understand that the lack of sustainability in agriculture was a reflection of the lack of sustainability in American society, which was rooted in the neoclassical paradigm of economic development. It was just easier to see and to understand in agriculture, where the critical connectedness of people with the earth and with each other is clear.

As I worked with and learned from others who were developing a new sustainable paradigm for agriculture, I could see that we were also developing a new sustainable paradigm for society in general. I accepted the responsibility to work most diligently on the economic dimension of sustainability because few economists seemed to take questions of sustainability seriously. I understood neoclassical economics because I had spent my whole career believing and teaching it. I understood where the skeptics of sustainability were coming from because I had been there.

I eventually came to understand that the new economics of sustainability had to be based on the principles of living systems, because only living systems are capable of self-renewal and regeneration. Sustainable agriculture is about living systems—soil microorganisms, plants, animals, and people—the life upon which the sustainability of human life on earth ultimately depends. Perhaps I was well qualified for this task.

It would be a mistake to categorize this book as a challenge to neoclassical economic thinking, although it certainly is that. But it is mostly a new vision of hope, not in "the conviction that something will turn out well, but the certainty that something makes sense, regardless of how it turns out."[1] Hope is a belief in the possibility of something good. This is a book about faith—in the abilities of people to work in harmony with nature and with each other to sustain a healthy and happy society. It is a book about love because the capacity to care for each other and for the earth must be based upon love. In faith and in love, there is always hope.

Endnote

1. Vaclav Havel, *Disturbing the Peace* (New York: Vintage Books, Random House, Inc., 1991).

ACKNOWLEDGMENTS

This book represents the culmination of nearly 10 years of directed thinking and a lifetime of learning. In the summer of 1996, I presented a paper at a national conference of agricultural economists in which I indicted neoclassical economics for its inadequacies in addressing the critical issues of sustainable agriculture. I was challenged by a colleague to develop a new economics of sustainability and thus began the directed thinking.

I will not attempt to name all the people who have directly contributed to that thinking because there are far too many, and most don't even realize that they have contributed. In reality, this book is the result of a lifetime of learning, influenced by virtually everyone I have ever known and everything I have ever read or experienced. I have always thought of those who claim to be "self-made men" as the most egotistical and unappreciative among us. I am not a self-made man, and I am not the sole creator of this book.

That being said, I do want to thank my family, my friends, and my many colleagues, scattered across the continent and around the world, who have shared their insights during development of the specific ideas expressed here. In particular, I want to thank my wife, Ellen, who has read virtually every word I have written for the past six years and who has read, reviewed, and proofed this particular manuscript at least a half-dozen times. Without her support and encouragement, this project would not have been possible. Together, I hope we have at least started the process of developing a new economics of sustainability.

CHAPTER ONE

THE NEGLECTED PRINCIPLES OF ECONOMICS

The Question of Economic Sustainability

With the fall of communism in the former Soviet Union, political leaders around the world declared victory for capitalism as the world's dominant global economic system. Even societies such as the People's Republic of China, although still clinging to political socialism, are increasingly turning to free markets to guide their economies. Admittedly, capitalistic economies around the world have achieved impressive records of economic growth and prosperity over the past two centuries. But as we enter a new century, serious questions are emerging concerning the sustainability of capitalistic economies.

Questions of sustainability persist because capitalistic economies inherently are extractive, with respect to the natural resources upon which they must depend for productivity, and are exploitive, with respect to the societies within which they must function. Ecological integrity and social equity must be imposed upon the capitalistic economy from the *outside*—by society, through public policies—to ensure that the economy functions for the long-run benefits of society. More and more, however, those who benefit from economic growth have been able to shape public policies to support maximum current growth, with little regard for future ecological or social sustainability. Environmental protection and social justice are increasingly viewed as impediments, rather than priorities, in the public policy process.

Regardless of the cause, new threats to ecological sustainability arise continually—water pollution, air pollution, acid rain, soil erosion,

1

loss of biological diversity, ozone depletion, global warming—and the list continues to grow.[1] Growing threats to social sustainability are no less menacing, although less appreciated: isolation, distrust, injustice, inequity, depression, litigation, confrontation, terrorism, and war.[2] Scientists, activists, and politicians all cite their selected statistics and debate the issues of economics versus the environment and society, and they continue to argue whether our society is better or worse today than in past decades. Very few people would argue that such questions and such debates are irrelevant in today's world.

However, the most important questions of sustainability cannot be answered with either statistics or logic. Most differences of opinion concerning sustainability arise from differences in *beliefs*, not *facts*. In general, those who are concerned about sustainability believe in the existence of inviolable laws of nature, including human nature, to which human actions must conform and comply if we are to sustain a desirable quality of life.[3] In general, those who are not concerned about sustainability believe that the current ecological limits and the social constraints on human activity are but temporary obstacles to progress that can be overcome with better science and technology. This latter belief dominates contemporary scientific and economic thinking today, although it is rarely articulated in such direct terms. We must realize that these different beliefs arise from fundamentally different worldviews. Different worldviews are rooted in different foundational beliefs, or *first principles*, which provide the starting points for all proofs and thus cannot be proved or disproved. The most fundamental questions of sustainability cannot be resolved by data, facts, or logic but instead must be resolved through a process of social and moral consensus concerning what is true and what is right regarding issues of sustainability. A new economics of sustainability, rooted in an appropriate set of first principles, is needed to address the questions, to inform the debate, and thus to provide a logical approach to reaching such a social and moral consensus.

Nothing suggests that our current economic and social systems will automatically evolve to accommodate the long-term needs of the natural ecosystem without societies making conscious, purposeful decisions to do so. In times past, humans were physically and technologically incapable of doing irreparable damage to the global ecosystem. People might destroy the ability of their little niche of the earth to support human life, and thus destroy their unique culture, but other people in other places were always able and willing to carry on the process of civilization. Left alone, the wounded earth eventually healed itself.

Today, however, humans clearly possess the ability and the apparent inclination to do things that eventually could make the earth uninhabitable by humans—if not through military conflict, then through overpopulation and overconsumption. The threat of nuclear annihilation may have lessened somewhat with the end of the Cold War; however, some nations still threaten the use of *all available means* either to defend themselves or to impose their will upon others. Despite the growing evidence of ecological destruction and societal decay caused by economic exploitation, the developed nations forge ahead in their pursuit of ever-greater economic prosperity. And despite the growing evidence of ecological destruction and persistent poverty caused by overpopulation, the peoples of developing nations continue their unbridled growth.

Some population experts argue that world population will begin to stabilize within the next fifty years and level off by 2100, as the developing nations become more economically affluent.[4] However, if economic affluency translates into greater resource use per capita, as has been the case historically, humanity's claims on Earth's resources will continue to grow indefinitely. No evidence suggests that human wants are ever satiated by increased wealth. Ultimately, humanity must accept its moral responsibility to those of future generations. The only real hope for long-term ecological sustainability is a global society that is committed to making conscious, purposeful decisions to caring for each other and to caring for the earth. A new economics of sustainability is needed to help shape and guide a social and moral commitment to sustainability.

The development of a new economics of sustainability will require more than just fine-tuning or restructuring current economic thinking. Society and the environment, which are currently treated as *external,* or outside of economics, cannot be *internalized* without destroying their integrity. Our relationships with each other and with the earth—which currently create a passive context within which decisions are made—must instead become active priorities in all economic decisions. Economics must be expanded to accommodate the social and ecological, in addition to the individual, if economics is to effectively address the critical issues of sustainability. A new economics of sustainability must be rooted in an appropriate set of principles, including first principles, from which all other truth and rightness are derived.

Before beginning to build a new economics, it may be wise for us to see what can be salvaged from the old economics, and we will do so by reexamining some of the recently neglected principles of *classical* economics.

The Economics of Happiness

The understood purpose of *classical* economic thinking was to assist individuals and societies in the pursuit of happiness. Early nineteenth-century classical economists, including such notables as Adam Smith and Thomas Malthus, considered happiness to be the ultimate goal of all economic activity. Smith clearly emphasized the pursuit of *wealth*, but his writings reflect a clear understanding that one's pursuit of wealth should not take precedence over one's social and moral responsibilities. Smith wrote in his classic, *Wealth of Nations*, "What improves the circumstances of the greater part can never be regarded as an inconvenience to the whole. No society can surely be flourishing and happy, of which the far greater part of the members are poor and miserable."[5] For his part, Malthus suggested that population growth would ultimately outstrip our ability to produce food—a concept that gave economics its initial label, *the dismal science.* But Malthus, commenting on the connection between wealth and happiness wrote, "Perhaps Dr. Adam Smith has considered the two inquiries as still more nearly connected than they really are."[6] While agreeing that wealth and happiness are related, neither Smith nor Malthus assumed that greater wealth was synonymous with greater happiness.

In the latter half of the nineteenth century, the focus of economics shifted toward satisfying individual human *wants*, as well as needs—with a clear understanding that human *wants* were affected by human relationships.[7] However, at the turn of the twentieth century, Vilfredo Pareto set about freeing economics from the subjectivity of sociology and psychology by focusing on the "revealed preferences" rather than on happiness.[8] To Pareto, all that mattered was whether a person consistently chose one thing over another. Obviously, rational persons would make choices consistent with their wants and needs. Economists should focus on consumer preferences and choices, he suggested, and should let the sociologists and psychologists worry about whether such choices actually made people happier. Pareto's theories were eventually adopted by other economists, presumably because the theories allowed economists to focus on observable and measurable human behavior, rather than on some intangible concept of human happiness.

The abandonment of happiness by economists laid the foundation for neoclassical economics. In the early 1900s, Alfred Marshall conceded that economics no longer dealt directly with human *well-being*, his term for "happiness," but rather with the "material requisites" of it. Later, twentieth-century economists largely ignored the economic boundaries set by Marshall and Pareto, as well by other early neoclassical economists, making little distinction between economic wealth and societal happiness. John Hicks and R. G. D. Allen replaced earlier theory, which relied on an assumption of measurable satisfaction or utility, with new consumer theory, which relied solely on ordinal preferences of consumers.[9] Paul Samuelson, beginning in the 1930s and having been joined by a host of other quantitative economists since, completed the process of rewriting the logic of economics into the language of mathematics and statistics. These neoclassical economists wanted to turn economics into a *hard* science, not a *social* science. Thus, they sought to define the whole of economics in terms of quantifiable economic variables in order to accommodate their mathematical and statistical models. However, neoclassical economists were not willing to restrict the realm of economics to individual, material self-interests. Maximizing wealth was equivalent to maximizing satisfaction, happiness, or well-being as far as neoclassical economists were concerned. Thus, *the new dismal science* of today was born.

Economists may feel secure with the assumptions underlying their mathematical and statistical models of individual and societal well-being, but the connections and conflicts between wealth and happiness have not been so easily resolved in the minds of many thoughtful people. Happiness has long been the subject of discussion and debate among the world's greatest philosophers. Historically, happiness was generally accepted as the motive of all purposeful human activity, as had been accepted by classical economists.

The hedonist philosophers equated happiness with sensual pleasures—to individual, personal, sensory experiences.[10] Another group of philosophers, however, including Aristotle, used the term *eudaimonia* for happiness.[11] Eudaimonia is not hedonism; it is instead broadly defined as "human flourishing." Happiness is an end in itself, whereas sensory pleasure and pain are physical indicators that motivate individual actions toward further ends. Eudaimonia also is inherently social in nature—it is realized by the individual, but only within the context of family, friendships, community, and society.[12] This social happiness was considered a natural consequence of positive personal relationships. In addition, eudaimonia was not something that could be pursued, but instead was a by-product of actions taken because they were intrinsically good. John Stuart Mill concluded that happiness could be attained only by focusing on the happiness of others or the improvement of humankind.[13] In essence, Aristotle and his followers believed that happiness was not something to be pursued, but instead was a natural consequence of righteous relationships.[14]

To the extent that neoclassical economics includes any remaining element of happiness, it most clearly is *hedonistic* in nature rather than *eudaimonic.* Economists commonly refer to overall well-being as the ultimate objective of economic activity, and, in contemporary psychology, "the terms *well-being* and *hedonism* are essentially equivalent."[15] The current pursuit of economic wealth is a pursuit of individual, hedonistic, sensory pleasure. And the pursuit of individual wealth, within this context, inevitably encourages the exploitation of others for individual gain and thus degrades the integrity of personal relationships. Accordingly, the pursuit of individual wealth quite logically might be expected to diminish eudaimonia or social happiness.

Perhaps no nation in modern times has been more committed to the pursuit of wealth than has the United States of America. And evidence of the inherent conflicts between the pursuit of wealth and the pursuit of social happiness can be found in the rising cost of law enforcement and increasing number of prisoners, the increasing number of lawyers and rising cost of civil litigation, and the rising poverty in single-parent homes and even in working households. These trends are symptoms of increasingly dysfunctional human relationships and declining social happiness, and all have occurred during a time of rising national wealth.

Robert Putnam, a Harvard University political scientist, clearly documents our growing social disconnectedness in his book *Bowling Alone.*[16] He provides statistical data to validate the trends toward increasing crime, civil conflict, and poverty in America. He also evaluates a multitude of measures of social involvement, ranging from voting in elections, to belonging to civic and professional organizations, to joining bowling leagues, to visiting friends and neighbors. He concludes that Americans, by a multitude of measures, are only about half as connected socially today as they were in the late 1950s.

As Aristotle might have predicted, this growing disconnectedness occurred while America was abandoning many of its social and moral constraints in the pursuit of greater individual wealth and maximum economic growth. During the early part of the twentieth century, Americans tempered their economic ambitions with concern for their fellow citizens. They restrained corporate greed at the turn of the century with their support of strong federal antitrust legislation. They supported Roosevelt's New Deal programs to care for the needy and help lift the nation out of recession. And most Americans supported the Civil Rights movement of the 1960s. But since the 1960s, there has been little societal or political restraint to the unbridled pursuit of individual economic self-interests.

Aristotle also might have predicted the consequences for our national happiness. Putnam points out that the rate of mental depression among the last two generations of Americans has increased roughly tenfold—these being the generations most socially disconnected. Furthermore, between 1950 and 1995, the rates of suicide among American adolescents more than quadrupled and among young adults nearly tripled. Less serious, but no less significant, the incidence of *malaise*—such as headaches, indigestion, and sleeplessness—show patterns similar to those associated with suicide and mental illnesses. Equally revealing, between the late 1970s and late 1990s, surveys indicate that each new generation, on average, has been unhappier than the previous generation. Whereas Putnam makes no claim of cause and effect, as each generation has become increasingly disconnected, the nation as a whole has become increasingly mentally ill and physically miserable. Americans have succeeded in extending their lifespan, but they have failed to sustain their quality of life. The United States has become a nation of greater wealth, but a nation of growing social unhappiness.

The Economics of Free Markets

Adam Smith also might have predicted that a nation preoccupied with the pursuit of wealth eventually would become a nation of increasingly unhappy people. Adam Smith and the other classical economists defended the potential benefits of the pursuit of self-interest but never suggested that the kinds of markets that dominate today's economy would function for the benefit of society as a whole. In his landmark book, *Wealth of Nations*, he wrote, "It is not from the benevolence of the butcher, the brewer, or the baker that we expect our dinner, but from their regard to their own interest. We address ourselves, not to their humanity but to their self love, and never talk to them of our necessities but of their advantages."[17] In referring to the benefits of free trade, Smith wrote, "he intends only his own gain, and he is in this, as in many other cases, led by an invisible hand to promote an end which was no part of his intention. . . ." "By pursuing his own interest he frequently promotes that of the society more effectually than when he intends to promote it."[18] These statements provide the foundation of the contemporary economic wisdom that the pursuit of individual self-interests is the best means of achieving societal good.

However, the full title of Smith's original book was *An Inquiry into the Nature and Causes of Wealth among Nations*.[19] Smith inquired into the nature of the economic world as it existed in the late 1700s and drew conclusions based on what he observed. He obviously wanted to influence the economic thinking and economic policy of his times, but he never claimed to have developed a new economic theory for all times. In fact, somewhat later, Karl Marx is said to have been the first to label Smith's economic theories as *capitalism*. Marx predicted that capitalism would degenerate into an exploitive, divisive society, resulting in growing unhappiness and, eventually, in revolution.[20] Smith likewise warned about the potential threats that industrialization and the division of labor would have on the social fabric of society. He wrote, "The man whose whole life is spent in performing a few simple operations . . . has no occasion to exert his understanding, or his invention in finding out expedients for removing difficulties which never occur. He naturally loses, therefore, the habit of such exertion, and generally becomes as stupid and ignorant as it is possible for a human creature to become. . . . His dexterity in his own particular trade seems, in this manner, to be acquired at the expense of his intellectual, social, and martial virtues."[21]

From Smith's observations, of 200-plus years ago, economists developed the fundamental assumptions that underlie neoclassical economic thinking even today. The assumptions, which characterized the society of the late 1700s, are no less essential to capitalistic economies today, if the pursuit of individual self-interest is to be transformed into societal good.[22]

The first of these necessary conditions is that markets must be economically competitive, meaning that the numbers of buyers and sellers are so large that no single buyer or seller has a large enough share of the total market to have any noticeable effect on prices. Any buyer must be able to double production or go out of business without causing prices to rise or fall. In such markets, profits are quickly competed away, and the benefits of more efficient production are quickly passed on to consumers. Most lists of essential assumptions also include homogeneous or indistinguishable products, so that no seller can command a higher price than can his or her competitors. But this simply means that sufficient sellers and buyers of the same basic product must exist to ensure competition.

In addition, it must be easy for new sellers to enter profitable markets and for existing sellers to get out of unprofitable markets, so that producers are able to respond to consumers' changing wants and needs by changing what is produced. Consumers also must have clear and accurate information concerning whether the things they buy will actually meet their wants and needs. And finally, the consumer must be sovereign—their tastes and preferences must reflect their basic values, untainted by persuasive outside influences.

Obviously, none of these characteristics exists in the dominant capitalistic economies of today. Most major industries are dominated by a handful of corporations at national levels, and domination by multinational corporations is growing even at the global level.[23] Any one such corporation's actions obviously have impacts on the market opportunities and pricing strategies of others. Corporations may compete for market share, but they do so in ways that tend to enhance profits for their industry as a whole, while retaining profits for corporate managers and stockholders rather than passing benefits on to consumers. Only in industries in which services are difficult to differentiate, as in air travel, do we see vigorous price competition. But even in such cases, consumer price benefits are short-lived as predatory price wars further reduce the number of competitors, moving such industries toward eventual monopolies.

The tremendous size of today's corporate competitors constitutes equally large capital barriers to new entrants. In addition, patents protect most important technologies and products today, effectively granting monopoly powers to patent holders for up to twenty years. Even without patents, many corporations have established brand names, which give them tremendous advantages over prospective new entrants into their markets. Most successful new entrants into today's capitalistic economies entered essentially new industries, such as microcomputers, rather than existing industries. The same factors that make market entry difficult also make it virtually impossible to liquidate a major corporation today without incurring unacceptable losses for stockholders. Most voluntary liquidations of corporations today result in corporate consolidations, which reduce, rather than increase competition. It is not easy to get into or out of business in today's capitalistic economy.

The economic assumptions of accurate information and consumer sovereignty are related, and neither exists in today's capitalistic economy. Advertising expenditure by U.S. businesses on mass media advertising alone amounted to $128 billion in 2003, with total advertising expenditures of more than twice that amount—about $2,500 per household.[24,25] The purpose of the vast majority of advertising today is not to inform consumers so they can make wise choices; instead, the intention is to persuade consumers to buy the advertised product, regardless of whether it will yield the satisfaction they have been led to expect. Much of today's advertising is targeted at children, turning impressionable children into naïve persuaders of parents. Most advertising today could be correctly labeled as *disinformation by design*.

Even more disturbing from an economic perspective, much of today's advertising is designed specifically to *create* wants that do not yet exist. Advertisers make us feel ugly so they can sell us something that will make us feel pretty. They make us feel old fashioned so they can sell us something to make us feel modern. They turn vulnerabilities into wants and wants into needs so that we will feel compelled to buy something we don't really need. Advertisers employ psychologists to explore our mental and emotional frailties so that we can be exploited for economic gain. Consumer sovereignty is based on the premise that our tastes and preferences are true reflections of choices that will make us happy—that is, tastes and preferences untainted by persuasion or coercion. Without consumer sovereignty, there is no assurance that economic resources will be guided toward the good of society, even if all the other assumptions of capitalism were valid.

Today's free markets are not competitive markets, at least not in the classical economic sense of competitiveness. Neoclassical economists often argue that the assumptions of perfect competition are no longer relevant. As long as the economy continues to produce ever-larger quantities at ever-lower prices, we are told that we should not be concerned about the assumptions of classical economics. However, without those classical assumptions, we have no assurance that a free market economy will serve the economic interests of society. We have no assurance that prices couldn't be even lower and that quantities couldn't be even higher. And certainly, we have no assurance that we are receiving the optimum assortment of goods and services to meet our true needs, rather than our created wants—if we still knew what our true needs actually were.

The *invisible hand* of Adam Smith's capitalistic economy is no longer capable of transforming individual self-interests into societal well-being. Today's economy may produce lots of cheap stuff, but there is no assurance that it is producing the right stuff in order to meet the real needs of today or to meet the needs of the future. Economic sustainability will require that we reaffirm the neglected principles of competitive free markets.

The Economics of Free Trade

Neoclassical trade theory is rooted in classical economic thinking of the early 1800s, primarily in the writings of David Ricardo, who might also have foreseen that a nation preoccupied with individual self-interest eventually would become a nation of increasingly unhappy people. Ricardo and the other classical economists defended the potential gains from free trade. He wrote, "It is quite as important to the happiness of mankind, that our enjoyments should be increased by the better distribution of labour, by each country producing those commodities for which . . . it is [better] adapted, and exchanging them for commodities of other countries."[26] But he never claimed the happiness and enjoyment of "mankind" would be increased by the kinds of transactions that dominate much of today's trade.

Ricardo's discussion of trade is based on the assumption that when two individuals freely choose to trade, each will be better off after the trade than before. People have different tastes and preferences and thus each person values the same things somewhat differently. So, if I value something that you now own more highly than I value something I own, and you value the thing that I own more highly than you value the thing you own, we will both gain by trading.

Ricardo used this same common sense concept to show the potential gains from trade associated with economic specialization.[27] For example, one farmer may be a more efficient producer of one crop, such as tomatoes, and another farmer may be a more efficient producer of another, such as green peas. If so, one farmer can then specialize in green peas and the other in tomatoes. The better tomato producer can then trade tomatoes for peas and the green pea producer can trade peas for tomatoes, and they both will be better off than if they had each tried to produce both peas and tomatoes.

Ricardo also demonstrated that potential gains from trade exist in cases in which one producer is more efficient than is the other in producing both commodities. For example, even if one farmer is a better producer of both peas and tomatoes, the other farmer will have a *comparative advantage* in producing one or the other. Let's say the first farmer could produce either 4 tons of green peas or 80 tons of tomatoes on a hectare of land using a given amount of labor and capital. Assume that a second farmer could produce only 3.3 tons of green peas or 60 tons of tomatoes on a hectare of land using the same amount of labor and capital—not as much of either crop as the first farmer could. If the first farmer decided to produce only peas, he or she would have to forgo 20 tons of tomatoes for each ton of peas produced (80 ÷ 4 = 20). However, if the second farmer decided to produce peas, he or she would have to forgo only 18 tons of tomatoes for each ton of peas (60 ÷ 3.3 = 18). In economic terms, this means that the second farmer has a *comparative advantage* in producing peas because his or her *opportunity cost* of producing peas is less. Using the same logic, the first farmer has a lower *opportunity cost* of producing tomatoes: 0.050 ton of peas per ton of tomatoes (4 ÷ 80), compared with 0.055 ton of peas per ton of tomatoes (3.3 ÷ 60). The *opportunity costs* for both crops are lower if the second farmer specializes in producing peas and the first farmer specializes in producing tomatoes.

Although the arithmetic gets a bit messy, if the second farmer specializes in peas and the first in tomatoes, and if they trade their surpluses to each other, both will be better off than if each produces some peas and some tomatoes. Ricardo wrote mostly about trade between nations rather than between individuals, but this simple two-producer, two-commodity example was the heart of Ricardo's economic theory of comparative advantage and trade.

In situations where trade between nations fits the assumptions of trade between two sovereign individuals, Ricardo's conclusions are quite reasonable and logical. However, trade between two independent individuals, or even between nations of the early 1800s, does not accurately reflect the reality of trade among nations in the early 2000s.

First, trade is truly free only if both partners are sovereign, if they are free to choose to either trade or not trade. In true free trade, neither partner can be dependent on the other; they must have an *interdependent* trading relationship. Interdependent people relate to each other by choice, not by necessity.[28] If one trading partner is dependent on another, the dependent partner is not free to choose to *not* trade. Interdependent relationships can be formed only between two otherwise independent entities—only when neither is compelled by the other to form or to maintain the relationship. Under such circumstances, each trading partner maintains their sovereignty—forming trading relationships only if beneficial to both parties, and continuing relationships only so long as beneficial for both parties.

Trading under conditions of coercion is not free trade, as when a weak nation trades with a strong nation under an explicit or implied threat of withdrawal of military protection. Nor is it free trade when one trading nation is dependent on the other for its economic survival, as when one nation owes large debts to the other. In general, poor nations are made dependent on rich nations by their lack of economic wealth, economic infrastructure, and technological advantages, regardless of their inherent worth to humanity. Trade, when one party sees no choice other than to trade, is not free trade. Coerced trade is not free trade.

Second, free trade assumes informed trade. Both parties must understand the ultimate consequences of their actions; otherwise, the perceived benefits of trade may never materialize. When a developed nation encourages a lesser-developed nation to produce for export markets, knowing that such production will lead to exploitation of their natural and human resources, but does not inform the people of these consequences, this is not free trade. The exploiters know the consequences, but the exploited do not. In some cases, the people of nations may be intentionally misled by their own leaders because actual benefits will accrue to specific individuals, but not to the nation as a whole. When the informed exploit the uninformed, such trade is not free. Uninformed trade is not free trade.

Third, free trade theory assumes that decisions are made by individuals—not by groups of people. Individuals presumably have no unresolved internal conflicts regarding the relative values of items to be traded and will trade only when trading will be beneficial to them overall. Nations, on the other hand, are made up of people with diverse preferences and priorities and thus cannot think with one mind or speak with one voice. Nations may make and carry out trade agreements to which a substantial portion of the nation's population is opposed, both before and after the trading takes place. In economics, the nation is assumed to benefit economically if the economy in total is made more profitable by trading. However, a more profitable economy does not ensure that all, or even most, of the individuals who constitute the economy have benefited from trade.

Neoclassical economics simply does not deal with personal relationships and thus does not deal with the social and ethical consequences of trade. In neoclassical economics, a nation is said to gain from trade if those who benefit *could* compensate those who lose and still have something left over. Of course, the gainers are under no legal obligation to compensate the losers, and they rarely, if ever, do so. It does not matter that the rich are made richer and the poor are made poorer as long as the economy grows. It does not matter how many people are made relatively worse off or relatively better off by trade, as long as trade results in greater total wealth and growth of the overall economy. In neoclassical economics, free trade does not address issues of social equity or justice.

Fourth, free trade theory is rooted in a barter economy, that is, people trading things rather than buying or selling them. In an international currency-based economy, comparative advantages in trade can be distorted by fluctuations in currency exchange rates that have nothing to do with relative productivity and, thus, with comparative advantage. Such fluctuations can cause the exports from one nation to become more or less costly to importers from another nation for reasons totally unrelated to production efficiency. Under such conditions, free markets do not result in efficient resource use. Trade theory assumes that differences in monetary prices reflect differences in real value, which may or may not be true in any given situation.

Finally, free trade theory assumes that both trading partners use their individual resources, such as land, labor, capital, and technology, to do more of whatever they do relatively more efficiently and, thus, to realize their *comparative* advantage. No consideration is given to the possibility that one nation might instead transfer some of its resources, such as capital and production technology, to another nation where those resources might generate even greater profits. The mobility of capital and technology eventually eliminates the *comparative* advantages of the higher-cost nations because increasing the importation from lower-cost nations devalues both land and labor in the higher-cost nation down to globally competitive levels. With full mobility of capital, technology, and labor, national markets eventually meld into a single global market. The classical economic concepts of comparative advantage simply did not anticipate the international mobility of capital and technology.

In summary, the free markets of today's capitalistic economy are no longer capable of ensuring mutually beneficial free trade. Because of growing inconsistencies between economic trade theory and economic reality, the theory of economic free trade does not reflect the reality of international free trade today. The elimination of all constraints and barriers to trade among nations undoubtedly would increase the level of economic activity and short-run profitability in the global economy. However, there is no assurance that free trade would be mutually beneficial to all traders or would enhance the overall quality of life of a global society. Indeed, there are logical reasons to believe that free trade, as is currently being promoted, would lead to further exploitation of the people and natural resources of the weak by the strong *among* nations and to further exploitation of the weak by the strong *within* nations. Economic sustainability will require that we reexamine and heed the neglected principles of competitive free markets.

The Economics of Capitalism

The economic concept of capitalism continues to evolve over time, reflecting changes in various economies that claim the capitalistic label. However, the basic economic principles of capitalism are deeply rooted in classical economic theory. Historically, capitalism has been defined as an economic system based on the private ownership of property and the private allocation of resources, through free markets. Communism, by way of contrast, is characterized by public ownership of property and government allocation of resources, through central planning.[29] Capitalism is further distinguished from communism by differing theories of value. Communists believe that all economic value results from the application of labor to natural resources, and all capital thus represents value previously appropriated from workers by the capitalists. Capitalists believe that economic value can arise from all factors of production—land, labor, management, and capital—and that profits legitimately accrue to those who risk diminishing the value of their capital, as they seek to enhance the value of capital, through investment.

One principle of capitalism frequently neglected is that capitalism depends upon people making economic decisions as individuals and accepting responsibility for the individual decisions they make. Communists, at least in theory, make all economic decisions collectively. Alexis de Tocqueville, in his historic four-volume work, *Democracy in America*, stated that the widespread participation of people, as individuals, in political affairs at local, state, and federal levels was a major strength of the American democracy.[30] Tocqueville warned, however, of the tendency toward excessive wealth and power in the "manufacturing" sector—today's corporate sector. He thought American society ultimately might well evolve toward a manufacturing aristocracy, within which people would lose both the incentive and ability to participate in public affairs.[31]

Adam Smith, in his *Wealth of Nations*, suggested that individuals must make their own decisions and accept personal responsibility if capitalism is to work effectively. Competition requires a large number of *independent* buyers and sellers in markets for all basic goods and services. Smith wrote, "the pretense that corporations are necessary for the better governing of a trade, is without any foundation." He also saw little legitimate use for "joint stock companies" and saw potential mischief in anything that allowed individuals to act collectively in the marketplace.[32]

The fears of both Tocqueville and Smith were well founded. Under capitalism, the processes of industrialization and corporatization have effectively dissuaded people from direct, personal participation in both economics and politics. The rising power of industrial corporations in America has fundamentally transformed both the American economy and the American democracy.[33]

Corporatism is defined in Merriam-Webster's *Collegiate* dictionary as "the organization of a society into industrial and professional corporations serving as organs of political representation and exercising some control over persons and activities within their jurisdiction."[34] Corporatism means that we participate in *society* as members of groups, which not only represent us but also exert control over us. Corporatism means that we participate in the *economy*, not as individuals but as members of organizations—as workers, owners, or managers of corporations. Corporatism means that we participate in the *political process*, not as individuals but as members of organizations—as members of labor unions, corporate business organizations, political action committees, or other special interest groups. Corporatism means that we let someone else make our economic and political decisions for us.

Corporatism is a naturally occurring stage of industrial development. The industrial paradigm of development is characterized by the processes of specialization, standardization, and consolidation. Specialization, with each person or unit performing fewer functions, allows each function or step of a production process to be performed more efficiently through the division of labor. Standardization allows the various specialized functions to be controlled and integrated into an efficient overall production process, as in assembly line production. Specialization and standardization allow, in turn, the efficient centralization of management and consolidation of control in order to achieve economies of scale. The evolution of social economies, from hunting and gathering to agriculture, from agriculture to manufacturing, and from manufacturing to services, simply reflects different evolutionary stages of specialization, standardization, and consolidation.

Incorporation facilitates functional specialization by allowing the ownership of an organization to be separated from management and labor. Public stock offerings allow people with large amounts of capital to specialize in owning companies that they neither manage nor work for, and it allows others to specialize by working for or managing companies that they do not own. The business practices of corporations owned by families and other close-knit groups may reflect the common values and ethics of the owners. However, the overriding motive for most investments in publicly traded corporations today, particularly those supported by investments made through pension funds and mutual funds, is to realize maximum dividends or growth in stock value. Thus, corporate ownership frequently seeks to remove all social and ethical constraints on a company's pursuit of ever-greater profits and growth. Anything that is legal is considered allowable, and if profitable, is deemed desirable, regardless of the social or ethical implications. Corporate acts of patriotism and altruism become nothing more than public relations strategies designed to minimize societal constraints on profits and growth.

In general, corporate ownership reduces capital constraints on growth, allowing business organizations to grow ever larger. Fewer, larger corporate firms are therefore able to gain greater market share and greater control over total industry output. As corporations become fewer and larger, they acquire increasing market power—thereby allowing them to enhance and retain profits—leading to further economies of size, meaning still greater market power, and chronically declining competitiveness of markets. Labor unions and other special interest groups have emerged to counteract the power of large industries to exploit their workers, civil society, and the natural environment, but thus far they have been unable to restrain corporate power and growth.[35]

This same industrial organizational paradigm now characterizes private for-profit corporations, special interest groups, and government organizations—all specialize, standardize, and consolidate power to achieve greater operational efficiency. Each organization, and each division, department, and work group within the organization, performs a specialized and standardized function. Control of the organization can then be centralized, allowing a few key decision makers to make most of the important decisions, thereby exerting control over the people within the organization while claiming to represent them to the outside world. The corporation speaks for its stockholders and employees, the labor union speaks for its members, and the political action groups speak for their contributors. People participate in society indirectly, through various types of corporate organizations—not directly, as independent individuals.

The natural tendency of capitalism is toward corporatism—toward the separation of decision making from ownership and responsibility. Thus, as capitalism evolves over time, it requires ever-increasing supplies of human and natural resources to support its continual need for corporate profits and growth, as suggested by Karl Marx.[36] In addition, the natural evolution from capitalism to corporatism systematically removes all moral and ethical constraints on the exploitation of both natural and human resources. Thus far, most political struggles between business corporations and the other countervailing corporate groups—such as labor unions, environmentalists, and advocates for social justice—seem to have been won by business corporations.

Corporate financing of political campaigns has become the lightening rod of corporate influence in politics, but the incestuous relationship between politics and economics goes much deeper than campaign financing. The public promotion of continued economic growth has become a dominant consideration in virtually every political decision. Neoconservative economics—first championed by the administrations of Ronald Reagan in the United States and Margaret Thatcher in the United Kingdom—has become the dominant economic philosophy of most capitalist countries. An increasing emphasis on removing all government restraints on the private economy and privatization of government functions has effectively neutralized the ability of governments either to constrain corporate consolidation or to protect natural resources and workers from corporate exploitation.

As corporate consolidation takes place globally, the numbers of multinational corporations grow and nations lose their ability to protect their resources and their people from corporate exploitation. As corporate consolidation takes place vertically—that is, consolidating the control of resources, manufacturing, distribution, and retailing—free market coordination is replaced by *corporate* central planning. Ironically, corporatism is transforming capitalism into a perverse form of communism, in which corporate ownership, rather than government ownership, is replacing individual private ownership and central planning by corporations, rather than government, is replacing free market allocation of resources.

The fundamental flaw in capitalism is its lack of attention to the need to continually renew, regenerate, and reproduce the natural and human resources that must support productivity over the long run. Economic investments today are investments in more efficient means of extraction or exploitation, not investments in renewal or regeneration of the natural and human resource base. In other words, any system that naturally encourages the exploitation of nature and of people is incapable of protecting nature and people from its exploitation. Even if neoclassical economics were to give adequate attention to antitrust laws in maintaining competitive markets, it still would be incapable of addressing issues of renewal, regeneration, and reproduction, which are the fundamental issues of economic sustainability.

Our pursuit of happiness has degenerated into a pursuit of wealth, the invisible hand of Adam Smith's free market capitalism is no longer capable of transforming the pursuit of individual greed into societal good, free trade is no longer free because too few are free to *not trade*, and free market capitalism is being replaced by centrally planned corporatism. Thus, the development of a new economics of sustainability will require far more than the fine-tuning of neoclassical economics. Social and ecological relationships must again become active priorities in all economic decisions, and not treated as some passive context of decision making. Society and the environment cannot simply be *internalized,* or made a part of the economy; the unique values or relationships and rightness must be given explicit consideration in the decision-making process. Economics must return to its philosophical roots if it is to contribute to a sustainable society.

The new economics of sustainability must be built upon the first principles of classical economics, upon principles relevant to the pursuit of happiness and societal well-being instead of the singular pursuit of wealth. Our common sense of those first principles tells us that our physical or material well-being is but one aspect of happiness or true quality of life. Our common sense tells us that our life is made better by relationships, even noneconomic relationships—within families, communities, and cultures. Our common sense tells us that life is made better by ethical and moral rightness in our thoughts and actions. We know intuitively that an economic system that relies on exploitation of the earth and of people is fundamentally incapable of sustaining human happiness. We will need to reexamine and rethink the foundational principles of economics if we are to find sustainable happiness.

Endnotes

1. Paul Hawken, Amory Lovins, and L. Hunter Lovins, *Natural Capitalism* (New York: Little, Brown, and Company, 1999).

2. Robert D. Putnam, *Bowling Alone* (New York: Simon and Schuster, 2000).

3. Donella H. Meadows, *Limits to Growth* (New York: Penguin Books, New American Library, 1977).

4. Joseph Chamie, *World Population Projections to 2150* (New York: Population Division, Department of Economic and Social Affairs, United Nations Secretariat, 1998).

5. Adam Smith, *Wealth of Nations* (Amherst, Mass.: Prometheus Books Great Mind Series, 1991, original copyright, 1776), 83.

6. Thomas Malthus, *An Essay on the Principles of Population* (London: Macmillan, 1966; London: St. Paul's Church-Yard, printed for J. Johnson, 1789).

7. C. Menger, *Grundsatze der Volkswirtsschaftslehre* (Vienna: Braunmuller, 1871), translated in Luigino Bruni, *The History of Happiness in Economics* (London: Routledge, 2004).

8. Vilfredo Pareto, *Manual of Political Economy* (New York: Kelly, 1971; original copyright, 1906).

9. John Hicks and R.G.D. Allen, "A Reconsideration of the Theory of Value," *Economica,* no. 1, (1934): 52–76.

10. Marco E. L. Guidi, *Pain and Human Action: Locke to Bentham* (Pisa, Italy: University of Pisa.) http://fausto.eco.unibs.it/~segdss/paper/guidi.pdf.

11. Aristotle, *Nichomachean Ethics* (Oxford, England: Oxford Press, 1980).

12. D. B. Rasmussen, "Human Flourishing and the Appeal to Human Nature," *Social Philosophy and Policy,* 16, no. 1 (1999): 473–480.

13. John Stuart Mill, *John Stuart Mill, Autobiography* (New York: Penguin Group, Putnam Penguin, Inc., 1989; original copyright, 1873).

14. Bruni, *Happiness.*

15. R. M. Ryan and E. L. Deci, "On Happiness and Human Potentials: A Review of Research on Hedonic and Eudaimonic Well-Being," *Annual Review Psychological*, 52 (2001): 141–166.

16. Putnam, *Bowling Alone.*

17. Adam Smith, *Wealth of Nations*, 7.

18. Adam Smith, *Wealth of Nations*, 199.

19. Adam Smith, *An Inquiry Into the Nature and Causes of Wealth Among Nations*, ed. Adam and Charles Black; and Longman, Brown, Green, & Longmans (London: J. R. McCulloch, 1828; original copyright, 1776).

20. Karl Marx and Friedrich Engels, *The Communist Manifesto* (New York: Pocket Books, Simon and Schuster, 1964; original copyright, 1848).

21. Adam Smith, *An Inquiry*, 550.

22. C. E. Ferguson, *Microeconomic Theory* (Homewood, Ill.: Richard D. Irwin, Inc., 1969), 222–225.

23. David Korten, *When Corporations Rule the World* (West Hartford, Conn: Kumarian Press, 1995).

24. TNS Media Intelligence, "TNS Media Intelligence News, March 8, 2004," TNS Media Intelligence, http://www.tns-mi.com/news/03082004.htm (accessed April, 2005).

25. Universal/McCann, *Insider's Report: Robert Coen's Presentation on Advertising Expenditures, June 2004*, Universal/McCann, http://www.universalmccann.com/Coen_Insiders_Report_0604_Color.pdf (accessed April, 2005).

26. David Ricardo, *The Works and Correspondence of David Ricardo*, ed. Piero Sraffa, (Cambridge, England: British Royal Society, 1951–55), 132.

27. Ricardo, *Works*, 134–136.

28. Stephen R. Covey, *The 7 Habits of Highly Effective People* (New York: Simon and Schuster, 1989).

29. *Microsoft Encarta Encyclopedia, 2003*, "Capitalism and Communism." (Redmond, Wash.: Microsoft Corp. 1993–2002).

30. Alexis de Tocqueville, *Democracy in America* (New York: Bantam Books, 2000; original copyright, 1835), 95–108.

31. Tocqueville, *Democracy*, 690–694.

32. Smith, *Wealth of Nations*, 482–484.

33. John Ralston Saul, *The Unconscious Civilization* (Toronto, Ontario: House of Anansi Press Limited, 1995).

34. Merriam-*Webster's Collegiate Dictionary, 11th edition*, "Corporatism." (Springfield, Mass.: Merriam-Webster Inc., 2003.

35. According to Korten (*Corporations*, 12), corporations and financial institutions that were once beneficial have been transformed "into instruments of a market tyranny that is extending its reach across the planet like a cancer, colonizing ever more of the planet's living spaces, destroying livelihoods, displacing people, rendering democratic institutions impotent. . . ."

36. Marx and Engels, *Communist Manifesto.*

CHAPTER TWO

THE PURSUIT OF ENLIGHTENED SELF-INTERESTS

Rational Economics

The discipline of economics provides a logical, rational means of evaluating alternatives and making choices.[1] The foundation for current economic thinking was laid during the Age of Enlightenment—an era rooted in the rationalism of such seventeenth-century philosophers as Galileo, Newton, and Descartes.[2] The French, including Montesquieu, Rousseau, and Voltaire, are credited with being the intellectual leaders of this period of revolutionary thinking, which spanned most of the eighteenth century. In addition to the French, Kant of Germany, Hume and Locke of England, and Franklin and Jefferson of America contributed significantly to the critical thinking of the time.

Perhaps the most important distinguishing characteristic of Enlightenment philosophy was an unwavering belief in the power of human reasoning. The general belief was that God had made the universe, put it in motion, and then stepped aside, leaving mortals to fend for themselves in a mysterious world. The universe, including the earth and everything upon it, was believed to function according to a set of immutable, unchangeable laws that governed everything, including the natural ecosystem and human society. However, these rationalists believed that human reasoning and logical thinking eventually could unravel the mysteries of the world, leading to unending human progress—not only in human understanding, but also in technical achievements and even in the ultimate perfection of human values.

New scientific methods based on human reasoning, they proclaimed, eventually would unlock the mysteries of the universe, revealing all of its secrets. They believed that humans could learn to manipulate nature for their own benefit, and that even human nature could be altered and improved through greater understanding and proper education. They accepted a Deist concept of God, believing in the existence of some higher or natural order of things, but they most soundly rejected Christian theology. Human efforts should be centered on improving current life, not on some promise of life hereafter in heaven. The scientific method, the Industrial Revolution, and neoclassical economics all have their roots in the Age of Enlightenment.

The "economic man," by assumption, is a rational being; he makes logically consistent choices calculated to bring him closer to his desired goals. Because economics assumes that human wants are insatiable and that economic resources are scarce, economic beings are always striving to get more of the things they value, while sacrificing less to get them. And because economic beings are rational, they naturally pursue their individual self-interests. If an economic being makes some sacrifice that benefits another person, it's only because he or she expects to receive some greater benefit in return. Economic beings may choose to act in ways considered moral or ethical, but they do so only because they expect to realize some greater individual benefit in return.

Most neoclassical economists rationalize acts of altruism by accepting Pareto's proposition that peoples' decisions can be driven by a variety of motives, some rational and some not. However, as long as people make consistent choices, it does not matter whether their decisions are driven by egotism or altruism; their choices will be consistent with maximizing whatever they value.[3] However, consistency of choice assumes that decision makers show no personal preference in choosing to deal with one person rather than another. Thus, economics becomes a science of individuals who exhibit no personal preference for other specific individuals, thus leaving no place for relationships of a purely personal nature. As Pareto wrote, "Science proceeds by replacing the relationships between human concepts (which [are the] relationships [that] are the first to occur to us) by relationships between things." He goes on to write, "Such a path is also the only one that can lead to the truth in political economy."[4]

Philip Wicksteed agreed with Pareto that economics was capable of dealing with the whole range of human motives, not exclusively with an egotistic concept of self-interest.[5] He argued that a person could be either selfish or unselfish without affecting the economic nature of any given relationship. But he wrote also, "As soon as he is moved by a direct and disinterested desire to further the purposes or consult the interests of particular 'others' . . . the transaction on his side ceases to be purely economic."[6] In other words, when a person shows favor or disfavor to particular persons for personal reasons, a business transaction is no longer economic, in that it may or may not be of benefit to the larger society. Wicksteed concluded that the critical characteristic determining whether a relationship is economic is not its *egotism* but instead its *non-tuism*, which in this context means engaging in relationships of a wholly impersonal nature. When *tuism* affects decisions to some degree, he states, transactions cease to be wholly economic.

In everyday terms, if a person freely chooses to purchase an item from a friend or neighbor at a price higher than would be paid for the same item from someone else, the buyer may be maximizing his or her individual satisfaction but is not making a rational *economic* decision. Or if a person freely chooses to work for a specific environmental organization at a salary less than he or she could earn for the same work elsewhere, the person may be making a rational decision, but it is not a rational *economic* decision. Such relationships are clearly *tuist*, there is a *specific other* involved, and thus such decisions are not *economically* rational. However, many economists fail to recognize that such choices, although logical in maximizing the overall well-being of individuals, are not consistent with the necessary conditions of a classical economy, in which the pursuit of individual self-interests is assumed to benefit the larger society.

Pareto's and Wicksteed's claims that revealed preferences are consistent maximum social welfare were based on the premise that individuals' altruistic choices are strictly impersonal. In other words, individuals might be willing to pay a higher price for a locally produced item, but the buyers could have no personal relationship with any particular local seller. If persons choose to work for an environmental organization at a lower wage, they must be willing to work for any other environmental organization at a similar wage. However, in a world in which peoples' decisions are affected by personal preferences, there is no logical reason to believe that individual choices will result in maximum benefits to society as a whole.

Pareto also concluded that pure economics deals only with "choices that the individual makes considering solely the things that he prefers," thus excluding from economics all actions "that the individual makes considering the effects that these choices will have on other individuals."[7] In economic choices, each person is expected to protect his or her own self-interest, and therefore the interest of others never enters into the decision. In economics, all relationships also are instrumental, meaning that they have no value other than as a way of acquiring something. Purely personal relationships have no instrumental value. One person cannot benefit economically by contributing solely to another person's success or happiness. No one can possibly benefit economically from anything that happens after his or her death because rational economic benefits must be experienced by the individual. Persons might do something for their children or their grandchildren because a child or a grandchild might reciprocate the favor while the parent or grandparent is still alive. But, it is irrational to do anything solely for the benefit of others, even nonspecific others of some future generation. There is simply no logical economic reason for such acts because one cannot possibly reap a rational, individual benefit. Thus, the individual choices that are made—either wholly or in part because of their anticipated effects on others, either present or future—are excluded from neoclassical economics.

Economists missed an opportunity to follow a quite different path in dealing with human relationships in economics. Unlike Pareto and Wicksteed, Alfred Marshall proposed limiting the realm of economic goods to include only those things that "can be measurable by a money price."[8] He shared a belief with classical economists, such as Smith and Malthus, who understood that wealth was related only indirectly to overall human well-being. Marshall treated income and wealth as simply the means of acquiring the material requisites of well-being. He thought it more appropriate to limit the discipline of economics to the material aspects of life and to deal with personal relationships and ethical principles within the disciplines of sociology and philosophy. The material, social, and ethical dimensions of well-being could then be synthesized into a unified concept of human behavior, he suggested. Most economists, however, seemed to want a single science of economics capable of encompassing the whole realm of human choices. So Marshall's suggestion for synthesizing economics with sociology and philosophy was never seriously pursued.

Instead, during the 1930s, John Hicks and R. G. D. Allen repositioned and formalized Pareto's rational choice theories and methodologies to develop *modern consumer theory*. In the process of repositioning and formalizing, they transformed a "subjective theory of value into a general logic of choice, extending its applicability over a wide field of human conduct."[9] In other words, they applied economic logic and reasoning with little regard for the limitations that had been imposed on choice theory previously by Pareto and Wicksteed. Samuelson, Hayek, Friedman, and other noted economists of the twentieth century undoubtedly were aware of the theoretical limitations of their discipline. However, they treated wealth as essentially equivalent to well-being and largely ignored the intrinsic importance of personal relationships and ethical behavior in determining overall human well-being. Such things as altruism, ethics, morality, sympathy, empathy, friendship, and love are all lumped together into the *consumer's preference structure*, which is accepted as predetermined or given. Society and nature are treated as *externalities*, as affecting preferences, but from outside the realm of economic decision making. The objective of all economic activity then becomes maximizing individual material well-being, within the constraints of predetermined preferences, with the implicit understanding that doing so will maximize individual and overall societal well-being. Intentionally or not, economists have encouraged people to believe that the pursuit of individual economic self-interest is the surest route, if not the only route, to maximum long-term societal well-being.

Common Sense

Our common sense tells us that relationships and ethics are too important to be treated as a passive context or preference structure, within which individuals pursue their individual material self-interests. Our common sense tells us that choices based on personal relationships—within families, communities, and cultures—are important determinants of our quality of life. An economic system that fails to recognize the existence and importance of such choices can hardly be expected to guide human society toward a better way of life. Our common sense tells us also that ethical and moral choices—including those affecting the future of humanity—are important determinants of our quality of life. An economic system that fails to recognize the legitimacy and importance of such choices will not guide human society toward a sustainable quality of life.

But, why should we listen to our common sense? After all, we are living in an age in which logic and reason must ultimately prevail. How can we possibly expect people to challenge the logic and reason of neoclassical economics with nothing more than common sense? We can because common sense must always provide the foundational principles upon which logic and reason are used to build understanding. These foundational principles, or first principles, must be used to test the truth of knowledge, that is, to decide whether we believe something to be true or false. And first principles must be used to test the morality of actions—to decide whether we believe something to be good or bad.[10] As Thomas Reid, the nineteenth-century philosopher wrote, "All knowledge and science must be built upon principles that are self-evident; and of such principles every man who has common sense is competent to judge."[11] These first principles provide a starting point, and, lacking a starting point, all logic and reasoning become circular, and thus, useless. For example, first principles of algebra, called *axioms*, or *laws*, are the foundation for all mathematical proofs. One such axiom is that *a* times *b* equals *b* times *a*. This may seem obvious, but that's the nature of first principles. First principles are common sense.

However, first principles are always subject to challenge. For example, if a number is somehow made more important by the fact that it comes first rather than second, then *a* times *b* would not be the same as *b* times *a*. For example, if we were using algebra to evaluate social status, where who comes first is always important, we would need to reexamine our axioms, or first principles, and ask whether algebra provides the appropriate logic for our evaluation. But at least for purposes of mathematical reasoning, the proposition that *a* times *b* equals *b* times *a* makes sense. So, we simply accept it as valid. However, it's important to remember that all scientific *proofs* are based on a set of *unproven* first principles, or axioms.

Common sense may have become an overused colloquialism in recent years, but it has deep philosophical roots extending back to the eighteenth century. The philosophy of common sense is sometimes called *Scottish philosophy* because it was most popular among Scottish philosophers. It arose largely in response to the *doctrine of ideas*, which John Locke had adopted from earlier work by Descartes. Berkeley's related theory of *pure idealism* attempted to explain the external world solely in terms of ideas, in the absence of external reality.[12] Hume, by contrast, had argued that there was no logical basis for assuming the existence of any mental substance capable of receiving ideas, believing the mind to be nothing more than a succession of different states produced by experiences. Between these two propositions, both subject and object disappeared, leaving no external world and no ideas, and thus degenerating in complete skepticism.

Thomas Reid disagreed with Locke's doctrine of ideas and set out to vindicate the common sense or natural judgment of common people.[13] He concluded that both ideas and the mind are real simply because people know they exist. He argued that if the existence of the external world or the human mind cannot be proven, it's not because they do not exist or are unknowable. The ultimate reality, he proclaimed, is found in human consciousness or knowledge of reality, which neither needs to be proven nor is capable of proof, but is itself the ground of all proof. Other Scottish philosophers, including Thomas Brook, William Hamilton, and James Mackintosh accepted Reid's basic premise of common sense, adding other refinements dealing with direct knowledge of morality as well as reality. According to this eighteenth-century philosophy, our common sense is our inner sense of first principles, which is common to all people, and by which we test the truth of knowledge and the morality of actions.

The foundation for the philosophy of common sense actually was laid much earlier, around 400 B.C., when Plato proposed the existence of *pure knowledge*. He argued that one can never gain *pure knowledge* of a thing through observation because anything that can be observed is always changing, whereas *pure knowledge* never changes.[14] He argued that we observe only imperfect examples of the true *form* of things— the order or architecture of pure knowledge. Thus, we can observe examples of *form* and we can visualize ideas of true *form* in our minds, but we can never actually observe true form or fully grasp pure knowledge because it exists only in the abstract. We can't prove the existence of pure knowledge, but we still know that it exists.

Plato's proposition suggested the existence of a set of unchanging principles, first principles, which define the architecture of pure knowledge. We can never prove the existence of these first principles because they exist at a level beyond the realm of our direct observation. These first principles, in fact, are the foundation for all scientific proof. We can see evidence of their existence in the world around us and in the lives of other people. However, our changing observations have meaning only because we have some intuitive knowledge of the unchanging form and the principles by which knowledge is defined.

Our understanding of *pure knowledge* must necessarily come from our insight, our intuition, or more precisely, from our common sense. Through observing the interrelationships among things in nature, including human relationships, we can gain insights into the nature of the higher order of things. But we can never fully understand it because it exists only in the abstract. Our only direct knowledge of ultimate reality must come from our common sense.

Neoclassical economics is based on conventional wisdom rather than common sense. Although the two are often used interchangeably, conventional wisdom is very different from common sense. Both tend to represent widely held opinions, but the sources of those opinions are quite different. Conventional wisdom is rooted in observation and experience rather than in first principles. Logic and reason are applied to observations and experiences in order to draw conclusions, and, when confirmed by further observation and experience, the conclusions eventually become conventional wisdom. Then conventional wisdom is passed from generation to generation and as such is generally not based on direct or first-hand experiences or observations, which allows each generation to add to the accumulation of conclusions. Consequently, the conventional wisdom of past generations may persist long after it is no longer consistent with current experience because few persons, if any, question its validity. Once something becomes conventional wisdom, it becomes unpopular to challenge it and difficult to change it, regardless of its validity.

Conventional wisdom includes many things that make common sense. However, because it is rooted in observations and experiences, which are inherently imperfect and ever-changing reflections of an unchanging reality, conventional wisdom often differs from common sense. Something truly makes sense only if it can be derived from first principles that we *know* to be true or right. Some people choose to deny their common sense, instead relying on their own observations and experiences, or more commonly, on conventional wisdom. But all people have access to common sense, if we choose to use it.

Even the Founding Fathers of the United States were capable, at times, of denying their common sense in favor of the conventional wisdom. The rightness of owning slaves, for example, was conventional wisdom until well into the nineteenth century—it had always been done. However, it has never made common sense that one person should own another person. Thomas Jefferson wrote and spoke out against slavery because he knew it was ethically and morally wrong.[15] Yet he helped draft a constitution that allowed slavery, and he personally owned slaves. Jefferson allowed the conventional wisdom of the times to take precedence over his common sense.

However, Jefferson and the other signers relied heavily on their common sense in developing the Declaration of Independence. They had no scientific basis for the bold assertion, "We hold these truths to be self-evident, that all men are created equal, that they are endowed by their Creator with certain unalienable rights, that among these are life, liberty, and the pursuit of happiness."[16] These truths were not derived by logic and reason or from experiments or observations, and this statement certainly did not represent the conventional wisdom of the times. They considered the truth of this statement to be self-evident, thus requiring no proof because it was known to be true. They were relying on their common sense.

Relying on common sense does not imply rejection of scientific inquiry as a means of knowing and understanding. But science must be rooted in common sense. Thomas Huxley, a noted English botanist, once wrote, "All truth, in the long run, is only common sense clarified."[17] Albert Einstein's popular quotation, "Common sense is the collection of prejudices acquired by age eighteen,"[18] obviously refers to conventional wisdom rather than common sense. He also wrote, "The whole of science is nothing more than a refinement of everyday thinking,"[19] which is clearly consistent with the philosophy of common sense. Science should be used to clarify and refine our common sense, but not to replace it. An economics of happiness and sustainability must be built upon a foundation of common sense.

Enlightened Self-Interests

As humans, we will pursue our self-interests. Doing so is inherent within the nature of being human. We don't need to prove it; it's common sense. We quite naturally defend ourselves when attacked and place a high priority on our physical health and personal security, even during times of safety and tranquility. We put a high priority on having enough food, clothing, and shelter to ensure our survival, but we also quite naturally enjoy the material comforts and pleasures of life. Our individual material well-being is an important aspect of our overall quality of life. Pursuit of individual self-interests is a common sense first principle upon which to build a happy, sustainable society.

However, concern for other people also is an inherent aspect of human nature. We are a social species; we need relationships with other people. We don't need to prove this either; it's just common sense. We need noninstrumental relationships with other people, relationships that are ends rather than means to some greater end. Such relationships are of intrinsic value; they enhance our quality of life in and of themselves. Love is not a means of acquiring anything else; it has intrinsic value. The apostle Paul wrote, "Love bears all things and believes all things; love hopes all things and endures all things. Love never ends. Faith, hope, and love abide, but the greatest of these is love."[20] A life without love is a life without quality. We can't prove it, but it does not need to be proven; we know it to be true. It's common sense.

Abraham Maslow, an American psychologist, recognized love as a basic human need, but argued that love becomes important only after our physiological and security needs are met.[21] However, this hierarchy pertains only in the short run. A baby without love may have no more chance of surviving to adulthood than does a baby without milk. Many thoughtful people will accept known risks to their personal health and safety through risky interactions that they deem necessary to maintain loving relationships with other people. Likewise, a person who feels alone and unloved may choose voluntarily to end his or her life. When we look beyond the present moment, we realize that our social quality of life ranks at least as high as our individual, material quantity of life. We do not need to prove this proposition; we know it to be true. It's common sense. Caring for and sharing with others represents a broader concept of self-interest than the individual material self-interest of neoclassical economics.

In addition, the search for purpose and meaning in life is an inherent aspect of human nature. We don't need to prove that life has purpose and meaning; it's just common sense. Logic and reason tell us that the purpose of anything can be determined only by seeing it within the context of the larger whole of which it is a part. Everything is a part of a larger whole and everything is made up of smaller parts of the whole, and the purpose of any part of a thing is inherently dependent upon the purpose of the larger whole. For example, a doctor may be able to describe the function of a human heart or brain—to transport blood or to process electrical impulses. But the purpose of these organs cannot be determined without considering the body as a whole. The human body represents the higher level of organization—the larger whole, which provides the heart and brain with a functional purpose.

Moving to the next higher level of organization, to human society, a person cannot possibly derive meaning or purpose for his or her life from relationships with other people or other parts of the natural environment. They are all at the same level of organization. The purpose and meaning of our lives must come from our relationship to, or rather our place within, some higher order of things, that is, the universal whole of which humanity is but a part. Our common sense is our only direct access to this higher order and therefore is our only direct access to purpose and meaning. We *know* life has purpose and meaning. We can't prove it, but we don't need to prove it; we know it.

Maslow considered self-actualization, which is the fulfillment of one's unique human potential, to be the highest human need. According to Maslow, after love comes self-esteem and then self-actualization. If life had no purpose or meaning, however, self-actualization would be impossible. There would be no potential to be realized. Again, any hierarchy of needs relates only to the short term because a life without meaning is hardly worth living. Thus, people strive to do what is right and resist what is wrong, even when such actions clearly are contrary to their narrowly defined, individual self-interest. For example, many people have willingly risked their lives for ethical causes, such as social and environmental justice, which Maslow's hierarchy would rank as self-actualization. People will do good for other people whom they have never known and will never know personally, including those of future generations, because it gives purpose and meaning to their lives. To judge what is *right* and *good,* they must use their common sense. Ethics and morality in our personal behavior and in our relationships with others reflect a self-interest that is higher than the individual material self-interests of neoclassical economics.

The uniqueness of the human species is not just a matter of our superior ability to reason or our ability to pursue animalistic pleasures by more logical and rational means. Our uniqueness is our ability to make conscious, purposeful decisions that reflect an understanding that we are but a part of a larger whole. We have the ability to understand that our own well-being is integrally interrelated with a universe far larger than the world of our observation and experience, a universe that spans both time and space. We understand intuitively that whatever we do affects other people, which in turn affects the whole of society, affects our natural environment, and ultimately affects us. Everything we do has meaning within some higher, unknowable order of things, which affects our sense of ethical and moral well-being. In our pursuit of a more *enlightened self-interest*, we must recognize the social, ecological, and moral implications of everything we do.

This is not some radical, *new age* idea. Such thinking has been around for a long time. For example, Alexis de Tocqueville, in his classic work *Democracy in America*, wrote of a similar concept of self-interest in the early 1800s—he called it "self-interest rightly understood."[22] Tocqueville believed that survival of the American democracy was critically dependent on deeply rooted religious beliefs, which constrained the early Americans' pursuit of individual self-interests. He suggested that if these strong religious beliefs were ever to erode, they would have to be replaced with a strong sense "that man serves himself in serving his fellow-creatures, and that his private interest is to do good." He wrote that early Americans believed strongly "that men ought to sacrifice themselves for their fellow-creatures . . . that such sacrifices are as necessary to him who imposes them upon himself as to him for whose sake they are made." Tocqueville believed that "self-interest rightly understood" reflected the fact that people benefit from fulfilling their proper role in the larger human society in ways that could never be linked directly to one's narrowly defined, individual material self-interest.

The pursuit of a *higher* concept of self-interest does not imply a return to the mysticism and superstition of the Middle Ages. It is a sensible theory concerning the functioning of the universe, which has been supported by philosophers, scientists, and common people throughout the whole of recorded human history. Humans have practiced religion since the beginning of civilization. Newton, Descartes, Voltaire, and Paine all believed in the existence of some higher order of things. The early economists, including Adam Smith and Thomas Malthus, gave great attention to issues of equity, justice, ethics, and morality. Thoughtful people throughout human history have known that a life lived without purpose and meaning is a life without quality.

The pursuit of a *broader* concept of self-interest is not carried out by studying the teachings of some radical cult movement. Throughout human history, people have sought out other people to form families, tribes, communities, nations, and civilized societies. It should be obvious to any observer, whether philosopher, scientist, or ordinary person on the street, that people benefit, directly and personally, from their relationships with other people. Certainly, some of these relationships are purely instrumental—simply a means of achieving individual benefits. However, there is clear and compelling evidence that people need other people for reasons that are not sensory, tangible, or even individual in nature. Love is one of the most thought-about, talked-about, written-about, and sought-after things in the world—and for good reason. People know that a life without love is a life without quality.

Our common sense tells us that humans are multidimensional. Throughout recorded history, people have referred to the body, the mind, and the soul. The body is the physical aspect of one's being, the mind is the thinking aspect, and the soul is the spiritual aspect. The physical, mental, and spiritual aspects of humans are not separate but instead are inseparable dimensions of whole people. We cannot take away any one of the three dimensions without destroying the essence of the whole. A being without a body, mind, or soul simply is not a person.

Since people are multidimensional, it should be no mystery that the quality of a person's life is likewise multidimensional. The tangible, sensory aspects of a person's life are fundamentally physical in nature. Thus, the individual, material quality of life—the quality arising from economic self-interests—is related to the physical dimension of one's being. Values that arise from human relationships are mental and emotional in nature. The sense of well-being that arises from positive relationships with another being is not something we can see, touch, hear, taste, or smell, but it is clearly something that affects one's mental and emotional well-being. Human values that arise from ethical and moral behavior are fundamentally spiritual in nature. The sense of well-being that arises from "doing the right thing" is not something tangible that can be sensed physically or even something that we can rationalize mentally. It is something we experience from deep within our being—in our heart and soul. The personal, relational, and spiritual dimensions are inseparable, and together they determine our overall quality of life. We can't prove these things, and we don't need to prove these things; we *know* them to be true. They are first principles; they are common sense.

Only within the past few decades has our economic system become disconnected from its social and ethical roots. Economics abandoned the pursuit of happiness for the pursuit of wealth because economists wanted their discipline to be accepted as a hard science—as are physics and chemistry. Economists wanted to reestablish the roots of their discipline in the logic and reason of revealed preferences rather than leave it rooted in the common sense principles of human relationships and righteousness. If economists had accepted Marshall's proposal to restrict economics to those things that can be valued monetarily, no great damage might have been done.[23] Monetary measures conform very well to the basic axioms of mathematics. Money can be added, subtracted, multiplied, and divided without distorting its value. Economics, sociology, and psychology could have been treated as separate disciplines dealing with the three inseparable dimensions of overall human well-being. The economic, social, and psychological implications of decisions could have been given equal importance in guiding both personal and public decisions.

However, economists were not willing to limit their discipline to those things that could be legitimately measured mathematically. They have attempted to internalize social and ecological externalities by devising ways to assess the monetary market values of relationships and stewardship. Market values, however, reflect only the *instrumental values* of social and ecological relationships; that is, they reflect their values as a means of creating economic value, and not their direct or intrinsic value in enhancing the quality of life. Reduced to their fractional economic values, the apparent values of social and ecological capital have become so diminished as to appear insignificant in relation to the values of economic capital and wealth. Thus, the economy has become driven by the pursuit of wealth, with little recognition of the real importance of relationships and ethics to overall societal well-being.

Economists have frequently relegated relationships and ethics to the role of providing the passive psychological context within which economic decisions are made. Lower prices or higher incomes allow people, as consumers or producers, to move to higher levels of overall satisfaction or utility. However, such changes in satisfaction result from changing *economic* variables—not from changes in the underlying social, ecological, or spiritual values. As an analogy, lower prices or higher incomes allow consumers to climb higher up the side of a hill called *utility*. But, the hill—a mound of social, ecological, and spiritual stones—is assumed to remain unchanged.

A better analogy may be to compare the pursuit of happiness to the act of flying an airplane. Neoclassical economics gives the pilot control of the throttle, which admittedly is a very important element of control. The throttle, like prices and income, allows the pilot to cause the plane to speed up or slow down. But the wing flaps and tail rudder, like consumer tastes and preferences, are assumed to be in fixed positions on the neoclassical economic plane. For any logical fixed position of flaps and rudder, the pilot can make the plane rise or fall by increasing or decreasing the speed of the plane. But it is difficult to change directions without being able to use the rudder to guide the plane into a turn. And it is difficult to take off or land without using the flaps, which allow the plane to remain aloft at slower speeds. It is not impossible to fly without controlling the flaps and rudder, nor is it impossible to fly faster, farther, and higher. But you cannot necessarily make the plane go where you want to go, and there is no way to come down once you get there—except with a dangerous crash landing.

An economy designed to facilitate the pursuit of happiness, rather than the accumulation of wealth, would give the pilot control of the flaps and a rudder, in addition to the throttle. It would help people make decisions designed to improve their social and ecological well-being as well as their individual material well-being. It would help people change the size and shape of the hill of utility, rather than simply climb up and down the hill. Building personal relationships and living with purpose would become important strategies for attaining and sustaining a desirable quality of life, rather than being considered as a passive psychological context within which decisions are made. People would be better able to understand and find ways to cope with the pervasive efforts of advertisers to reshape their tastes and preferences and create economic wants for which no real needs exist. People would diligently seek ways to build relationships and to act with moral courage. An economics guided by relationships and ethics, as well as income and wealth, would help people balance the economic, social, and spiritual dimensions of their lives so they could get to where they want and need to go, rather than feel compelled to go faster and higher in whatever direction the economy is headed.

Our common sense tells us that the happiness and well-being of people within a society are not determined solely by their collective wealth, but as much or more by the quality of their personal relationships and the rightness in their ethical relationships. Our common sense tells us that an economic system that compels us to pursue our narrow individual self-interest will not enhance our overall quality of life. Our common sense tells us that an economic system designed for the pursuit of happiness and sustainability must encourage us to care for each other and to care for the earth.

The most widely embraced of moral first principles is the Golden Rule, which directs us to treat other people as we would have them treat us. This principle is a fundamental part of every major enduring religion of the world and has been an important element of virtually all of the great philosophies throughout the history of humankind. The Golden Rule also is the foundational principle of sustainable development, of meeting the needs of all in the present while leaving equal or better opportunities for all in the future. Sustainability simply requires that we extend the Golden Rule across generations, treating those of future generations as we would have them treat us, if we were of their generation and they were of ours.

As Benjamin Franklin, who was a religious skeptic during much of his life, in his later years wrote, "He loves such of His creatures who love and do good for others." He wrote also, "since without virtue, man can have no happiness in this world, I firmly believe He delights to see me Virtuous because He is pleased when He sees me happy." Franklin concluded "that none but the virtuous are wise . . . that man's perfection is in his virtue."[24] The Golden Rule is not only the first principle of virtue, but also the first principle of happiness, the first principle of sustainability, and first principle of wisdom. Living with balance and harmony among the personal, interpersonal, and spiritual aspects of life is the key to happiness today and to sustainability tomorrow. The pursuit of happiness and sustainability reflects a *more enlightened* concept of self-interest—a self-interest that is firmly rooted in the wisdom of common sense.

Endnotes

1. Paul Heyne, *The Economic Way of Thinking* (Chicago: Science Research Associates, Inc., 1973).

2. *Microsoft Encarta Encyclopedia 2003*, "Enlightenment, Age of." (Redmond, Wash: Microsoft Corp., 1993–2002).

3. Luigino Bruni, *The History of Happiness in Economics* (London: Routledge, 2004).

4. V. Pareto, "Sul Fenomeno Economico, Lettera a Benedetto Croce," *Giornale degli Economisti,* 21 (1900):162, translated in Luigino Bruni, *Happiness.*

5. Philip H. Wicksteed, *The Common Sense of Political Economy* (London: Routledge, 1933, original copyright, 1910), 165.

6. Philip H. Wicksteed, *Political Economy*, 173–174.

7. V. Pareto, "Sunto di Alcuni Capitoli di un Nuovo Trattato di Economia Political del Prof. Pareto," *Giornale degli Economisti*, no.10, (1900): 223, translated in Bruni, *Happiness.*

8. Alfred Marshall, *Principles of Economics* (London: Macmillan, 1946; original copyright, 1890), 27.

9. J. R. Hicks and R. Allen, "A Reconsideration of the Theory of Value," *Economica*, no.1 (1934): 128.

10. William Hamilton, *Essays in Edinburgh Review* (Edinburgh: Edinburgh Review, 1829), 32.

11. Thomas Reid, *Works of Thomas Reid*, ed. William Hamilton, Thoemmes (Bristol, England: Continuum Press, 1863), 422.

12. *Catholic Encyclopedia*, "Philosophy of Common Sense," New Advent, http://www.newadvent.org/cathen/04167a.htm (accessed May 2005).

13. *Catholic Encyclopedia.*

14. *Microsoft Encarta Encyclopedia 2003*, "Plato: Theory of Forms."

15. Thomas Jefferson, "Nunc Dimittis on Slavery, letter to James Heaton, May 20, 1826," in *Thomas Jefferson Writings* (New York: Penguin Putnam Inc., 1984), 1516.

16. *U.S. History*, "The Declaration of Independence," U.S. History.org, http://www.ushistory.org/declaration/ (accessed June, 2005).

17. Thomas Huxley, *On A Piece Of Chalk* (New York: Scribner's, 1967; 1st Edition, 1869).

18. Albert Einstein, *Mathematics, Queen and Servant of the Sciences*, quoted by E. T. Bell, in *Men of Mathematics* (Washington, D.C.: Math Association of America, 1987; original copyright, 1937).

19. Chemistry Coach, "Common Sense, Albert Einstein," Bob Jacobs, http://www.chemistrycoach.com/common_sense.htm.

20. *The Holy Bible*, Corinthians, Chapter 13.

21. Abraham Maslow, *Motivation and Personality* (New York: Harper and Row, 1970).

22. Alexis de Tocqueville, *Democracy in America* (New York: Bantam Books, 2000; original copyright, 1835), 646–649.

23. Marshall, *Economics*, 27.

24. Benjamin Franklin, *Benjamin Franklin, The Autobiography and Other Writings* (New York: Penguin Group, Penguin Putnam Inc., 1961), 328–333.

CHAPTER THREE

THE CHALLENGE OF SUSTAINABLE DEVELOPMENT

The Rise and Fall of Capitalism

Before the Industrial Revolution, the only significant form of business organization on the European continent was the guild. Guilds were associations made up of people with common interests; they included business, charitable, religious, and social organizations. But the most important of the preindustrial organizations were merchant and craft guilds.[1] Merchant guilds were organized to protect local merchants when they traveled, to ensure common privileges among guild members, and to maintain or enhance profits of guild members. Through guild membership, merchants could buy in larger quantities, and, thus, at lower prices. Merchant guilds enhanced members' profits by prohibiting anyone other than members from selling competing products in local markets, thus limiting outside competition. Guild members collaborated in setting prices and standards of quality for their products, and members agreed on the wages to be paid to their workers.

Craft guilds included organizations of bakers, goldsmiths, tailors, weavers, and other similarly skilled workers. Craft guilds established rules much like those of merchant guilds, protecting their members against outside competition. They controlled the quality and quantity of production and collaborated in setting prices. Craft guilds attempted to allocate shares of local markets among members and discouraged individual members from attempting to increase sales at the expense of other guild members.[2]

41

Most guilds were located in towns and villages, and the sphere of economic influence of any specific guild was geographically limited. At the peak of their popularity, guilds, like today's corporations, became important political and social forces within their communities. Guilds often built town halls and market places and made large contributions to churches and civic projects.

Guilds initially benefited society, but, as they gained power, they eventually created virtual monopolies in local markets, exploiting local consumers through high prices and exploiting local workers through low wages. Consumers and workers also were deprived of opportunities for higher-quality products and better employment opportunities, which might have arisen from outside competition. By the time of the Industrial Revolution, in the eighteenth century, guilds had lost much of their initial effectiveness in serving public interests and thus had lost public support. The widespread acceptance of Adam Smith's laissez-faire economic philosophies was, in no small part, a public reaction to the previous abuse of power by merchants and crafts guilds. Society had failed to restrain the economic and political power of the guilds, and widespread corruption and exploitation were the inevitable results.

The acceptance of laissez-faire economics was also a rejection of the preindustrial economic philosophy of mercantilism. Mercantilism was championed by England, France, and other major trading nations of the world from the 1500s to the beginning of the Industrial Revolution. Under mercantilism, national governments strictly regulated economic affairs to enrich the national treasury, especially by ensuring that exports exceeded imports. Mercantilism was based on two basic beliefs. First, mercantilists believed a nation's well-being could be measured by its stock of gold and silver, and by its wealth rather than by its standard of living. Second, mercantilists believed the world had a limited supply of wealth, and so any nation could grow rich only at the expense of another. [3]

Nations that did not have gold or silver mines believed they had to rely on foreign trade for their wealth. They pursued government policies designed to create an excess of exports over imports, which they termed as a "favorable balance of trade." At that time, gold was the chief form of payment in international trade. So a nation that exported more than it imported collected the difference in gold from the importing countries, thus increasing its national wealth. Some nations prohibited the sale of gold and other precious metals to foreigners in order to maintain their national coffers. Mercantilist governments often exacted high tariffs and other restrictions on imports and encouraged the growth of domestic industries to produce for export markets. Many nations also engaged in colonization to open up new markets for exports and find new sources of raw materials.[4]

Mercantilism was an extractive and exploitive system of economics. Nations prospered at the expense of others—other nations, their colonies, and their own citizens. In their pursuit of greater wealth through trade, government officials became corrupt and ineffective in developing and implementing trade policies. Their preoccupation with exports deprived domestic workers of the full potential benefits of their own labor. Restrictions on imports deprived local citizens of the potential benefits of lower costs and higher-quality products from other countries. Mercantilism was the international equivalent of local merchant and craft guilds. Thus, the people of those times were willing to read and to believe Adam Smith when he wrote about how a merchant, when "pursuing his own interest, frequently promotes that of the society more effectually than when he really intends to promote it."[5]

The Industrial Revolution and the rise of capitalism served to repudiate the preindustrial economics of local guilds and international mercantilism. Restrictions were placed on guilds and on other forms of monopoly, and local markets were opened to competition among all existing and potential suppliers and workers. Consumers benefited from lower prices and a greater variety of products from which to choose. Entrepreneurs were encouraged and rewarded for bringing forth a constant stream of new production technologies and product innovations, leading to continual improvement in overall economic standards of living. Productive resources, including workers, were able to move freely from one geographic location to another, seeking their most productive economic employment.

Free interregional trade within nations eventually led to *freer* trade, if not free trade, among nations. Nations quickly came to understand and accept the potential economic benefits of international trade—not just in accumulating gold and silver, but also in enhancing standards of living. As Smith proclaimed, internationally free trade contributed to greater wealth among all trading nations—not simply benefiting some at the expense of others. However, nations persisted in their rights to choose their trading partners and to choose their terms of trade. Export subsidies and import restrictions remained a reality of economic life through the twentieth century, in spite of the success of international trade negotiations, as reflected in the General Agreements on Tariffs and Trade, or GATT.[6]

The tremendous societal benefits attributable to industrial capitalism are undeniable. However, its impacts have not been universally beneficial, particularly during the last half of the twentieth century. Early concerns about capitalism centered on the treatment of factory workers, including long hours, crippling physical work, dangerous working conditions, slave labor, child labor, low wages, and lack of benefits. Labor unions were authorized and encouraged by governments to help counteract the power of industrial corporations. Later, concerns shifted to the negative ecological and political impacts of industrialism, as capitalism was transformed into corporatism, as explained in Chapter 1. Today, negative evidence continues to mount, supporting the indictment of corporate organizations as having become abusive, destructive, and counterproductive to society as they have grown in economic and political power—just as the guilds did before them.[7] Corporations are the primary polluters of the natural environment and extractors of nonrenewable resources. Corporations are the primary exploiters of workers and disrupters of local economies. Transnational corporations are the primary sources of the concern held by participants of a growing number of global environmental and social justice movements. Neoclassical capitalism, like mercantilism before it, has been transformed into an exploitive, extractive, oppressive economic system, as social and moral constraints to economic growth have been systematically removed. The nature of this transition from competitive capitalism to exploitive corporatism is the subject of much of the rest of this chapter.

A strong case can be made that the societal usefulness of the industrial era has passed. Evidence continues to accumulate that any economic benefits no longer outweigh the rising ecological and social costs. The most impressive era of economic progress in the history of humanity appears to be nearing an end. All previous economic systems, including communism and socialism, eventually have become extractive and exploitive, rather than productive and supportive. They have degraded and depleted the natural and human resources upon which they were ultimately dependent. Eventually, the systems all benefited only the few at the expense of the many and benefited the present at the expense of the future. The fundamental flaw in all previous economic systems has been their intrinsic lack of sustainability. In an increasingly crowded world of scarce natural resources and destructive technologies, a new sustainable approach to economic development is imperative.

Sustainable Development

The term *sustainable development* is most commonly defined as development that meets the needs of the present while leaving equal or better opportunities for the future. This widely accepted definition of sustainability emerged in a 1987 report of the United Nations Commission on Environment and Development, commonly referred to as the *Bruntland Commission*.[8] A preceding United Nations conference, held in Stockholm in 1972, had first focused international attention on environmental issues, especially those relating to the depletion of nonrenewable resources and "transboundary pollution."[9] Although definitions of sustainability may vary with respect to specific wording, more than a decade of dialogue has led to a consensus, at least among its proponents, that sustainable development must address the needs of both present and future generations.

Some critics have interpreted *sustainable* as meaning tolerable, passable, or bearable and have suggested that "sustainable isn't good enough." However, *sustainable* also means enduring, supportable, and livable, and, thus, anything less than sustainable, quite simply, is not acceptable. Others consider the term *sustainable development* to be an oxymoron, interpreting *development* to be synonymous with *continuing growth* or *expansion*. However, the term *development* also suggests progress, advancement, or evolution rather than continuing growth, either exclusively or necessarily. So sustainable development, as a unified concept, means enduring progress, supportable advancement, or livable evolution. It means meeting the needs of people today, both individually and collectively, while preserving opportunities for those of the future.

To a society accustomed to unending promises of "more" and "better," promises of sustainability may not seem very inspiring. Sustainability suggests we may have to settle for *enough* rather than *more* because *more* may not always be possible and *less* may sometimes be better. Thus, sustainability may seem limiting, restricting, and almost pessimistic in tone. Admittedly, many people are more easily inspired by optimistic promises of unlimited and unrestricted growth in wealth and material well-being. But the fundamental flaw in today's economy and society is not a lack of quantity or quality of products, nor even a lack of income or wealth. The flaw, instead, is the inability of today's economy to sustain continuing growth in production and the inability of greater wealth to sustain greater individual or societal well-being.

Eventually, *sustainability* may be replaced with another word, some word that better identifies the more optimistic and hopeful aspects of this movement. But the movement currently is being driven by growing concerns for the long-run sustainability of today's dominant paradigm of economic development and growth. Thus, sustainability will remain the guiding transformational principle, at least until more people discover that the keys to sustainable development also are the keys to sustaining happiness and a more desirable quality of life.

Public concerns for the lack of sustainability of industrial development, as reflected in growing environmental and social justice movements, are validated by some of the most basic laws of nature. For example, the first law of thermodynamics, generally referred to as the *law of conservation of mass and energy*, might suggest that sustainability is ensured.[10] Matter and energy may change forms—matter may be converted to energy, or energy converted to matter—but the total of energy plus matter remains unchanged. Einstein's theory of relativity equation, $E = MC^2$, states that mass and energy are equivalent.

However, the second law of thermodynamics states that each time the form of energy and matter is changed, and each time matter is converted to energy or energy to matter, some of the "usefulness," the ability of energy to do "work," is lost.[11] This loss in usefulness is reflected in the concept of entropy, "the ultimate state reached in degradation of matter and energy; a state of inert uniformity of component elements; absence of form, pattern, hierarchy, or differentiation."[12] The second law of thermodynamics suggests an inevitable tendency to progress toward entropy and thus suggests that sustainability is impossible.

However, the first and second laws of thermodynamics relate to "closed systems," systems for which nothing is lost to the outside and nothing comes in from the outside. With closed systems, entropy *is* inevitable. Thus, the possibility of long-run sustainability of life on Earth is a consequence only of the earth's openness to the inflow of energy from the sun. Sustainable development is possible only because the earth, as an open system, is capable of capturing and storing sufficient amounts of new *useful* solar energy to offset the declining usefulness associated with the inevitable tendency toward entropy.

This dependence of life on Earth upon solar energy implies that sustainable development is dependent upon living systems. Only living organisms are capable of capturing energy from the sun, converting it, and concentrating it into more diverse and useful forms and, thus, are capable of offsetting the inevitable degradation of usefulness of energy and matter associated with nonliving systems. Scientists have experimented with synthetic solar energy collectors of various types, and energy captured from wind and water are indirect forms of solar energy. However, the leaves of living plants remain the only significant, practical collectors and concentrators of sufficient quantities of solar energy to support the earth's current living systems, including humanity. Plants depend upon other living organisms, and other living organisms depend upon plants. Thus, sustainable development is dependent upon the sustainability of living systems, including microorganisms, insects, plants, animals, and people.

The natural tendency of living systems is toward diversity in structure, form, hierarchy, and pattern—away from entropy. Natural ecosystems evolve through successive stages of increasing diversity until they achieve relatively stable "climax communities," made up of diverse but mutually supportive biological elements.[13] A sustainable human society must conserve, recycle, and reuse materials and energy if it is to succeed at slowing, rather than accelerating, the natural degeneration toward entropy. And ultimately, human population and per capita consumption must accommodate the "carrying capacity" of the earth.[14] But the global carrying capacity depends at least as much on our effective use of living systems to capture, concentrate, and store solar energy as on our efficient use of the stocks of energy and material with which the earth is endowed. Sustainable development is a living process.

A Question of Boundaries

Cells are the fundamental structural unit of all living organisms. All living cells are surrounded by membranes, which separate the water-rich cytoplasm inside the cells from their significantly different outside environments. These membranes, which define the boundaries of each cell, are semipermeable—they let some things pass through but keep some things in and some things out.[15] Cells that are permeable or nonpermeable, rather than semipermeable, cannot support life. If a cell did not keep anything out or in, its inside would become like the outside. It would become indistinguishable from its nonliving environment; it would die. If a cell did not let anything out or in, it would become isolated from its environment; it would die from lack of nourishment. If the walls of living cells were not semipermeable, they would not be able to retain moisture or minerals; they would not be able to metabolize food, release energy, eliminate waste—or live.

The natural devolution toward entropy results from the natural tendency of energy to disperse or to become less concentrated.[16] For example, the natural tendency of air in a balloon is to escape—to move from an area of higher concentration to an area of lower concentration. As the air escapes, energy is released, until the energy stored in the balloon is depleted. Energy can be restored by reinflating the balloon. However, the restoration process uses energy to reconcentrate energy and, in most cases, energy to reconstruct new membranes to hold the reconcentrated energy. All living organisms are made up of biological "balloons," called *cells*, within which solar energy is concentrated and stored. All living organisms, like living cells, are defined by selective, semipermeable boundaries.

The boundaries that define living organisms include such things as skin, bark, leaf surface, and scales. As with cells, the boundaries of organisms must be semipermeable or selective with respect to what they allow to pass through and what they keep in or keep out. The human skin, for example, protects the body against all sorts of physical and biological threats, but it must also be permeable to allow for respiration and perspiration. The human skin also has openings for the selective intake of food and selective elimination of wastes. The leaves of plants exchange oxygen and carbon with the air, plant roots exchange their stored nutrients for nutrients needed from the soil, and the boundaries of leaves and roots are very selective in what they let in and let out. The boundaries of living systems are necessary because living systems must be selective regarding what they take in and let out.

The sustainability of living things, such as plants, animals, insects, and bacteria, arises from their ability to renew, regenerate, and reproduce. To accomplish this miracle of life, organisms must create new forms and structures, which are defined by newly created boundaries. The natural tendency of living systems to progress toward biological diversity implies a tendency toward the production of more boundaries—more species, more varieties, more variations of organisms. For example, after a field has been stripped of all vegetation, the first life to return will likely be a single species, or perhaps a few species of weeds. The weeds will mature, reproduce, and die, but their rotted residue will create a favorable environment for other plant species. As the succession of regeneration processes continues, an increasing diversity of plant species will create a favorable habitat for an increasing diversity of microorganisms, insects, and animals, until a mutually supportive community of organisms is achieved. This increasing diversity of form and structure is defined by a multitude of new boundaries.

On the other hand, the natural tendency of *nonliving* things to degrade toward entropy implies a tendency toward the dissolution or destruction of boundaries. Again, the ultimate state of entropy is characterized as "a state of inert uniformity . . . absence of form, pattern, hierarchy, or differentiation," meaning an absence of boundaries. The reference to "degradation of energy and matter" in the definition of entropy relates to the fact that boundaries are destroyed as energy is released from matter and new energy is required to rebuild boundaries and reconcentrate energy in the form of new matter defined by boundaries. The energy required to rebuild boundaries and reconcentrate energy is not useful energy, in the sense that it is not available to do *work*. Therefore, each transformation from matter to energy and from energy back to matter leaves systems with less ability to support useful work than before—thus, the tendency toward entropy.

This important concept may be clearer when related to everyday events. For example, when an oak log is burned, energy is released from the wood in the form of heat and the structure of the wood is turned to ashes. The boundaries, or cell walls, that once defined the structure of the log are destroyed to the release of energy. The thermal energy released is made available for some useful purpose, such as warming a human body. The released energy eventually may be reconcentrated to form new matter, but some useful energy inevitably will be lost in the transformation process. In this case, the energy released is stored solar energy. The human body converts food to energy by a similar process, digesting or breaking down the physical structures of the things we eat. Some of the usefulness of food energy inevitably is lost through digestion, excretion, and reconstitution processes. In both cases, however, the energy consumed is renewable because new energy can be collected from the sun to build new boundaries, creating new living organisms, which can concentrate and store new energy for later use.

Living organisms are uniquely capable of renewal, reproduction, and regeneration, but only because they can extract energy from *non-living* things, including dead things that were once living. Lacking the daily infusion of new energy from the sun, all systems, living and non-living, eventually would lose their ability to restore boundaries and reconcentrate energy into matter and, thus, would slowly lose their ability to store and release the energy necessary for new life.

Contrasts between living and nonliving systems, and between sustainability and entropy are equally relevant to cultural, political, and economic systems. The dissolution of boundaries among cultures increases the efficiency of social and political processes, releasing the energy previously bound by the constraints of cultural differences. The dissolution of political boundaries, likewise, releases the energy bound up by conflicting laws, regulations, and other political constraints. The dissolution of economic boundaries removes constraints to economic specialization, standardization, and consolidation, thus allowing industrialization and maximization of productivity and economic efficiency. Thus, strong political and economic incentives exist to remove all cultural and social boundaries.

Agriculture, being a biological production process, provides a convenient illustration of this general principle. In farming, tremendous gains in productivity and economic efficiency have been achieved through the removal of boundaries. The diversity of crops and livestock enterprises that once defined the structure of typical family farms was abandoned to achieve greater specialization. Farmers then removed fences that had separated their fields, as they moved toward more mechanized and standardized systems of farming. Some farms specialized in livestock, others in crops, then single species of livestock or single crops, and even single phases of crop or livestock production—homogeneous monocultures. The landscapes of many farms were left without form, pattern, hierarchy, or differentiation.

These new, "more efficient" farming methods also allowed farms to become larger, through consolidation, thus removing the boundaries of ownership and identity that once defined farms within communities. As farms became larger, farmers reached beyond the boundaries of the local communities, marketing their products and purchasing their inputs outside their local communities because it was more efficient to do so. The economic and social boundaries of rural communities became blurred, and, in some cases, communities completely lost any meaningful identity.

This transformation, this industrialization of agriculture, resulted in tremendous gains in agricultural productivity and economic efficiency. The number of farmers in the United States dropped from more than 6 million during the 1930s to about 2 million in 2000,[17] whereas the U.S. population more than doubled[18] and the percentage of consumers' disposable incomes spent for food declined from approximately 20% to 10%.[19] The biological, economic, and social boundaries that once defined different fields, enterprises, farms, and communities were removed. Stored energy was released, allowing increases in productivity, but nothing was done to renew or restore the boundaries or to reconcentrate and store new energy for the future. Today, the sustainability of American agriculture is in doubt. To understand the concept of sustainability, we ask, "How will those of future generations meet their energy needs, once the usefulness of previously stored energy—in fossil fuels, uranium, hydrogen, and so on—has been depleted?" The industrial model of development has no answer for this question.

Industrial development is a *dead paradigm*. It provides a very efficient means of extracting stored energy—from land, water, air, plants, animals, and people; however, it must destroy boundaries in order to achieve its efficiency. Industrial development provides no incentive for restoring boundaries, reconcentrating energy, or recreating new matter and thus provides no means of renewing energy resources for the future. Incentives for investments in an industrial economy are limited to investments in the means of extraction and exploitation, not investments in resources for the future. In economics, all investments are evaluated in terms of their "net present value," not their value to future generations.

The amounts of fossil energy being used up by today's industrial systems far exceed the amounts of useful solar energy being captured from the sun. For example, the fundamental purpose of agriculture is to capture solar energy and transform it into food and fiber for human use. However, David and Marcia Pimentel estimate that America's industrialized food system consumes ten calories of fossil energy for every calorie of food energy it produces.[20] This industrialized system, like all such systems, inherently tends to progress toward entropy, that state of inert uniformity, without form, pattern, hierarchy, or differentiation. A lifeless desert is a system about as close to entropy as most people have seen here on Earth, whereas photos of the landscapes of the moon, Mars, and Venus reflect systems that appear to be even nearer to ecological entropy. Such would be the ultimate result of industrial development here on Earth, if we do nothing to stop it. An industrial system of economic development quite simply is not sustainable.

A Matter of Relationships

Semipermeable boundaries allow for *interdependent* relationships among living organisms. The dynamics of interdependence are fundamentally different from those of either *dependence* or *independence*. The word *dependence* connotes a parasitic relationship between two organisms—one feeds off the other. The dependent organism lives by exploiting its host, and thus the host organism's boundaries must be permeable to the parasite, leaving it vulnerable to exploitation. *Independence* connotes an absence of relationships—one doesn't need the other. An independent organism's boundaries are impermeable; it is self-sufficient and thus invulnerable. Interdependent relationships are imbued with mutual dependence or, more accurately, as symbiotic relationships between two potentially independent organisms, each benefiting from the other. An interdependent organism's boundaries must be semipermeable; it accepts some level of vulnerability in return for potential gains from relationships with others.

With respect to human relationships, interdependence extends the concept of semipermeable boundaries to matters of choice. [21] An independent person's boundaries are impermeable, accepting nothing from others and giving nothing to others—by choice. A dependent person's boundaries are permeable, as a matter of necessity—not by choice. Presumably, a person would not willingly leave himself or herself open and vulnerable to exploitation. In the case of interdependent relationships, both persons' boundaries are semipermeable and each relates to the other by choice, not necessity. The boundaries between two interdependent individuals are selective or semipermeable, as a matter of conscious choice.

These same basic concepts of dependence, independence, and interdependence relate to relationships among collections of individuals—among families, communities, regions, states, or nations, as well as among individuals. Interdependent relationships provide the conceptual foundation for sustainable development, in the sense that the health, survival, and sustainability of all living organizations—including economies and societies—depend upon mutually supportive relationships.

Interdependent relationships create opportunities for synergy, in which the whole of something becomes greater than the sum of its parts. The whole of a living organization is something more than the sum of its individual parts. This *something more* in the whole arises from the nature of relationships among its parts. Interdependent relationships, across healthy boundaries, allow organizations to maintain their health and diversity and to renew, reproduce, and evolve, thereby sustaining themselves over time. Dependent relationships within organizations are exploitive; one gains at the expense of another. Independent relationships within organizations are barren; nothing is gained and nothing is lost, except what is lost to the inevitable progression toward entropy. Interdependent relationships are holistic and synergistic; they renew life and maintain diversity. To maintain interdependent relationships, people must make conscious, purposeful choices that will lead to mutually beneficial outcomes. Living organisms and organizations can do useful work without exploiting, degrading, or depleting and without being exploited, degraded, or depleted. Sustainable organizations extract usefulness or utility from both living and nonliving resources to meet the needs of the present, but, at the same time, they are able to renew, restore, and regenerate the resources needed to meet the needs of the future. People within sustainable organizations must make conscious, purposeful decisions to maintain mutually beneficial relationships.

An economy is a living organization, or *organism*, defined as "a complex structure of interrelated elements whose relationships and properties are largely determined by their function within the whole."[22] The generic purpose of any economy is to provide a means of facilitating functional relationships among people and between people and their environment. Economic relationships, as with organizational relationships, can be dependent and thus exploitive, or can be interdependent and thus synergistic.

The natural tendency of economic industrialization, however, is to move toward exploitation—toward entropy. In the early stages of industrialization, relationships between the industrial organization and its workers and its customers may be interdependent and synergistic. Each is free to associate or not associate with the other. Such is the assumed nature of relationships in the purely competitive model of economic capitalism, as rooted in Adam Smith's, 1776 *Wealth of Nations.*[23] A truly competitive capitalistic economy is synergistic by design. Mutually beneficial relationships among buyers and sellers are ensured, but only so long as no buyer or seller has the ability to exploit any other buyer or seller.

Unfortunately, capitalism has a built-in incentive for ever-greater production and consumption, in the sense that the economic wants of humans are insatiable—more is always preferred to less.[24] This need for continuing growth in productivity, coupled with greater economic efficiencies of scale and size,[25] inevitably leads toward larger business organizations and greater concentrations of economic power among fewer, larger organizations. As businesses become larger, they require more capital and increasingly choose the corporate form of organization in order to secure the capital necessary to maintain growth. As explained in Chapter 1, this corporatization of organizations separates the function of management from the social and ethical responsibilities of ownership, thus freeing the corporation from any internal constraints on profits and growth. Freed from internal constraints, the corporation automatically sets about removing all external social and political constraints or boundaries as well. Such is the nature of the large publicly held corporations of today.

At some point in this process, it becomes far easier for a corporation to hire another acceptable worker than for a worker to find another acceptable job. The worker becomes dependent upon the corporation and thus becomes subject to exploitation. In addition, at some point, it becomes far easier for the corporate firm to find another customer than for the customer to find an acceptable alternative product. The customer becomes dependent upon the corporation and thus becomes subject to exploitation. At this point, economic relationships become dependent, rather than interdependent, thus accelerating the tendency toward socioeconomic entropy.

Clearly, the corporate organization is dependent on its workers and customers in total. But the corporation is not dependent on any particular worker or customer, and thus it has the power to dominate and exploit individuals. Unfortunately, corporations frequently find it more profitable to exploit their workers and customers, rather than to maintain synergistic relationships, at least in the short run. Because the lifeblood of corporate management is economic progress from fiscal quarter to quarter, rather than from generation to generation, the behavior of corporations rarely reflects long-run considerations, as will be explained further in Chapter 4. The uniquely human sense of moral and ethical responsibility for the equitable treatment of other people is essentially lost once the ownership of an organization is separated from its management. The corporation becomes a parasite; its workers and customers become its hosts. Thus, corporate-based capitalism invariably leads to the exploitation and degradation of human resources.

The only effective constraint to corporate exploitation is for workers and consumers to act collectively and thereby equalize their powers with the power of the corporation. They can accomplish collective action either by forming unions to bargain for wages and prices or by supporting laws and government regulations that restrain corporate consolidation, thus maintaining competition in the marketplace. Lacking the willingness or ability on the part of the people to claim this power of the collective, however, corporate industrialization inevitably leads to exploitation of both workers and consumers.

This drive toward exploitation is even more direct and evident in relationships between the industrial organization and the natural environment. The industrial paradigm was designed explicitly to extract economic value and wealth from an abundant stock of natural resources. In fact, the history of industrialization is rooted in the discovery of the means of harnessing fossil energy. The steam engine came first, powered first by wood but later by coal. The internal combustion engine came later, fueled by petroleum—diesel and gasoline. Thus, industrialization has been powered by natural resources extracted from the earth, with little if any attention given to the renewal and regeneration of energy resources for future generations. Even today, the most popular "fuels of the future" seem to be other natural resources, such as hydrogen, which are more plentiful, but are still nonrenewable.[26]

The relationship between the industrial corporation and the earth is almost purely exploitive. The industrial organization clearly depends upon a finite natural resource base, just as it depends on its workers and customers. However, nature has no means of protecting itself from exploitation, at least not in the short run. Minerals are mined from the earth, their usefulness extracted, and the waste left on the surface to foul the once-natural conditions. Petroleum is pumped from the earth and its energy is extracted, thereby releasing its wastes to pollute both air and water. Forests are harvested for lumber, stripping the land of its ability to absorb water and retain topsoil and leaving bare earth on which nature struggles to restore life. Once-fertile farm-lands are mined of their nutrients to produce food and fiber, making agricultural productivity dependent on nonrenewable chemical inputs and leaving the long-run ability of humanity to feed itself increasingly in doubt.[27]

Historically, the primary restraint on the economic exploitation of nature has been a sense of human responsibility for stewardship of the earth. Today, in an economy dominated by large, publicly owned cor-porations, there is little investor tolerance of environmental steward-ship whenever it conflicts with the corporate bottom line—as is the case with extractive production processes. Thus, the only effective constraint to corporate exploitation of the environment is for people to act collectively, through laws and government regulations designed to protect the environment. In a society conditioned to believe that their quality of life depends on unending economic growth, the ethic of stewardship has struggled to survive. Lacking a global commitment to environmental stewardship, a corporately dominated, industrial glo-bal economy will continue its relentless exploitation of the natural environment—again, leading inexorably toward entropy.

Sustainable development depends upon the creation of a new glo-bal culture, committed to caring for each other and caring for the earth. Sustainable development depends on a commitment to main-taining interdependent relationships with each other and with the earth—relationships that renew, restore, and enhance, rather than exploit and degrade. Sustainable development depends on the redis-covery of the potential value of positive relationships, not only to offset the natural tendency to move toward entropy but also to sustain a more desirable quality of life.

Conflicts, Consequences, and Challenges

Sustainable development cannot be achieved by fine-tuning indus-trial development, by improving the efficiency of resource use, by reducing wastes, by substituting resources, or by developing new technologies. Such strategies may slow, but cannot stop, the inevita-ble course toward entropy. The fundamental principles of industrial development are in direct conflict with the principles of sustainable economic development.

Industrial development and economic capitalism are inseparable aspects of the same whole. Adam Smith, in *Wealth of Nations*, provided the common conceptual foundation for both industrialism and capitalism. Smith wrote of the tremendous potential gains in productivity associated with specialization. He suggested that three men, specializing in specific functions and working together, could produce "two hundred and forty times" as many straight pins as could the same number of men working independently.[28] One would cut the wire, another would sharpen the point, and the other would make the head. The gains were the result of the specialization of each worker as he or she focused on a single narrowly defined activity and thus became skilled and efficient through practice and repetition.

Specialization of function, however, requires standardization of process. Each specialized worker on an assembly line, whether for straight pins or automobiles, must perform a specific task within the standardized process so that the next specialized worker will also have a specific task to perform. Only through standardization can a group of specialists produce a final product of uniform quality. Specialization and standardization greatly simplify the production process, thus making possible the consolidation of decision making and control, resulting in larger production units. The ultimate gains from industrialization, specialization, standardization, and consolidation of control arise from economies of scale. The reduced costs associated with larger scales of operation arise directly from the economic efficiencies of specialization, standardization, and consolidation of control.

Specialization, standardization, and consolidation of control are the cornerstones of the industrial paradigm of development. Smith's conception of a competitive economy, what Marx would later label as *capitalism*, provided the means by which a specialized, standardized, hierarchically controlled economy could be effectively coordinated. A competitive, free market economy, Smith claimed, was the most efficient means of realizing the undeniable potential benefits of industrialization. Yet Smith was not oblivious to the risks of industrialization. He warned of the dangers of a potential de-skilling of the workforce and a concentration of power by corporations and monopolies. But in the early days of the Industrial Revolution, these seemed but distant possibilities; by contrast, the potential gains from industrialization were immediate. Concerns over the potential negative consequences of industrialization were deferred.

Now, however, the time to be concerned with the negative consequences of industrialization is upon us. Industrialization must destroy boundaries to extract usefulness, but sustainable development must rebuild boundaries to renew usefulness. Industrial development demands specialization but sustainable development requires holism. Industrial development demands standardization, but sustainable development requires diversity. Industrial development requires consolidation of control and creates dependent relationships of necessity, but sustainable development empowers individuals, thus creating interdependence relationships of choice. Industrial development is inherently and inevitably in conflict with sustainable development.

This is the nature of the challenge. The old paradigm of industrial economic development must be replaced with a new paradigm of sustainable economic development. The new sustainable economy must provide a desirable quality of life for those of the present while leaving equal or better opportunities for those of the future. It must be economically viable, socially just, and ecologically whole. The new sustainable economy must support mutually beneficial relationships among people and between people and their natural environment, by maintaining healthy boundaries. The new economy must allow us to take care of ourselves, but also to care for others, including those of the future, as we would have them care for us. It's about sustainability, but also about human happiness and quality of life.

Endnotes

1. *Microsoft Encarta Encyclopedia 2003*, "Guilds." (Redmond, Wash.: Microsoft Corp., 1993–2002).

2. Robert Lekachman, "Medieval Economics," in *A History of Economic Ideas* (New York: Harper and Row Publishers, 1959).

3. Adam Smith, *Wealth of Nations* (Amherst, N.Y.: Prometheus Books, 1991, original copyright, 1776), 326–347.

4. Robert Lekachman, "Merchantilism," *Economic Ideas*.

5. Smith, *Wealth of Nations*, 352.

6. *World Book, 2002 Standard Edition*, "General Agreements on Tariff and Trade." (Chicago: World Book, Inc. 2001).

7. David Korten, *When Corporations Rule the World* (West Hartford, Conn.: Kumarian Press, 1995).

8. The World Commission on Environment and Development, *Our Common Future*, ed. Gro Bruntland (Oxford, England: Oxford University Press, 1987).

9. Donella H. Meadows, *Limits to Growth* (New York: Penguin Books, 1977).

10. *Encarta*, "Conservation Laws."

11. *World Book*, "Thermodynamics."

12. *Webster's New International Dictionary*, Unabridged, "Entropy." (Springfield, Mass., Merriam-Webster, 1993).

13. *World Book*, "Succession."

14. William E. Rees and Mathis Wackernagel, *Our Ecological Footprint, Reducing Human Impact on Earth* (Gabriola Island, British Columbia: New Society Publishers, 1996).

15. *World Book*, "Osmosis."

16. Frank L. Lambert, "Disorder—A Cracked Crutch for Supporting Entropy Discussions," *Journal of Chemical Education*, 79, no. 2 (2002): 187.

17. United States Department of Agriculture, National Agricultural Statistics Service, *Farms and Land in Farms*, February 2002 (Washington, DC: U.S. Government Printing Office, 2002).

18. United States Census Bureau, Population Division, *2000 Census of Population and Housing* (Washington, D.C.: U.S. Government Printing Office, 2002).

19. United States Department of Agriculture, Economic Research Service, *Food Cost Review*, 1996, Agricultural Economics Report 761, ed. Howard Elitzak (Washington, D.C.: U.S. Government Printing Office, 1996).

20. David Pimentel and Marcia Pimentel, eds., *Food, Energy, and Society* (Boulder, Colo.: University of Colorado Press, 1996).

21. Stephen Covey, *Seven Habits of Highly Effective People* (New York: Simon and Schuster, 1989).

22. *Webster's New Collegiate Dictionary*, 1973 edition, "Organism."

23. Smith, *Wealth of Nations*, 20.

24. C. E. Ferguson, *Microeconomic Theory* (Homewood, Ill.: Richard D. Irwin, Inc., 1969), 14.

25. Karl E. Case and Ray E. Fair, *Principles of Economics* (Englewood Cliffs, N.J.: Prentice Hall, Inc., 1989), 259–261.

26. Paul Hawkens, Amory Lovins, and L. Hunter Lovins, *Natural Capitalism* (Boston: Back Bay Books, Little, Brown, and Company, 1999), 22–47.

27. Worldwatch Institute, *State of the World 2004* (New York: W. W. Norton and Company, 2004).

28. Smith, *Wealth of Nations*, 11.

CHAPTER FOUR

THE INADEQUACIES OF ECOLOGICAL ECONOMICS

The Economists' Response to Sustainability

In addressing issues of ecological integrity, neoclassical economists have argued that markets are capable of allocating resource use over time, that market incentives will ensure adequate resources for future generations, and that free markets can therefore ensure long-term sustainability.[1] As nonrenewable resources become increasingly scarce, their prices in the marketplace will rise, and higher prices will limit current consumption as well as provide motives and create opportunities for the development of substitutes. We will never completely run out of anything of value, they say, because prices will continue to rise until increasingly scarce commodities become economically unattractive relative to substitutes that provide the same basic benefit at a lower cost. For example, industrial economies are heavily dependent on fossil fuels because fossil fuels are abundant in supply and cheap in cost, at least relative to alternative sources of energy. As fossil energy reserves are depleted, prices will rise, utilization will decline, and energy from alternative sources will become economically competitive. So the neoclassical answer to questions of sustainability is simply to let the markets work.

It's true that economics deals specifically with the management of scarcity. Resources have no economic value unless or until they become scarce and their economic value is directly related to the degree of scarcity. As a result, however, economics provides no guidance in the use of resources until supplies are depleted or quality is

61

degraded to a point at which the resource becomes scarce. In addition, the economic rate of the use of scarce resources is determined by their value to individuals, their private value—not their value to society in general, and certainly not their value to future generations. For example, clean air and water had no economic value until water and air became sufficiently polluted as to make clean air and clean water scarce. Even today, direct payments for water are mostly payments for the convenience of having water when and where we want it rather than payments for the water itself, although the recent sales of bottled water indicate an increasing scarcity of safe drinking water. Current prices and utilization of fossil fuels reflect only their current contribution to economic productivity, not the social and political costs of maintaining access to known oil and gas reserves or the potential costs of alternative energy to future generations. Certainly, expected future costs and returns affect current supply and demand. But the economic planning horizon is simply too short to address issues of ecological sustainability.

In addressing issues of social equity, some economists have proposed calculating the *marginal utility* of consumers' incomes, that is, the satisfaction gained from additional increments of income. Consumers with lower incomes presumably would receive greater benefits from a given income increment. Differences in marginal benefits associated with different levels of income could be given specific consideration in optimizing social welfare.[2] In addition to obvious measurement problems, this approach ignores potential impacts of changes in *relative* incomes—the rise or fall of one person's income relative to others' incomes. Social welfare is not simply the summation of individuals' welfare—relationships matter. Neoclassical economics simply does not address the value of personal relationships, which constitutes the essence of social well-being. In reality, economists rarely go beyond simply calculating net economic gains or losses in calculating social welfare. If the gains of those who gain are greater than the losses of those who lose, the welfare of society is assumed to have increased.

A new group of economists, calling themselves *ecological economists*, admits that *private* costs and returns may be different from *social* costs and returns, and thus, maximizing economic wealth or growth may not result in maximum social welfare in the long run.[3] They attempt to deal with both social and ecological issues by internalizing them—by bringing them into the private economy. They propose to internalize environmental costs and benefits by calculating their economic value and then using public policy to impose taxes or other economic penalties to reflect environmental costs and to offer subsidies or other economic incentives to reflect environmental benefits. Some have proposed buying and selling pollution rights, allowing those who degrade the environment to pay the economic cost of their degradation and those who protect or enhance the environment to receive an economic reward.[4] Internalizing costs at least places some value on the natural environment and society, and the concept has thus gained widespread support among advocates of ecological economics. However, irresolvable social and ethical problems arise when social and ecological costs and benefits are brought into the private economy. Once ecological and social resources have been assigned an economic value, the markets will allocate them to their most profitable alternative uses, without consideration of the full social or ethical implications of how they are allocated.

The inadequacies of neoclassical economics in addressing issues of sustainability are intrinsic and systemic and cannot be solved by tinkering around at the edges of the discipline. Sustainability is rooted in the concept of intergenerational equity, to meet the needs of both present and future, equitably. Economics is rooted in the present—the individual here and now. In neoclassical economics, individual self-interests are pursued by seeking pleasure and avoiding pain. One simply cannot realize sensory pleasure or pain as a consequence of their consideration, or lack of consideration, of the well-being of future generations. Ecological economics does not resolve this inherent inadequacy by substituting dollar values for social and ethical values. If economics is to address the most fundamental issues of sustainability, economists must venture beyond the individual market economy.

Economic Planning Horizons

Many competent and caring economists have spent their careers trying to help their discipline better address the most important ecological and social issues of their times. The work of these dedicated professionals—welfare economists, ecological economists, and others—cannot be lightly dismissed. Although their work may have fallen short of fulfilling its suggested purpose, it's important to understand where their work fits within the broader framework of a unified theory of economic sustainability.

During the early 1970s, which were the early days of the environmental movement, a small group of economists and ecologists came to the realization that their respective disciplines seemed to be pulling society in opposite directions. Economics was promoting maximum growth, whereas ecology was warning of the natural limits to growth. In an effort to bridge a growing gap between the two disciplines, the two groups began a series of meetings, which in 1988 led to the formation of the International Society for Ecological Economics.[5]

Ecological economics reflects an attempt to bring together analyses from the economic, social, and natural sciences to respond more effectively to growing worldwide concerns for the sustainability of current approaches to resource development. It's important to recognize, however, that "ecological economics does not constitute a new single unified theory for or of sustainable development."[6] It represents instead a new approach to the *practice* of economics.

First, a major justification for a new approach to the practice of economics is based on the realization that markets are fundamentally incapable of allocating resources efficiently between current and future generations. Market values are inherently *present* values. In considering the future, investors rely on the concept of discounting in order to estimate the "net present value" of expected future costs and returns.[7,8] Discounting is the inverse of compounding. In compounding, interest earned on an investment is added to the principal after a specific period of time, and interest for the next period is earned on the principal plus the earned interest, which again is added to the principal, and so on. Compounding tells the investor how much an investment made today will be worth at some time in the future, and discounting tells the investor the present value of a future payoff or return. The larger the interest rate or discount rate, the greater the difference between present and future values, and the greater the value placed on the present relative to the future.

Market-derived interest rates are a major component of discount rates because they represent returns that investors must forgo when they invest in a risky venture instead of simply allowing their money to earn interest in an insured account. Market interest rates reflect the scarcity of money: the willingness of savers to lend relative to the willingness of investors to borrow. Lenders must be rewarded for deferring the use of their money, but investors reward lenders for their sacrifice because they expect to earn more than enough by using the money. The fact that loans may be paid back with *cheaper* dollars, after adjusting for currency inflation rates, also is reflected in market interest rates. Furthermore, individual risk preferences and assessments of risks may have significant impacts on the discount rate that an individual investor finds acceptable.

With the exception of the high-inflation period of the 1970s, market interest rates for long-term government securities have generally averaged between 5% and 8% over the past several decades.[9] So a *discount* rate of 7% is both reasonable and convenient in illustrating the affects of time on market-derived values. With a *compound* interest rate of 7%, an investment will double in value over a period of approximately 10 years. So a $2 payoff made 10 years from now is worth only $1 today. Discounting future costs uses the same process to answer a different question: how much money would need to be set aside today to meet a future cost commitment. At a 7% interest rate, $1 set aside today will pay off a $2 commitment 10 years from now. So markets generally place a significant premium on the present relative to the future.

When net present values are discounted over the multigenerational long run, say, over 200 to 300 years, it becomes readily apparent why economic decisions seem to reflect little concern for future generations. For example, if a decision today is expected to generate a benefit of $1 million but the payoff will not come until 200 years in the future, the discounted net present value is only $1.34 using a 7% discount rate. Or if a decision will result in a $1 billion cost, but the cost will not be incurred until 300 years in the future, the discounted net present value of the cost is only $1.54. So it's easy to understand why economic investments seemingly give little consideration for the multigenerational long run. Something expected to happen a couple hundred years in the future really doesn't matter much, at least not economically, no matter how large the expected future costs or returns.

The economic logic supporting this result is quite clear. Markets value things only to the extent that they contribute to the narrow self-interest of individuals. Individuals' self-interests determine the supply and demand for money and thus largely determine the discount rates used in discounting future returns to net present values. Obviously, individual self-interests must be realized during the lifetime of the individual. Economic self-interest places significant values on costs and returns expected within a decade because at any point in time most investors expect to live at least that long. Economics places much less value on benefits or costs deferred between a decade and a normal life span because most investors have less than a full lifetime left to live. Economics values the future still less during the lifetimes of our children or grandchildren because the economic benefits we receive individually in these instances will be received indirectly through our relationships with our children and grandchildren. With a 7% personal discount rate, for example, the net present value of a future return is only 1% of it's future value when the total payoff is deferred for 70 years. Beyond the average lifespans of our children and grandchildren, the present value of future costs and returns become economically insignificant.

Business investors also must discount future returns to account for risks, such as technological obsolescence, shifting consumer preferences, increased competition, and rising input costs. Each additional risk adds to the discount rate and reduces net present value.[10] At a discount rate of 20%, it takes a $6 payoff 10 years from now to be worth $1 today. In reality, effective economic planning horizons for businesses rarely span more than a decade. Nothing that might happen beyond a decade from now is considered particularly significant to today's business decisions.

The Native American Great Law of Peace exhorts leaders and elders to evaluate each decision with consideration given to its potential impacts for those of seven generations in the future.[11] Economic sustainability requires planning horizons that span *all* generations in the future. However, a planning horizon that spans even seven generations makes no neoclassical economic sense. An economics that addresses sustainability must look beyond market-derived concepts of time-related values.

Sustainable Social Discount Rates

As early as the 1920s, some economists recognized the inadequacies of markets in allocating resources for the long-term benefit of society.[12] They suggested substituting "social discount rates" for market discount rates to reflect more accurately the true societal value of time.[13] Social discount rates could be imposed on decision makers through public policy. Although their suggestions have been largely ignored, social discount rates are still worthy of consideration.

The appropriate social discount rate for decisions related to sustainability logically would be zero, since benefits and costs of current and future generations are to be valued equally. This does not suggest the current generation must refrain from using nonrenewable resources, or even refrain from consuming total stocks of some resources. We have every right to meet our needs, as long as we ensure, to the best of our ability, that future generations will have an equal opportunity to meet their needs as well. One generation should not have to sacrifice so that another might prosper; each should have an *equal* opportunity to succeed.

However, if we are to err, we should err on the side of leaving more opportunities for the future rather than less. The social and ecological systems of the earth are living systems, and for living systems, errors tend to multiply with time and may not be reversible. A 1992 United Nations declaration stated this "precautionary principle" as follows, "Where there are threats of serious and irreversible damage, lack of full scientific certainty should not be used as a reason for postponing cost effective measures to prevent environmental degradation."[14] Thus, a lack of scientific proof regarding the nature or magnitude of future ecological or social costs should not be used as a reason for discounting the future relative to the present, at least not whenever potential negative consequences are large and possibly irreversible.

A society truly committed to sustainable development could simply choose to use a social discount rate of *zero* for all public investment decisions made by government. By placing no premium on current consumption and thus placing no priority on current resource use, no economic incentive would exist to value the present over the future in implementing public policies and thereby no preference would be given to the current generation over future generations. Such an approach would essentially remove public investments from the realm of economics, which, until now, American society has not been willing to consider.

Questions of appropriate social discount rates become far more complex when evaluating investments that are best made in the private sector, that is, through markets rather than government policies. The central planning of an entire economy has been shown to be an unworkable, unacceptable approach to allocating most resources. Thus, the vast majority of all investment decisions must remain in the private sector. Any attempt to calculate appropriate private discount rates to guide the optimal allocation of nonrenewable resources among generations would likely result in frustration and bureaucratic waste. The challenge would be similar to that of the central planning of an entire economy—tempting in theory but unworkable in practice.

Another alternative would be to limit nonzero social discount rates to use in allocating nonrenewable resources. Conceivably, severance taxes, similar to those currently levied on coal, oil, and minerals in some states, could be calculated for each nonrenewable resource. A severance tax that would just offset the time-value component of the market discount rate for each resource theoretically would equalize the economic incentive for the use of nonrenewable resources among current and future generations. But calculating such a tax would require knowledge of the socially optimum use pattern over time for the remaining stock of each nonrenewable resource. Uncertainty regarding current stocks of nonrenewable resources, future technological efficiencies, future substitutes for existing resources, future consumer needs and preferences, and a host of other relevant factors make the calculation of optimal social discount rates for nonrenewable resources impractical, if not impossible.

A more logical alternative might be to tax each nonrenewable resource just enough to encourage the development of renewable alternatives. Eventually, all nonrenewable resources would be either depleted or abandoned—regardless of how long it took. Thus, each generation might logically assume an obligation to those of the future to do their part in encouraging the development of renewable alternatives to replace all nonrenewable resources. Severance taxes on fossil fuels, for example, would only need to be high enough to encourage the development of alternative energy sources. Revenues from such taxes could be used to subsidize the research and development of renewable energy alternatives. The fact that such taxes would discourage current consumption—saving more energy for the future—might be a positive side effect of the tax. As renewable energy becomes more competitive with fossil energy, severance taxes could be reduced and eventually eliminated, allowing solar energy to replace fossil energy as remaining stocks decline. Similar strategies could be developed for all nonrenewable resources. Again, however, calculating actual values for "taxes sufficiently high as to encourage renewable alternatives" could prove to be an impractical if not impossible task.

The major obstacle of all such policies and taxes based on social discount rates would be achieving the social consensus necessary to support development and implementation. In addition, social discount rates do nothing to alter the distribution of benefits or costs within generations and thus do not address issues of intragenerational social equity. Therefore, the social discount rate concept is not the key to ensuring a sustainable economy, but instead, at best, it is a policy tool for potential use within the context of a more comprehensive theory of economic sustainability.

Internalizing Externalities

Among ecological economists, internalization of social and ecological costs and benefits probably has been the most popular approach to addressing the issue of sustainable development. Externalities can be defined as costs or benefits imposed upon or granted to people by an economic activity in which they are not directly involved. Because those affected by externalities do not participate in the decision-making process, they have no ability to express their preferences. The purpose of internalizing the externalities is to force economic decision makers to consider the full economic impact that their decisions have upon others.

Externalities can be internalized via a number of means, including government-imposed taxes and subsidies, private negotiation, legal rules and regulations, marketable permits, and direct government prohibitions.[15] Regardless of the means, internalization requires that all external costs and benefits first be assigned economic values. Economic values of externalities can be calculated in a variety of ways, as follows. In cases involving private property, estimates of external costs or damages can reflect diminished market values for the affected property. In cases involving persons, estimates of external cost or damages can reflect diminished earning capacity for the persons affected. Some economists use contingent valuation, or "willingness to pay," surveys to estimate the value of external economic impacts. They ask people directly how much they would be willing to pay to avoid some external cost or to receive some external benefit.[16,17] In some cases, courts may assess additional damages to punish violators of the law, or may compensate victims for pain and suffering as well as economic losses. However, *economic* externalities are intrinsically limited to economic costs and benefits.

Regardless of the method of calculation, the purpose in evaluating externalities is to assess economic values. Herein lies the problem with internalization. Many external costs and benefits simply are not economic in nature, but instead, are social or ethical costs and benefits. Even in instances in which ecological economists attempt to assess the value of social equity, they tend to value only those aspects of social relationships that affect economic productivity or material well-being.[18] Social and ethical costs and benefits can be neither accurately assessed nor adequately compensated by using economic measures of value. And even if social and ecologically values could somehow be expressed in economic terms, once they were internalized, they would be allocated by markets, without further consideration of the social or ethical consequences of their allocation.

Three Measures of Value

The three dimensions of human well-being—individual, social, and ethical—reflect different kinds of value arising from different belief systems. The values associated with individual material well-being arise from a belief in the inherent ability of the individual to succeed through hard work and creativity. The *enterprise belief system*, which dominates neoclassical economic thinking, has been built upon this principle. John Brewster, an economic philosopher, summarizes this belief system, paraphrased as follows: Successful proprietorship and accumulation of capital are the rewards of work ethic virtue . . . striving for excellence in employment is the highest distinction. The failure to achieve proprietary status and the failure of people to meet their total security needs reflect a life-long distaste for work and a lack of work ethic virtue and they make people undeserving of social acceptance. A businessperson's highest social responsibility is maximizing profits to his or her business. Free market competition automatically generates work opportunities and fair pay for all who are willing and able to work.[19]

Under the enterprise belief system, society has three major obligations to all individuals: to provide opportunities for the fullest development of their potential abilities, to offer opportunities to utilize and to maintain their abilities, and to give each a fair return for his or her contribution. According to Brewster, the enterprise belief system in America grew out of an earlier *work belief system* during the nineteenth century. It was both epitomized and extolled by Abraham Lincoln when he wrote, "I want every man to have a chance . . . in which he can better his condition—to be a hired laborer this year and the next, work for himself afterward, and finally to hire men to work for him. This is the true system."[20] The enterprise belief system is at least as popular among neoclassical economists today as it was in the days of Lincoln.

A belief in the accuracy of economic value as an adequate measure of true costs and benefits reflects a belief in the enterprise system because under this system economic value reflects one's ability to contribute to, and to be rewarded by, the free enterprise system. Economic value can be accurately assessed in terms of dollars and cents, regardless of whether the costs and benefits are internal or external. Decisions that reflect both internal and external economic costs obviously provide a more complete accounting of all individual material costs and benefits. Thus, internalizing economic externalities adds valuable information, which can be used in assessing the overall performance of an economy. However, whereas social and ecological resources can be used to create economic value, most of their contribution to overall quality of life and societal welfare is ignored when they are measured solely in terms of economic values, even when both market or non-market economic values are included.

Social values cannot be measured in dollars and cents. The values associated with social well-being arise from a belief that all people are created equal and that a life of quality can be achieved only through a personal commitment to equity and justice for all. Brewster summarizes the *democratic belief system,* which has traditionally dominated the American political system, and his summary is paraphrased as follows: All men are equal in dignity and worth. None, however wise or good, is wise or good enough to have arbitrary power over any other. Each person is entitled to a voice in making rules, which all must observe.[21] The democratic belief system is intrinsically rooted in a belief in a *creator*—that is, in a higher order, be it a belief in some natural order or a belief in God. People cannot be considered equal—not in wealth, ability, creativity, wisdom, or by any other measure—in any sense other than their inherent value within a higher order. Thus, the equal dignity and worth of all is a *first principle*. It cannot be proven, but does not need to be proven; it is accepted as a self-evident truth.

The writers of the American Declaration of Independence did not attempt to prove, or even to provide logical reasons for, their assertion that "all men are created equal, that they are endowed by their Creator with certain unalienable rights, that among these are life, liberty, and the pursuit of happiness." They simple stated, "We hold these truths to be self-evident," as a matter of common sense. In spite of the current dominance of the enterprise belief system, in politics as well as economics, the U.S. Constitution remains rooted in this system of democratic beliefs.

A belief in the necessity of assessing social values separate from economic values when measuring true social costs and benefits reflects a belief in the democratic system. In assessing social values under the democratic belief system, each person is equal in dignity and worth, and thus, the values of each person must be given an equal weight in the valuation process. Obviously, people have unequal impacts on economic values because they have unequal abilities to contribute to and benefit from the economy, being inherently unequal in ability, energy, creativity, and wealth. Free enterprise will not reward people equally, no matter how efficient the system. Consequently, social values must be measured through the political process, where values are weighted equally, according to the individual's value to society rather than his or her value to the economy. In other nondemocratic cultures and societies, the power to influence public decisions may not be distributed equally to all, but it nonetheless will be distributed differently from the power to influence economic decisions. Social value quite simply cannot be measured in terms of economic value.

A belief in the necessity of assessing ethical or moral values as separate from economic or social values is derived from a belief in the existence of a set of inviolable principles, which define what is good or bad. A belief in such principles, as explained in the previous chapter, is derived from a belief in a higher order of things within which human society must function, and to which human society must ultimately conform. Ethics, like science, is rooted in first principles that cannot be proven because they are the foundation for all proofs. Science is rooted in beliefs concerning what is true or false, whereas ethics is rooted in beliefs regarding what is good or bad. Both are rooted in beliefs, not facts.

Moral or ethical values provide the philosophical roots for both economic and social values. The moral and ethical values of a society reflect a consensus of what is considered acceptable or unacceptable behavior within that society. Government derives its basic authority from a consensus of the society it governs, and the economy must function within the bounds set by government. Thus, both government and economy are the creations of society and must therefore conform to the ethical and moral standards of society, if they are to serve it well. Ethical values are more deeply rooted than are either social or economic values and thus must be assessed by yet another process.

Ethical values, like other first principles, can never be known with *scientific* certainty. The ethical values of a society arise from a common sense among members of the society concerning what is morally good or bad and right or wrong. Ethical or moral values cannot be assessed by markets, by political majorities, or even supermajorities. The moral and ethical values of a society must be defined by a process of consensus.

Under most forms of government, the social and ethical values of a society are encoded in its constitution, which defines the basic structure of government and the principles by which it must function. The processes by which constitutions are constructed and amended provide useful insights into the process of reaching consensus. A consensus does not necessarily require unanimous agreement, but it requires sufficient agreement to convince those who disagree of the wisdom of agreeing to abide by the consensus. Consensus results from an earnest seeking of common beliefs and values, not from vote swapping, compromises, or coercion. Article V of the U.S. Constitution states that amendments may be proposed when deemed necessary by two-thirds of both houses of Congress or by the legislatures of two-thirds of the states, and must be ratified by the legislatures or by constitutional conventions of three-fourths of the states. Proposed constitutional amendments are not likely to make it through this process, unless they are supported by a consensus of the people.

Consequently, ethical or moral values cannot be measured in dollars or cents or even by a simple vote of the people. Obviously, something that is ethically wrong cannot be made ethically right, no matter how much one might be willing to pay to make it so. What is perhaps less obvious but equally true is that when something is ethically wrong it cannot be made ethically right by even a supermajority vote of the people or their elected representatives. A free enterprise economy is fundamentally incapable of either defining or assessing an appropriate value for either ethical or unethical behavior. A democratic system of government is capable of defining ethical and unethical behavior, but it is fundamentally incapable of assigning an appropriate numerical value to either.

Through government, societies develop constitutions, which define the principles of acceptable or unacceptable behavior, but they cannot accurately assess the value of either conforming to or violating those constitutional principles. Without a constitution, or some similar set of defining principles, there is no society, and thus no definable entity to which to assign costs or benefits. Violation of a constitution represents a direct attack on a society, which cannot be compensated and thus cannot be tolerated. Accordingly, laws that violate the Constitution of the United States are declared invalid, regardless of the size of the majority by which they were passed by Congress. Likewise, actions that violate constitutional principles cannot be excused legislatively or compensated economically; they must be prohibited. Moral values simply cannot be measured through either economic or political processes.

Therefore, economic, social, and ethical values must be defined and measured separately in addressing sustainability. Socially and ethically acceptable behaviors have some fractional economic values, which can be assessed through means currently used by ecological economists. However, the total value of an equitable and moral society far exceeds the society members' fractional contributions to the economy and consequently their total contribution cannot be measured in dollars and cents. The inadequacies of neoclassical economics in addressing issues of sustainability simply cannot be solved by internalizing social and ecological externalities.

Addressing Economic Inadequacies

Much of the remainder of this book is devoted to outlining the dimensions of a unified theory of economic sustainability. At this point, it may be useful, even necessary in some cases, to reassure the reader that such a major undertaking is both necessary and feasible.

First, the theory of economic sustainability is rooted in the pursuit of a more desirable quality of life, which is fundamentally different from the neoclassical economic pursuit of wealth, as was discussed in the previous chapter. And, as will be shown in the following chapter, the pursuit of wealth is not sustainable.

Second, the theory of economic sustainability integrates economic, social, and ethical values, without redefining or distorting the inherent nature of their contribution to societal sustainability or individual quality of life. Whereas neoclassical economics treats social and ethical values as external constraints on economic growth and development, the following chapter will further validate the necessity of integrating economic, social, and ecological values when addressing issues of sustainability. The purpose here is to demonstrate that this integration is both possible and practical, even though it may not be quick or easy.

An economy cannot be sustained without a solid foundation of social responsibility and ecological integrity. Ideally, the ethical principles of sustainability should be written into the constitution, or other defining principles of a society, within which the sustainable economy is to function. The Constitution of the United States currently focuses primarily on defining the *social* principles of a *democratic belief system*. In addition to defining the basic structure of government, the Constitution provides a bill of rights, written to ensure that all are granted equal dignity and worth, that none shall have arbitrary power over any other, and that each person has an equal voice in the processes of governance. In essence, the U.S. Constitution defines the principles of social equity and justice of the nation. However, social equity and justice make up but one of the four ethical cornerstones of sustainability.

The nation must recognize three additional basic types of rights of all people in order to ensure sustainability. First, all people must be afforded a basic right to be protected from economic exploitation. No person has a right to benefit economically at the expense of another. Second, all people must be afforded a basic right to a clean and healthy natural environment. No person has the right to foul the environment within which another must live. And third, people of future generations must be afforded social, economic, and environmental rights equal to the rights afforded to people of the current generation. As with social equity, these rights are self-evident, fundamental first principles, matters of common sense. These four ethical cornerstones, social justice, economic security, ecological integrity, and intergenerational equity, provide the moral foundation upon which a sustainable economy must be built.

Regardless of whether these principles are encoded in the constitution or simply written into laws, these principles cannot be violated without threatening the sustainability of a society. In practice, these principles should be defined to reflect *minimum* standards of behavior, which must be followed by everyone, everywhere, and at all times. To achieve the consensus necessary for implementation, such principles must logically apply equally to all. Interpreted as fundamental ethical or moral principles, they should be considered strict prohibitions or requirements, which cannot be compromised and cannot be compensated, and thus must be obeyed by all. All other laws and economic practices then must conform to these fundamental principles of sustainability, just as all laws and economic practices today must be *constitutional*. Within this framework of ethical and moral principles, a society would be free to allocate the resources over which it has control—economic, social, and ecological—to achieve and sustain a desirable quality of life—individually and socially, across generations.

Sustainable resource allocation and development requires two types of decisions: individual or private decisions, and collective or public decisions. In regard to the latter, societies must make collective decisions concerning the allocation of resources to which all have been deemed to have an equal right because each person must be given an equal voice in deciding how such resources are to be used. The private market sector of the economy reflects individual decisions motivated by self-interests. Thus, private markets allocate resources according to ability, productivity, or wealth, which inherently are distributed *unequally* among people. Thus, collective or public decisions are necessary to ensure social equity.

People may choose to allocate resources collectively for a variety of reasons, including efficiency and convenience, as will be discussed in a later chapter. However, public decisions are most clearly defined, and are most obviously necessary, in cases where all people are to be afforded equal rights and opportunities. If all people are to be granted an equal right to life and liberty, the right must be ensured collectively, through a system of criminal laws. If all people are to have equal opportunity to pursue happiness, that right likewise must be ensured collectively, through government. This is not communistic or socialistic philosophy. The U.S. Declaration of Independence, after naming several unalienable rights of all, clearly states, "That to secure these Rights, Governments are instituted among Men. . . ." The commitments of the U.S. government to provide public services, such as military protection, public education, public roads and highways, and Social Security and Medicare are all based on the principle of ensuring that all have equal opportunities to acquire and benefit from those things to which they have equal rights.

A sustainable society must extend the realm of public choice beyond ensuring social equity and justice to ensuring the rights of all to protection from economic exploitation, the rights of all to a clean and healthful environment, and the rights of future generations to be equal to those of the present. Beyond the *minimum* requirements and prohibitions of sustainability, people still should be encouraged to act collectively in their pursuit of the common good. Specifically, individual states and communities within nations should be encouraged to do more than is required by minimum national standards to protect the natural environment. Sustainability is inherently individualistic, site-specific, and dynamic, and the requirements for sustainability will therefore differ across various ecosystems and communities at different times. In addition, individual states and communities should be encouraged to strive to enhance, not just sustain, the quality of life in their states and communities through the pursuit of the common good. National requirements and prohibitions simply lay the foundation upon which sustainable local economies, ecosystems, and communities can then be built.

In other words, the citizens of states and communities must retain the right to exceed *minimum* national standards of ecological integrity, economic fairness, and social well-being. In such cases, public costs and benefits may be reflected in various types of taxes and subsidies, or even allocated through marketable permits, because the *unalienable* rights of all will have already been protected through a system of inviolable national *minimum* requirements and prohibitions. But in all such cases, each person must be granted an equal voice in the decision-making process, because each shall have an equal responsibility to bear the costs and an equal right to receive the benefits.

To ensure sustainability, all people also must be afforded the right to pursue their individual self-interest, as long their private benefit is not achieved at the expense of others. The primary purpose of the suggested national *minimums*, augmented by state and local enhancements, would be to create a framework within which individuals could pursue their self-interest without infringing upon the well-being of others, including the well-being of future generations. The enterprise belief system must be expressed through the private economy within the ethical and social context of sustainability. Within such a framework, free markets would once again function for the public good, as in the days of Adam Smith. The free market economy once again would reflect the principles of classical capitalism, and the new capitalistic system would be sustainable.

One's first reaction to the call for a new economic system might be to claim that we already have such a system in place. We already have a constitution, a set of laws, and a private economy. It's true that we already have the basic institutions in place to ensure economic sustainability, but we do not yet have a national consensus to secure fundamental economic and ecological rights for all people or to secure equal rights for current and future generations. Much of the public sector of society today is preoccupied with largely politically motivated subsidization of individual and corporate economic interests, rather than the protection of individual rights or the pursuit of the common good. In addition, the private sector of today's economy is not truly competitive, and thus it does not ensure economic fairness in the individual pursuit of self-interest. Nor do we have a system for integrating ecological, social, and economic decisions into a holistic pursuit of sustainability, happiness, and quality of life. Today, society and the environment are viewed as constraints on economic growth, not as cornerstones for long-term economic viability. Sustainability will be possible only when economic, social, and ecological values are understood and treated as three distinct but inseparable aspects of the same whole.

All of these things are necessary for sustainability, and few if any are either facilitated or encouraged by our current approaches to economic investing, social discounting, or internalizing externalities. Our current system of economics, including ecological economics, has inherent inadequacies that continue to encourage and support decisions and actions that threaten economic sustainability. A new economics of sustainability is both necessary and feasible, and it's mostly a matter of common sense.

Endnotes

1. Harold Hotelling, "The Economics of Exhaustible Resources," *Journal of the Political Economy*, 39 (1931): 137–175.

2. E. N. Blue and L. Tweeten, "The Estimation of Marginal Utility of Income for Use in Agricultural Policy Analysis," *Agricultural Economics*, 16 (1997): 155–169.

3. C. E. Ferguson, *Micro-economic Theory* (Homewood, Ill.: Richard D. Irwin, Inc., 1969), 460–464.

4. R. Hahn and G. Hester, "Marketable Permits, Lessons for Theory and Practice," *Ecology Law Quarterly*, 16 (1989): 361–406.

5. Robert Costanza, "The Early History of Ecological Economics and the International Society for Ecological Economics (ISEE)," *Internet Encyclopedia of Ecological Economics*, International Society for Ecological Economics, http://www.ecoeco.org/publica/encyc.htm (accessed October, 2004).

6. European Society of Ecological Economics, "What is Ecological Economics," ESEE, http://www.euroecolecon.org/whatis.htm (accessed February, 2005).

7. Karl E. Chase and Ray C. Fair, *Principles of Economics* (Englewood Cliffs, N.J.: Prentice-Hall, Inc., 2nd ed., 1992), 323–326.

8. Milton Friedman, *Free to Choose* (Chicago: Aldine Publishing Company, 1962).

9. The Federal Reserve Board, *Statistics, Releases, and Historical Data*, the Federal Reserve Board, http://www.federalreserve.gov/releases/ (accessed October, 2004).

10. Paul Heyne, *The Economic Way of Thinking* (Chicago: Science Research Associates, Inc., 1973).

11. Leon Shenandoah–Tadodaho, speaker of the house, Grand Council of the Six Nations of the Iroquois Confederacy: "The Great Law of Peace imparted at Onondaga Lake instructed leaders and elders to always consider how their actions and decisions will affect the Seventh Generation of their offspring. This wisdom says we don't own the Earth, but borrow it from our children and grandchildren." http://www.onondagalakepeacefestival.org/Sustainability.htm (accessed February, 2005).

12. F. Ramsey, "A Mathematical Theory of Savings," *Economic Journal*, 38 (1928): 543–559.

13. R. Solow, "The Economics of Resources or the Resources of Economics," *American Economic Review Papers and Proceedings*, 64 (1974): 1–14.

14. United Nations, "Rio Declaration on Environment and Development," *ILM 874*, June 14, 1992.

15. Case and Fair, *Principles*, 452–456.

16. R. E. Just, D. L. Hueth, and A. Smitz, *Applied Welfare Economics and Public Policy* (Englewood Cliffs, N.J.: Prentice-Hall Inc., 1982).

17. Ecosystem Valuation, "Contingent Valuation Method," Dennis M. King and Marisa Mazzotta, http://www.ecosystemvaluation.org/contingent_valuation. htm#over (accessed February, 2004).

18. Neva R. Goodwin, "Equity," *Internet Encyclopedia of Ecological Economics*, International Society for Ecological Economics, http://www.ecoeco.org/publica/encyc.htm (accessed October, 2004).

19. John Brewster, *A Philosopher Among Economists*, eds. Patrick Madden and David E. Brewster (Philadelphia: J. T. Murphy Co. Inc., 1970), 60–61.

20. John Nocolay and John Hay eds., *The Complete Works of Abraham Lincoln* (New York: Francis E. Tandy Co., 1894), 360–361.

21. Brewster, *Philosopher*, 60.

CHAPTER FIVE

ECONOMICS AS A LIFE SCIENCE

The Evolution of Economics

Historically, the discipline of economics has been referred to as a social science—suggesting a science of society, of human relationships. Over the years, however, economics has become a mechanistic science of individual self-interest. In the neoclassical economics of today, a society is considered to be nothing more than a collection of self-seeking individuals. However, this certainly is not how economics began, as has been suggested in previous chapters. The founding fathers of classical economics, including Adam Smith,[1] Thomas Malthus,[2] David Ricardo,[3] and John Stuart Mill,[4] were very much concerned about the social connectedness of people, particularly about issues of social equity and justice. They were concerned about the distribution of wealth and the economic welfare of ordinary working people and of the hungry, the poor, and the oppressed. They saw economics as a means of helping to build a stronger society, not simply a means of maximizing material well-being. They were concerned about the pursuit of happiness, not just about earning, spending, and accumulating wealth.

Adam Smith believed that the *invisible hand* of a "laissez-faire" economy would transform the pursuit of individual self-interests into societal economic well-being, but he never suggested that a strong economy meant a strong society, as is the conventional wisdom of today.[5] Classical economists, such as Smith, understood that an economy is but one part of society. They understood that a strong economy must rest upon a solid social and moral foundation. They understood that issues of social responsibility and moral consensus must be

81

addressed by societies as wholes, not just by individuals. They treated land as a unique resource upon which all life, including human life, ultimately must depend.[6] They understood economics as a life science. They understood that the pursuit of individual self-interests was not synonymous with the pursuit of happiness, and that competitive markets would not ensure a moral and just society. The *classical* economists were true social scientists.

Around the turn of the nineteenth century, the trend toward mechanistic economic thinking began with those who are now called *neoclassical economists*, including Walras,[7] Pareto,[8] Marshall,[9] Wicksteed,[10] Edgeworth,[11] and Fisher.[12] They wanted to add precision and quantitative rigor to economics—to make it more like the physical sciences, such as chemistry and physics. However, they had no apparent intention of taking the life out of economics; they just wanted to make economics more rigorous and thus more scientific. They brought together the concepts of diminishing marginal productivity and diminishing marginal utility to define the concepts of market supply, market demand, and equilibrium market price. They developed the economic concept of revealed preferences, or consistent choice, which freed them from the difficulty of measuring consumer utility or value. They began to use charts, graphs, and mathematical equations to define these new economic relationships. The more precise logic of mathematics could then be used to derive conclusions and to either prove or disprove economic propositions. Once economic values could be quantified, economic relationships could be evaluated statistically, thus accommodating the inherent imprecision of economic data. Over the years, the social science of classical economics was reshaped into the mathematical and statistical science of neoclassical economics.

Through quantitative data, mathematical logic, and statistical analysis, however, economists created only the illusion of stable, separable, generalizable, and predictable economic relationships. Such relationships simply do not exist in living systems—particularly in human society. Living systems, unlike contemporary economic models, are dynamic, holistic, individualistic, and evolutionary.

The Economy as a Living System

To create a sustainable economy, we must embrace the concept of the economy as a living system, as was explained at length in Chapter 3.

Sustainable systems must be regenerative; they must be capable of maintaining their productivity and usefulness indefinitely. Living organisms, being inherently regenerative, possess the only logical means of offsetting the inevitable tendency of all nonliving systems toward entropy.

All systems, both living and nonliving, can be characterized by pattern, structure, and process.[13] The pattern of a nonliving system is the organizational concept—the plan or blueprint by which it is constructed. The pattern of a living system is encoded in its DNA—the genetic code, which guides its development process. The structure of both living and nonliving systems is the physical embodiment of pattern. The structure is the thing that you can see, feel, touch, or otherwise perceive using your physical senses, such as the plant, animal, machine, or factory. The process of a system is the means by which the system performs the functions necessary for the system to fulfill its purpose—the means by which it works. Something useful or meaningful results from the processes of both living and nonliving systems—both are able to perform work.

The primary difference between living and nonliving systems relates to the processes by which their structures are made. Nonliving systems must be constructed, according to some plan or blueprint, but living systems are self-constructed. Once built, the structure of nonliving systems remains constant. Nonliving systems may break or eventually wear out, but their basic structure remains unchanged. Nonliving systems can be remodeled, rebuilt, or redesigned, but they cannot remodel, rebuild, or redesign themselves. Living organisms, by contrast, are not built or rebuilt; instead, by their nature, they make and remake themselves, according to their genetic code. They are born, mature, reproduce, grow old, and eventually die—by nature. The physical structure of a living system is continually renewing and changing, although its genetic pattern remains constant, at least during its lifetime. The cells of living organisms are replaced continuously, even in mature organisms, thus creating essentially new structures, often many times during a single life span. Of course, when a living organism dies, the processes of renewal and regeneration cease—it becomes a self-made dead system. Furthermore, whereas the pattern of an individual living organism remains unchanged, species of organisms are capable of evolving genetically, from generation to generation, to accommodate their changing environments. Living and nonliving systems may both perform useful and productive work, but part of the process of any living system is the remaking of its structure and the regeneration of its species.

Unfortunately, economics is no longer a living discipline; it was killed by neoclassical economists. Economics is no longer a social science because it became a nonliving, mechanical science. Contemporary economics is reductionistic, whereas living systems are holistic.[14] Economics attempts to take systems apart, piece by piece, to gain an understanding of the whole by examining the parts. For example, the fundamental principles of neoclassical economics were created via the concept of *ceteris paribus*—a Latin adverb meaning "other things being equal or unchanged." Cause-and-effect relationships in economics, such as changes in quantities demanded in response to changes in price, are isolated by assuming that all other relevant factors, such as consumer preferences, remain unaltered. In contrast, when any component or part of a living system is changed, the whole is changed, and thus ceteris paribus conditions never actually exist. In living systems, the effect of every cause becomes the cause of another effect, essentially changing the nature of the whole. Even the simple acts of observation and experimentation can change the context and thus change the nature of relationships. Living systems are holistic and require a holistic approach to scientific inquiry.

Contemporary economics is static, whereas living systems are dynamic. Economists have attempted to develop dynamic economic models, but the theories behind economics are rooted in static paradigms. *Econometrics* is a popular branch of economics that expresses economic relationships in mathematical form and uses statistical methods to estimate the nature of the relationships. Statistical methods allow economists to address the inevitable variability observed in the data used to test hypothesized economic relationships. Statistical analysis is based on the assumption that the structure of the system remains constant—at least long enough to identify and quantify structural relationships. However, the structures of living systems are continually changing, even in the absence of direction, influence, or interference from outside the system. Thus, statistical conclusions, even when relevant to some economic structure of the past, may have little relevance to economic structures of the present or future.[15]

Contemporary economics is a search for generalizable truth, but living systems are individualistic. Economists attempt to generalize about the actions and reactions of individuals and groups, using conclusions drawn from the observation of other individuals and groups.

They attempt to anticipate future trends in one economy, based on past observations of another economy. However, all living systems are unique. For instance, no two living organisms are identical, even if they have identical DNA.[16] Individual reactions to unique life experiences cause each individual to be different from any other living individual. Furthermore, each group of living individuals is different from any other group of individuals; each community or each economy is a unique whole. Relationships observed within one living system will never be the same as relationships within another living system even if everything else were identical. Thus, economic generalizations are inherently limited in scope, restricted in nature, and, more typically, essentially lacking in credibility.

Living Organizations

An economy is, in fact, a living system. An economy is the physical embodiment of a specific pattern of economic relationships, and those relationships exist among living entities. Economies are created by societies to meet the needs of societies, and societies are made up of people. People—as workers, consumers, and citizens—are, of course, living organisms, not machines. Living organisms, including humans, are essential elements of the natural ecosystem, which is the ultimate source of all economic resources. An economy is alive, not dead. The paradigms of neoclassical economics quite simply are not appropriate for managing systems made up of people, societies, and natural ecosystems. And nonliving paradigms most certainly are not appropriate for dealing with uniquely human issues, such as values, culture, equity, justice, ethics, and morality.

Obviously, the contemporary paradigm of industrial economic development has facilitated the generation of many material benefits for humanity. But the benefits have come largely from resource extraction and exploitation, rather than from sustainable production. As long as both natural and human resources were both plentiful and productive, the consequences of their exploitation were not so obvious. But after decades of exploitation, the sustainability of both the natural environment and civil society quite clearly are being threatened. As long as humanity maintained a strong sense of community and held solid ethical and moral values, the negative impacts of using dead paradigms for living systems could be minimized. But after decades of the intentional dismantling of social and ethical constraints to the pursuit of individual self-interest, the negative impacts of dead thinking on a living society have become clear. Virtually all of the ecological and social problems confronting human society today are direct consequences of using dead paradigms of economic and resource development to guide the actions of a living society. Ecological degradation, in general, is a direct consequence of the extraction and exploitation of natural resources motivated by maximum short-run economic gain. Social and moral decay, likewise, are direct consequences of the unethical exploitation of the economically weak by the economically powerful. Living things are not like machines or factories; their exploitation has inevitable ethical, social, and, ultimately, economic consequences.

The economy is alive, life is necessary for sustainability, and thus a new sustainable economy must be designed to function as a living organization. To *organize* means to put together into an orderly, functional, structured whole; to arrange in a coherent form; to systematize for harmonious or coordinated action.[17] Hence, any orderly, functional arrangement of things or people is an organization, including businesses, nonprofit groups, churches, political parties, governments of all types, and even such things as factories and machines or communities and families. All organizations have a purpose; otherwise, there is no reason for arranging things rather than simply allowing things to function individually, without order, coherence, or coordination. The purpose of an organization always suggests an appropriate structure for the organization and an appropriate set of principles by which the organization should function. Any *purposeful* arrangement of things—including money, machines, materials, and people—is an organization.

Therefore, an economy is an organization. Economies, in general, allow people to move beyond self-sufficiency; to specialize, individually and geographically; and to trade. But the purpose of any specific economy must be identified by the society that the economy is to serve—an economy is a subset of a society. Accordingly, existing or imposed economic structures and processes should not be allowed to determine the purpose of an economy. Instead, economic structures and processes should be designed or redesigned as appropriate for a socially determined purpose.

All economies are systems, in that they have patterns, structures, and processes. With nonliving mechanistic organizations, such as machines and factories, the purpose of the organization can be designed into the structure. The various components of the structure can be designed and arranged in such a way that the purpose of the organization will be achieved, if it functions according to its structural pattern. For example, if an automobile is properly designed and assembled, and then is filled with fuel, it will start, run, and take the driver wherever a car can go. As long as its mechanical structure remains intact, the car will fulfill its purpose. Its purpose is built into its structure.

For living organizations, however, the purpose of the organization must be encoded in its operational principles, rather than designed into its organizational structure. The purpose of a living organism is encoded into its DNA. The structure of a living organization is dynamic; it continually renews and regenerates itself. The genetic code of a living plant or animal includes all the information needed for the organism to germinate or to be born; to renew its cells; and to grow, mature, and reproduce. The guiding principles or conceptual DNA for an organization must be developed by those whom the organization is designed to serve. The living organization's principles, its DNA, must include all of the information needed for the organization to be self-making. The living organization must be able to renew, to grow, to mature, to reproduce, and to evolve without losing its sense of purpose.

A Matter of Purpose and Principles

The generic purpose of any economy is to sustain a desirable quality of life by facilitating relationships among people and between people and their natural environment. The capitalistic economy became prominent during a period of history when a higher economic standard of living was likely the most effective means of achieving a higher quality of life. Among the social, ethical, and economic dimensions of well-being, the economic was the most lacking. Thus, it's understandable why the purpose of the capitalistic economy might drift from enhancing the quality of life to promoting material well-being. This redirection of purpose may well have seemed reasonable during the early stages of industrialization, when most people lived lives of hard physical labor, constant drudgery, and deprivation of opportunity. Many people struggled with hunger, pestilence, and disease before dying an early death. For the masses of that time, a lack of the physical, material, and personal necessities of life was almost certainly more detrimental to the quality of life than any lack of social connectedness or moral purpose.

Over time, however, the balance of priorities among the material, social, and ethical dimensions of well-being has shifted. The tremendous gains in productivity brought about by industrial development eventually led to the systematic degradation of social relationships and ethical values—not necessarily intentionally, but nonetheless, undeniably. Thus, over time, the true priority of human needs has shifted from the material to the social and ethical. For most people in the United States, for example, acquiring more material goods and services is no longer the key to a more desirable quality of life, as was discussed in Chapter 1. In defining the purpose for a sustainable economy, we must to return to the roots of economics, to the pursuit of happiness and quality of life.

Quality of life is multidimensional; it has individual, social, and moral dimensions. People have physical, emotional, and spiritual needs that must be met to sustain the body, the mind, and the soul. It's true that man does not live by bread alone, at least not very well. People need connectedness with other people; people need to love and to be loved. People need to live lives of purpose and meaning; people need a sense of spiritual connectedness with something that transcends self and others.[18] But, it's also true that man does not live *without* bread, at least not very long. People need food, clothing, shelter, health care, and at least some material comforts of life. In the new sustainable economy, therefore, economic structures designed to facilitate the pursuit of individual self-interests must be replaced with a new set of economic principles designed to facilitate the pursuit of happiness. The new economy must be guided by an enlightened concept of self-interest, by the pursuit of happiness and quality of life.

Even though an understanding of the generic purpose of an economy is important, each individual economy should be based on a specific statement of purpose. And because an economy is a subset or component of a society, the purpose of an economy should be derived from the purpose of the society of which it is a part. Only then can a set of guiding principles be derived that will be appropriate for the specific purpose of a particular economy within a specific society. This process of defining the purpose and principles for an economy is not as abstract or esoteric as it might seem at first. A general application of this process to the U.S. economy should not only make the nature of the process more clear, but also provide a point of departure in design-ing the pattern for a sustainable U.S. economy.

A purpose statement for the United States is embodied in the Declaration of Independence and in the preamble to the U.S. Consti-tution. The Declaration of Independence begins, as quoted previously, "We hold these truths to be self-evident, that all men are created equal, that they are endowed by their Creator with certain unalienable Rights; that among these are Life, Liberty, and the pursuit of Happi-ness.–That to secure these rights, Governments are instituted among Men, deriving their just powers from the consent of the governed." The preamble to the U.S. Constitution also begins with a statement of purpose. "We the People of the United States, in Order to form a more perfect Union, establish Justice, insure domestic Tranquility, provide for the common defense, promote the general Welfare, and secure the Blessings of Liberty to ourselves and our Posterity, do ordain and establish this Constitution for the United States of America." The pur-poses embodied in these two documents seem to have served the country well for more than 200 years.

Any statement of purpose for the U.S. economy should be consis-tent with these historical purposes for instituting and constituting the United States of America; alternatively, the nation's purpose should be redefined. Thus, the U.S. economy must facilitate the individual pur-suit of happiness, without infringing upon the opportunities of others for life, liberty, and happiness as well. In addition, the economy must generate the financial means of providing for national defense and law enforcement, but at the same time, must promote the general welfare, ensure justice, and secure freedom and liberty for those of both cur-rent and future generations.

Fortunately, these constitutional preconditions for the United States are entirely consistent with the purpose of sustainable eco-nomic development. Sustainable economic development must meet the needs of all members of the current generation, while leaving equal or better opportunities for those of the future. Sustainable eco-nomic development must be economically viable, socially just, and ecologically responsible. Sustainable economic development must facilitate the pursuit of happiness—individual, social, and spiritual happiness. Sustainable economic development is about attaining and sustaining a desirable quality of life—personally, interpersonally, and ethically. Even though the purpose of the U.S. economy may be stated in terms of the pursuit of happiness or quality of life, the historical guiding principles of the nation are entirely consistent with the principles of a sustainable, living economy.

To achieve sustainability, the U.S. economy must be economically viable—meeting the material needs of the present while conserving and renewing adequate natural and human resources to sustain future economic viability. Thus, economic *viability* must replace economic *growth* as a guiding economic principle. The U.S. economy may well continue to grow, as it becomes more efficient in using nonrenewable resources and becomes increasingly effective in utilizing renewable sources of energy. But economic viability must be its guiding principle if the economy is to make the necessary transition from extraction and exploitation to sustainable economic development. Capitalism, defined as private ownership of property and market allocation of resources, probably will continue to be the most appropriate model for most economic development activities, at least for the seeable future. But a capitalistic economy must function in harmony with the society and the natural ecosystem that supports it in order to remain economically viable over time.

To achieve sustainability, the U.S. economy must be socially equitable and just. Economic equity and justice do not imply that each person should be rewarded equally for their efforts, regardless of their productivity or economic contributions to society. Economic justice does mean that everyone has a right to enough food, clothing, shelter, education, and health care to ensure their survival and physical, mental, and spiritual development. Economic equity also means that everyone has an equal right to pursue economic opportunities of their choosing and to be protected against the oppressive, exploitive, or coercive economic actions of others. A socially just economy also must ensure the rights of all people to obtain accurate, unbiased information and to be protected against attempts by others to manipulate or subversively influence their thoughts, expressions, or actions for economic gain. And finally, a socially just economy must ensure the rights of people to collaborate, organize, and pursue joint economic activities, but only to the extent that such organizations and associations clearly contribute to the overall societal quality of life. The specific list of guaranteed rights obviously is debatable. Such a set of social economic principles would be consistent with the purpose of U.S. society, would protect people from economic exploitation, and thus would help to ensure mutually beneficial economic relationships and a sustainable economy.

To achieve sustainability, the U.S. economy must be ethical and moral. Economic ethics and morality do not suggest a set of economic principles based on any particular religion or philosophy, but instead suggest principles based on common sense. Among the most common of these common sense principles is, "Do unto others as you would have them do unto you." For economic sustainability, we must extend this moral principle to those of future generations, as well as to our neighbors today. Aldo Leopold's "land ethic"[19] and the Native Americans' consideration of the "seventh future generation" are but two expressions of the common sense of intergenerational equity. An ethical and moral economy must ensure that those of the future have opportunities equal to those of the present—to be protected, to grow, and to develop. To fulfill these responsibilities, those of the current generation must be able to obtain and distribute information concerning the responsibilities of stewardship and potential threats to the natural environment, without harassment or censorship. People in a sustainable economy also must accept the responsibility to pass on a culture that values stewardship of the earth, from each generation to the next. Such a set of ethical principles would be consistent with the purpose of U.S. society. In addition, such principles would not only ensure the long-term sustainability of the economy, but would also ensure the righteousness of relationships with each other and with the earth necessary for the well-being and happiness of any generation.

In addition to these foundational principles of economic viability, social equity, and ecological integrity, a sustainable economy must embody operational principles consistent with those of living systems. The sustainable economy must be managed as a whole, rather than as individual economic enterprises, industries, or sectors. The connections, arrangements, and relationships should receive as much or more attention than the individual economic entities. The sustainable economy must be managed to maintain diversity. Healthy, selective economic boundaries must be maintained among enterprises, communities, states, regions, and nations, not only to facilitate economic competitiveness, but also to maintain the biological and cultural diversity necessary for sustainability. The management of a sustainable economy must be individualistic, site specific, and dynamic—thereby respecting the inherent uniqueness of people, places, and specific points in time. The management of a sustainable economy must be decentralized—thus promoting interdependent relationships among sovereign entities. Mutually beneficial relationships are the ultimate payoff of holism, diversity, and uniqueness, allowing the whole to be greater than the sum of its parts. However, true interdependence in human relationships is always a matter of choice.

These foundational and functional principles of a sustainable economy will be addressed in more detail in later chapters. Chapter 6, Managing the Sustainable Organization, explains how the principles of holism, diversity, and interdependence can be used to manage sustainable organizations. And Chapter 7, The Three Economies of Sustainability, addresses the individual, social, and moral economies and suggests how the three might function together for economic sustainability. Organizing and managing for economic sustainability are mainly matters of organizing for purpose and managing by principles.

A Return to Economic Philosophy

The economics of sustainability must be a true social science, a life science, and thus economics must return to its roots in economic philosophy. "Philosophy is a study that seeks to understand the mysteries of existence and reality. It tries to discover the nature of truth and knowledge and to find what is of basic value and importance in life. It also examines the relationships between humanity and nature and between the individual and society."[20] The economics of sustainability is inextricably related to questions of basic human values, relationships between humanity and nature, and relationships among individuals within society. Any system of economics that ignores these basic issues, quite simply, is not sustainable. History has shown that the pursuit of individual economic self-interest will systematically remove all social and moral obstacles that stand in the way of continuing growth. Thus, guidance and control of a sustainable economy must come from the inside. Social values and ethical principles must be brought *inside*; they must become an integral part of economics.

An economy driven solely by the pursuit of individual self-interests is like a cancerous tumor. Cancer is a disease in which once-healthy cells begin to multiply wildly, destroy healthy tissue, and endanger the life of their host. In all healthy organisms, cells multiply according to complex chemical instructions that ensure that cells divide only when needed to support life and health. However, when this finely tuned control system becomes damaged, cells begin to multiply without control, the tumor grows and spreads, and displaces or damages vital organs until the tumor ultimately destroys the life upon which it had depended.[21]

Social and ethical values once provided the complex set of instructions necessary to ensure that the character and rate of economic growth was consistent with the requirements of a healthy human society and regenerative natural ecosystem. The classical capitalistic economy certainly wasn't perfect, but it was reasonably productive and socially supportive, as long as its growth was guided and controlled by strong social and ethical instructions. For the most part, those controls were internal. People simply didn't do everything they could have done to maximize their income and wealth; many things weren't considered socially acceptable or ethical. Those who ignored such guidance were ostracized by their family members and neighbors and were condemned by their church. They may have become wealthy, but they became social outcasts in the process.

On occasions when abuses of ethical and moral principles outgrew the realm of control of family and community, society reacted collectively, through government, to reestablish responsible social and ethical controls. The Progressive Movement of the 1890s and early 1900s was a direct response to widespread perceptions of socially and morally unacceptable economic behavior. Industrial monopolists, dishonest politicians, city slums, and poor working conditions in factories and mines were all seen as unhealthy consequences of rapid economic growth in the United States during the 1800s.[22] The economy had to be brought back under control. Antitrust laws, tax reforms, federal trade regulations, labor unions, direct election of senators, and voting rights for women were all eventual results of the peoples' attempts to regain social and ethical control of their economy.

Social and ethical values continued to influence, if not control, the character, size, and power of economic institutions and organizations throughout much of the twentieth century. The Great Society programs of the 1960s and the environmental programs of the 1970s both grew out of a strong sense of national commitment to social equity and environmental stewardship, regardless of their ultimate effectiveness. However, the 1980s seemed to bring a change in the tide of public sentiment in the United States. At first, a slim majority of Americans seemed to feel that the economic costs of social equity and environmental protection were simply too high, or perhaps, that government programs were inherently incapable of addressing such issues. Since then, antitrust laws have become largely ineffective,[23] labor union membership has dropped from 20% of the workforce in 1982 to only 13% in 2003,[24] and the share of total tax revenues from corporate income taxes has dropped from more than 16% in the late 1970s to less than 10% in the early 2000s.[25] During the late 1990s and early 2000s, social welfare and environmental programs have been significantly weakened by those who view such programs as unnecessary economic constraints.

Economics, as a discipline, also seemed to cling to its social and ethical traditions well into the twentieth century, in spite of the early shift to neoclassical economics. Keynesian economics,[26] as advocated by the "Harvard school," still dominated macroeconomic thinking through the 1970s, in spite of growing opposition from Milton Friedman's "Chicago school" of free market economics.[27] But a distinct shift to economic conservatism in the 1980s essentially completed the transition of economics from a philosophy to a science, or at least to a political science. Freed from the constraints of true competitiveness and human cultural responsibilities, corporations gained increasing market power and political influence, transforming capitalism into corporatism. Today's corporatist economy has many of the characteristics of a cancer; it multiplies wildly, destroying the natural environment and civil society, and threatening the sustainability of human life on Earth.

The call for a return to economic philosophy does not suggest some nostalgic longing for a return to earlier, simpler times. The sustainability of the global economy, society, and ecosystem clearly are at risk. A return to economic philosophy is necessary, not to reclaim the past, but instead to meet the critical challenges of the future. The future will be different from the past—things never remain the same. But if the future is to be better than the past, perhaps even if there is to be a future, the economy must return to the inviolate philosophical principles that have always have been, and will be, necessary to sustain human progress on Earth.

A return to economic philosophy suggests a return to the economic purpose and principles of earlier times. Conveniently, the basic framework of competitive capitalism is as relevant today as in the days of Adam Smith. However, constructive competitiveness must be valued as a living paradigm capable of guiding the private economy, not simply revered as a set of sacred theoretical assumptions.

"Atomistic" competition—meaning so many small buyers and sellers than no individual exerts any significant pressure on total quantity or price in a market—is a prerequisite for a sustainable economy.

Short-run tradeoffs may exist between the size of business organizations and economic efficiency; however, many of the economies of scale of industrial organizations today arise from the economic exploitation of consumers, workers, and the natural environment, rather than from economic efficiency. As the private economy becomes guided by the principles of ecological integrity and social responsibility, many of the economic advantages of bigness, of economic and political power, will be greatly diminished. Sustainable systems must accommodate the niches within culture and within nature, and most such niches are far smaller than are today's corporations. If economic enterprises are kept appropriately small, benefits from gains in productivity and efficiency will be shared equitably among consumers, workers, investors, and entrepreneurs. If enterprises are kept appropriately small, no one will have the power to capture and retain benefits for themselves or to exploit others. In a constructively competitive economy, economic entities must be diverse and interdependent.

Freedom of entry and exit is another basic prerequisite for competitive capitalism. It must be easy to establish new enterprises when consumers need more of something than is currently produced and easy to get out of enterprises whenever consumers need less than is being produced. This condition is necessary to ensure that the economy can evolve to meet the changing needs of a dynamic, living society. Industrial economies of scale or size, again, have created financial barriers to entry and exit in the form of large investments in buildings, equipment, and infrastructure. Patents and copyrights, designed to facilitate the development of industrial technologies, also have placed legal constraints on getting into business. In general, the corporate industrial model is the root cause of the entry and exit problems that exist in today's economy. A truly competitive economy is dynamic by nature; it must be easy for the old to die off and for the new to be born.

With true competition, accurate information ensures that neither consumers nor workers are misled into making commitments that they will later regret. Reasonably accurate information is necessary not only to prevent exploitation, but also to prevent the misallocation of resources in a competitive economy. Information problems are related directly to the corporate industrial model of economic development. Specialization of various levels of production and distribution adds spatial and functional complexity to the economic system as a whole, resulting in frequent miscommunication between producers and consumers. The obvious solution is less specialization of function, more niche marketing, more localized production systems, and, thereby, direct communications between producers and consumers. In a truly competitive economy, producers and consumers are able to maintain interdependent relationships of choice, which create benefits for the whole of society.

Consumer sovereignty is the cornerstone of competitive capitalism. In economic theory, consumers' tastes and preferences are accepted as given, as if genetically encoded or assigned from "on high," and are assumed to be untainted by outside persuasive influences. Consumer sovereignty is necessary to ensure that resources are allocated to meet the true wants and needs of consumers and of society. Workers also must have sovereignty in making decisions concerning the use of their labor and management abilities. Many workers feel trapped into working for whatever corporation will hire them. In today's economy, consumer sovereignty, rather than being protected, is attacked every hour of every day, all around the globe, with a constant barrage of persuasive corporate advertising. The purpose of much of this advertising is not to inform, but to persuade—to bend and shape consumers' preferences so as to enhance corporate profits and growth. In a truly competitive economy, consumers and workers must be sovereigns; economic transactions must be matters of choice, free of outside influence or coercion.

A return to the classical principles of competitive capitalism is a necessary condition for economic sustainability, but it is not sufficient. Economics must reintegrate questions of philosophy back into the discipline: "what is of basic value and importance in life and in relationships between humanity and nature and among individuals within society?". Sustainability is holistic; its individual, social, and ethical dimensions are inseparable; the individual economy cannot be treated as *internal* to economics and the social and ethical economies treated as *external*. If the institutions of science are unwilling to accept economic philosophy as a discipline, then perhaps science ultimately can be restored to its rightful place as simply a means of clarifying or refining common sense.

Economists must once again be willing to address issues of equity and justice, along with issues of employment, income, and wealth. Economists can no longer ignore the critical impact that the distribution of economic and political power has on economic sustainability. Economists must once again be willing to address issues of ethics, morality, and intergenerational equity, along with issues of economic growth and development. Economists can no longer ignore the vital ecological and social implications of doing what is good and bad or right and wrong. An economy that is socially unjust or unethical is simply unsustainable. The individual economy must be integrated with the social and moral economies in achieving economic sustainability.

Once the purpose and principles of economic sustainability become established within a society, the people will be free to pursue their individual economic self-interests without threats of exploitation or degradation. The private markets again will be *free*, the power of the *invisible hand* will have been restored, and the pursuit of a more enlightened concept of self-interest will lead to a sustainable quality of life. However, maintaining competitive capitalism in the private economy will require constant intention of action and attention to results; the economy is a living system that must be cared for, nurtured, and encouraged if it is to remain healthy and productive. It cannot simply be redesigned, rebuilt, and again left to function on its own, according to some new design. Life is a process.

Economic theories of sustainability, if they are developed, will be quite different from the scientific theories of today. Today's science is based on a mechanistic worldview—a stable, separable, generalizable, predictable world of causes and effects. This is not the world of economic sustainability. The science of economic sustainability must be based on an organismic worldview—a dynamic, holistic, individualistic, evolutionary world of interdependence. Only when science is able to move forward, embracing the realities of a living world, will science become capable of addressing the most important issues of sustainability. Only then will the economics of sustainability become accepted as a science rather than a philosophy. The science of economic sustainability must be a true life science.

Endnotes

1. Adam Smith and Herbert Wallace Schneider, *Adam Smith's Moral and Political Philosophy* (New York: Hafner Publishing Company, 1948).

2. James Bonar, *Malthus and His Work* (New York: Macmillan Publishing Company, 1885).

3. J. R. McCulloch, *The Works of David Ricardo* (London: John Murray, 1826).

4. John Stuart Mill, *Essays on Some Unsettled Questions of Political Economy* (New York: Hafner Publishing Company, 1948).

5. Adam Smith, *Wealth of Nations* (Amherst, N.Y.: Prometheus Books, 1991; original copyright, 1776), 351.

6. Henry George, "The Single Tax: What It Is and Why We Urge It," *Christian Advocate*, 1890 (New York: Robert Schalkenbach Foundation, 1990).

7. Leon Walras, *Elements of Pure Economics*, translated by William Jaffe (New York: Irwin Publishing Company, 1954).

8. Vilfredo Pareto, *Mind & Society* (New York: Dover Publishing Company, 1935).

9. Alfred Marshall, *Principles of Economics* (New York: Macmillan Publishing Company, 1920).

10. Philip H. Wicksteed, *Common Sense of Political Economy* (London: Routledge and Kegan Paul, 1934).

11. F. Y. Edgeworth, *Mathematical Physics* (London: Kegan Paul, 1881).

12. Irwin Fisher, *Mathematical Investigations into the Theory of Value and Price* (New Haven, Conn.: Yale University Press, 1892).

13. Fritjof Capra, *The Web of Life* (New York: Anchor Book, Random House Publishers 1996).

14. John E. Ikerd, "The Question of Good Science," *American Journal of Alternative Agriculture*, 8, no. 2 (1993): 91–93.

15. Sidney Siegel, *Nonparametric Statistics* (New York: McGraw-Hill Book Company, 1956), 1–5.

16. Richard Lewontin, *The Triple Helix* (Cambridge, Mass.: Harvard University Press, 1998).

17. *World Book, 2002 Standard Edition,* "Organize."

18. Victor Frankl, *Man's Search for Meaning* (New York: Washington Square Press, 1984; original copyright, 1946).

19. Aldo Leopold, *A Sand County Almanac* (New York: Ballantine Books, 1949), 237–261.

20. *World Book,* "Philosophy." (Chicago: World Book, Inc. 2001).

21. *Microsoft Encarta Encyclopedia 2003,* "Cancer." (Redmond, Wash.: Microsoft Corp., 1993–2002).

22. *World Book,* "Progressive Movement."

23. David Korten, *When Corporations Rule the World,* (West Hartford, Conn.: Kumarian Press, 1995).

24. U.S. Department of Labor, "*Current Population Survey: Union Members Summary, January, 2004* (Washington, D.C.: U.S. Government Printing Office, 2004).

25. U.S. Office of Revenue System, *Internal Gross Revenue Collections by Type of Tax, Service Data Book, Publication 55b* (Washington, D.C.: U.S. Government Printing Office, 2003).

26. J. M. Keynes, *General Theory of Employment, Interest, and Money* (New York: Harcourt Brace, 1936).

27. Milton and Rose Friedman, *Free to Choose* (New York: Harcourt Brace, 1979/1980).

CHAPTER SIX

MANAGING THE SUSTAINABLE ORGANIZATION

Industrial Management Transformation

Industrial management is a term used to describe the techniques and expertise involved in organizing, planning, directing, and controlling the operations of a business.[1] Peter Drucker, in his classic 1950s' book, *The Practice of Management*, is generally recognized for giving credibility to management as a legitimate academic subject.[2] Drucker's approach to "management by objectives," with its emphasis on corporate planning and accountability, remains a cornerstone of management science. Drucker's later writings distinguish between *managers*, who affect the efficiency of an organization, and *executives*, who affect the capacity of an organization.[3] Drucker suggests that organizations relying on *knowledge* workers, as opposed to relying on manual laborers, need both managers and executives. Using Drucker's distinction, sustainable organizations, which are inherently knowledge-based organizations, must rely more on the executive functions of leading, nurturing, and empowering and less on the management functions of planning, directing, or controlling.

The new paradigm for managing sustainable organizations is already being developed by visionary executives in all types of organizations. During the 1980s, several futurists began to write about the fundamental transformation from an industrial to postindustrial society. In his book *Power Shift*, Alvin Toffler proclaimed that industrial models of economic progress were becoming increasingly obsolete and that industrial measures of efficiency and productivity were no longer sufficient.[4] He suggested that customized goods and services, targeted to niche markets; continuous innovation; and value-added products were the trends of the future. The most important new productive resource had become knowledge.

Peter Senge, in his book *The Fifth Discipline*, wrote about the necessity for systems thinking in managing the twenty-first century organization as a whole, rather than simply relying on new management tools.[5] Production systems of the future will embody enormous complexity with simultaneous and dynamic linkages among a multitude of interrelated factors, he wrote. Humans can deal *consciously* with only a very small number of different things at the same time. Yet humans are able to perform enormously complex tasks quite easily by using their well-developed *subconscious* minds. Our subconscious mind can solve problems without our even thinking about them. Senge believes people are perfectly capable of becoming systems thinkers.

Peter Drucker also writes of the "postbusiness" society in his book *The New Realities*.[6] He states that the most significant development of his lifetime is the shift to the knowledge society. He explains some important and fundamental differences between knowledge work and industrial work. Industrial work is a mechanical process, whereas the basic principles of knowledge work are biological. This difference has important implications in determining the *right* size for business organizations. In a mechanical world, greater efficiency is generally associated with greater size; there are economies of scale. But in a biological world, efficiency results from fitting size to function. "It would surely be counterproductive for a cockroach to be big, and equally counterproductive for the elephant to be small,"[7] Drucker writes.

Robert Reich, former U.S. Secretary of Labor, labels knowledge workers as "symbolic analysts" in his book *The Work of Nations*.[8] Symbolic analysts are the problem solvers, problem identifiers, and strategic brokers and hold positions such as design engineers, public relations executives, investment bankers, doctors, lawyers, real estate developers, and consultants of all types. The futurists seem to agree that the postindustrial era will be dominated by knowledge workers and that knowledge-based organizations will require a fundamentally different approach to organization and management.

Even though the numbers of knowledge-based organizations are growing, most of today's corporate managers exhibit little evidence of a transformation in management philosophy, in spite of the corporate rhetoric extolling reengineering, restructuring, and constant innovation. Dee Hock, founder of Visa Corporation, wrote in 1999, "The Industrial Age, hierarchical, command-and-control structures . . . that have grown to dominate our commercial, political, and social lives are increasingly irrelevant. They are failing not only in the sense of collapse, but also in the more common and pernicious form—organizations [are] increasingly unable to achieve the purpose for which they were created, yet [they are] continuing to expand as they devour resources, decimate the earth, and demean humanity."[9] These archaic industrial organizations are no longer capable of meeting the critical social, ecological, or economic challenges of today.

Most corporate managers, even those in knowledge-based organizations, still cling to the industrial philosophy of management and thus continue to manage unsustainable organizations. Industrial managers seek organizational efficiency through specialization, standardization, and centralization because they have been led to believe that efficient organizations must function according to those principles. However, the greatest current threats to ecological integrity, social equity, and even economic viability can be traced directly to overspecialization, overstandardization, and overcentralization of control. Thus, the greatest threats to sustainability are directly related to the industrial approach to organizational management.

Specialization, standardization, and consolidation are not necessarily extractive or exploitive strategies, if they are guided and limited by natural controls and restraints. They are simply general principles that can be used, or misused, in managing all types of organizations, biological as well as mechanical. Charles Darwin observed that living organisms appear to evolve in ways that allow them to perform specialized functions within their particular ecological niches.[10] Furthermore, living organisms, although unique, function according to clearly defined, or standardized, chemical and biological processes. And hierarchies of influence and control exist among many insect and animal species within nature. So even healthy living organisms and organizations may be specialized, standardized, and centrally controlled by their very nature.

A fundamental difference, however, is that living species survive and succeed by evolving to accommodate the ecological and social systems within which they exist, rather than by changing their ecological and social environment to accommodate their particular species.

Every species attempts to alter its environment in order to maximize its advantage relative to other species, even when it is to the apparent detriment of other species. But when a species succeeds in altering its environment, it then must adapt to the environment it has altered.[11] For example, when any particular species becomes dominant within its niche, it begins to encounter natural ecological or social constraints; it runs out of food, develops diseases, or encounters deadly conflicts with other species. These natural constraints reduce its numbers and force the once-dominant species back into harmony with its ever-evolving ecological and social niche. In other words, nature has effective means of limiting specialization, standardization, and consolidation of control.

Eventually, the forces of nature also may place natural constraints on industrial organizations that devour resources, decimate the earth, and demean humanity, as they attempt to maximize their current economic advantage. Many people believe that Malthus ultimately will be proven right, that the expansion of world population eventually will place overwhelming demands on the world's natural resources, and the human species will be devastated through starvation.[12] In addition, along with exploding human populations can come new diseases, such as AIDS and Ebola, that could wipe out large segments of humanity. Other living organisms—viruses, bacteria, insects, and even rats and roaches—have always found ways to compete with humans, in spite of our superior technologies. And of course, humans are not immune to the possibility of self-annihilation. Humans still seem incapable of resolving their cultural differences without wars. Some nations still view military action as a means of imposing their will on others, and modern weapons of mass destruction, if used en masse, could threaten the future of human life on Earth.

However, sustainable development ultimately will require that human societies recognize and respect the laws of nature and the limits of nature. Society must recognize the power of nature to limit any species, including the human species, that attempts to appropriate the total resources of the earth for its own benefit. Sustainability requires that we manage both natural and human resources in ways that are in harmony with their basic nature. Sustainability requires that humans voluntarily and purposefully choose levels of specialization, standardization, and centralization to accommodate the laws of nature and, thereby, to maintain the integrity of the social and ecological environment upon which human life on earth ultimately depends.

The value of diversity in creating synergistic organizations and the appropriate limits on specialization are readily apparent when the manager takes a holistic approach to management. Appropriate limits on standardization become apparent when the manager shows an appreciation for uniqueness and customizes the organization to accommodate the natural differences in people and places. Collaboration and cooperation place appropriate limits on the consolidation of control when the manager recognizes the value of interdependent relationships among sovereign individuals. Managers of sustainable economic organizations must learn to manage by a new set of management principles, which value diversity, individuality, and interdependence.

Managing Sustainable Organizations

All organizations must have a purpose, or a logical reason, for bringing people, money, and other resources together. Because the industrial organization is designed to operate like a mechanism, its purpose is embodied in its organizational structure. An industrial organization is structured so that specific functions, procedures, and responsibilities, if carried out properly, will ensure that the purpose of the organization is achieved.

A well-run industrial organization works like a well-oiled machine. Each machine is designed to fulfill a purpose, which may be as simple as drilling a hole or as complex as assembling the body of an automobile. Each part of a machine is designed to carry out a specific process, and all parts function in synchronization so that the machine can fulfill its purpose. Each machine is controlled by an operator, who may do something as simple as flipping a switch or as complex as guiding the machine through a series of intricate maneuvers. However, the role of the operator is matched with the design of the machine; together they perform a specific function.

A machine must be maintained in order to continue performing effectively; otherwise, it breaks down too often and wears out too soon. But even under the best of care, individual parts eventually wear out and have to be replaced. Machines having interchangeable or replaceable parts can be serviced and thus have a tremendous advantage over machines that are manufactured as single units. Eventually, however, any machine will become obsolete; it will no longer be able to fulfill its purpose, at least not as well as some newer design. Eventually any machine must be either redesigned or discarded and replaced with a newer model.

The people in an industrial organization become a part of the mechanism. Each position in the organizational chart, from chief executive officer to production line worker, performs a specific function in furthering the purpose of the organization. And like a machine, the industrial organization requires constant maintenance to ensure that each person in the organization performs his or her function in support of the overall organizational purpose. But even in the best of organizations, individuals eventually *wear out*. Eventually, they become disabled, obsolete, or simply lose their commitment to the organization. They get fired, or they resign or retire—voluntarily or otherwise—and have to be replaced. However, a *new* person can always be hired to fulfill the specific responsibilities of the *old* person— in industrial organizations, the people are interchangeable—and the organization will continue to function as before.

If the industrial organization becomes obsolete— unable to perform its purpose as effectively as some competitive organization—it must be reorganized, restructured, or redesigned so as to make it run more effectively. The ultimate responsibility for redesign lies with those who own the organization, the stockholders in the case of a corporation, but this responsibility typically is delegated to top-level management. Regardless, someone must decide when an organization has become obsolete and must therefore be redesigned or discarded.

The management paradigm for a sustainable organization, by contrast, is that of a living organism rather than an inanimate mechanism. Dee Hock provides an example of an appropriate management paradigm for sustainable organizations, and he refers to it as the management of *chaordic organizations*.[13] A chaordic (*cha-* from "chaos" and *-ord* from "order") organization, like any other organization, must have a purpose. In the chaordic organization, however, the purpose plays a continuing role in organizational management, and thus it cannot simply be designed into the structure. In the chaordic organization, the purpose must be instilled in the hearts and minds of every person in the organization. In living, chaordic organizations, the focus is on the people who fill the positions, rather than on their position descriptions, and the people must remain personally committed to the purpose of the organization.

The essence of the chaordic organization is embodied in its princi-ples of operation rather than its organizational structure. These organi-zational principles are expressed as a set of standards for individual and collective actions, which may include both structural and operational values. The principles chosen must be both necessary and sufficient to ensure that the organization fulfills its purpose. If a principle is not nec-essary for the functioning of the organization, the organization's ability to adapt to changes in its environment will be unnecessarily con-strained. If the set of principles is not adequate or appropriate, the orga-nization may not function effectively in pursuing its purpose.

The structure of a living organization is dynamic rather than fixed. Positions, departments, divisions, and organizational units change over time. They are continually evolving, forming, and dissolving as the orga-nization transforms and renews itself to meet the ever-changing demands of a dynamic marketplace in an ever-changing economic, social, and natural environment. This is the *chaotic* part of Hock's cha-ordic organizational model. The *order* part is embodied in the principles that guide the organization's processes or functions. The purpose and principles of the organization—the conceptual DNA, so to speak—remain unchanging, thus allowing the structure to evolve as needed to maintain both the effectiveness and efficiency of the organization.

For the people who work in sustainable organizations, principles are fundamentally different from the functions that make up a position description. A person in a living organization may still have specific responsibilities, but he or she will be free to meet those responsibilities by any means consistent with the principles of the organization. The person in the position, not the position description, will determine the most appropriate means of pursuing the purpose. And the person may change their means of fulfilling their responsibilities at any time in order to adapt to different situations or changing organizational envi-ronments. Thus, the management of sustainable organizations is focused on purpose, principles, and people rather than on planning, directing, and controlling.

Holistic Management

As indicated previously, the sustainable organization must be man-aged holistically. Any organization—business, social, or political—is defined as much by the *arrangement* of its components as by the nature of the components that make up the organizational whole. Gains from specialization result from greater efficiency in the functioning of individual components, whereas gains from holism come from greater efficiency in the functioning of the whole—including greater coherence among individual components. Thus, holistic management deals with the arrangement of diverse components and functions, across space, over time, and among individuals, so as to improve the effectiveness with which the components work together to fulfill their shared purpose. Holistic management is synergistic; it sees the organization as something more than the simple sum of its parts.

Economic organizations, by their very nature, involve human resources, ecological resources, and economic resources. The purpose of any economic activity is to allocate scarce resources so as to meet the needs of people, and all *economic* resources are extracted from either human or ecological resources. In industrial management, the depletion of ecological and social capital can be largely ignored because the business organization has no obligation for regeneration, unless the obligation is imposed via government regulations. As indicated in Chapter 4, contemporary economists consider society and the natural environment to be *externalities*, which are only managed in cases in which they have been *internalized* through public policies or social pressures.

In managing sustainable organizations, in which quality of life is always a primary consideration, the social and ecological dimensions of organizational performance are as important as the economic. And equally important, both people and nature, in the form of social and ecological capital, are integral aspects of the sustainable economic organization. In sustainable management, nature and society are not external to the organization; they are integral and inseparable aspects of the organizational whole.

On the surface, holistic management, with its emphasis on interrelationships, might seem quite complex. Once understood, however, it is mostly just common sense. Alan Savory's book *Holistic Resource Management* provides an excellent framework for managing holistically.[14] The basic principles and strategies of holistic management are quite straightforward. Savory refers to the holistic organization's purpose as a "three-part holistic goal," which includes economic, social, and ecological dimensions. Nature, including human nature, functions according to fundamental and unchangeable principles—a fact often ignored by industrial managers. Thus, the manager of a holistic organization must recognize and respect the fundamental economic, social, and ecological principles by which sustainable organizations must function.

All of the interconnections among the various components, including ecological and social components, are important to the organizational whole. Once the holistic manager has a thorough understanding of the whole under management, decisions can be made incrementally to improve organizational performance, without having to consider all of the interconnections at the time of any particular decision. In economics, this approach to management is called *partial budgeting*.[15]

Partial budgeting begins with the current organizational situation. The manager then asks a series of questions regarding the consequences of a potential change, the answers to which, taken together, indicate the advisability of the proposed action. First, what will be the potential *direct economic* benefits and costs of the change? Next, what are the potential *indirect economic* benefits and costs—that is, changes in costs or returns *elsewhere* in the organization brought about by the proposed change, considering all affected interconnections? Direct and indirect costs are then subtracted from direct and indirect benefits to derive the *net economic benefit* of the potential change.

The process is the same conceptually for estimating economic, ecological, and social impacts of change—the ecological and social impacts are just more difficult to quantify. In the case of ecological and social estimates, the distinction between direct and indirect costs and benefits also may seem less clear. Regardless of the process, the holistic manager must assess the *net social benefit* and the *net ecological benefit*, which are to be balanced with the *net economic benefit*.

Therefore, in holistic management, the final step in the partial budgeting process is to consider the balance among net economic, social, and ecological benefits. Unfortunately, no objective means exist for calculating an expected net total benefit—the problem that led to the economic abandonment of happiness. For this, the holistic manager will simply have to rely on his or her insight, intuition, or common sense to decide what is best for the organization. However, with an understanding of the organizational whole and the purpose and principles by which it must operate, along with a thoughtfully derived set of potential net economic, ecological, and social benefits, such decisions are made easier.

In any case, the manager will never be able to anticipate all the ultimate consequences of his or her choices. Thus, the holistic manager must constantly monitor the performance of the organization in relation to its purpose and principles, must be quick to admit mistakes, and must be slow to conclude success. Savory refers to this as "assuming that you are wrong" until proven right. Most industrial managers seem to assume the opposite and thus deny their mistakes until it's too late to reverse course. Holistic managers must recognize the fundamental laws of nature, including human nature, within which the sustainable organization must be managed, and they must attempt to work with nature rather than against it, knowing that nature always has the last word.

Diversity

Diversity among distinct entities, across space and time, is essential in sustaining all living processes—biological, social, and economic. Thus, management of diversity is an essential element of managing any sustainable organization.

Economic diversity is necessary to sustain the economic gains achieved through *appropriate* levels of specialization. Economic synergy depends on gains from trade among diverse economic entities—individuals, businesses, or nations—each of which has a different comparative advantage. No potential gains from trade would exist if all economic entities were identical or lacked diversity. Economic diversity is necessary also to ensure the stability and strength of an organization. Beyond some point, increased specialization and increased standardization leave the industrial organization more vulnerable to economic adversity. For example, an organization that produces only one product, using a single production process, and for a single customer is extremely vulnerable. The organization that markets a diverse line of products, to a large number of different types of customers, and using a variety of production processes is far more secure. The diverse organization may be less efficient, but the loss of a single customer, product, or process will have minimal impact on the overall performance of the organization.

The same principles of synergy, diversity, and sustainability apply to the ecological and social dimensions of an organization. Every human organization has an impact on the natural ecosystem of the bioregion in which it is located and on the ecosystems from which it procures raw materials or markets its products. Such impacts are obvious for organizations involved with farming, forestry, mining, or other natural resource–based enterprises. However, every organization depends on resources of the earth, which is the basic source of all physical inputs—including minerals, chemicals, and energy—and the ultimate *sink* for all wastes. The organization's choices of inputs, its conservation of resources, and its methods of waste disposal all have impacts on the natural environment. Impacts are not limited to the environment of the organization's workers and neighbors, but indeed may be felt across nations and around the world for generations into the future.

Ecosystems with greater diversity provide more opportunities for synergistic relations, both among organisms and between organisms and their environment, thereby resulting in greater natural productivity and regenerative capacity. When natural ecosystems lose their diversity, they lose their health and their ability to renew and reproduce. Those living organisms most capable of complex behavior tend to dominate their ecological environment, implying an advantage also for diversity within organisms.[16] Diversity within ecosystems also contributes to resistance, resiliency, and thus to their capacity to endure adversity. Diverse living ecosystems can withstand and recover from the diminished or lost contribution of any one species. However, the loss of a single species within a less diverse system may trigger a process of ecological degradation, leading toward irreversible decline. The sustainable organization must accept its ethical and moral responsibility for ecological integrity, and, in so doing, it ensures its own long-term productivity, strength, stability, and regenerative capacity.

The relationship between sustainability and social diversity is perhaps less well understood than is economic or ecological diversity, but is no less important. Diversity among individuals not only creates opportunities for economic synergy, but also is necessary for the happiness that arises from positive human relationships. If all people in an organization have the same values, ideals, attitudes, aspirations, and lifestyles, they will have little to contribute to each other and will have no one to challenge their thinking. The inherent value of any human relationship arises from the opportunity to share one's life with various people. Obviously, diversity can result in conflicts as well as collaboration and can be destructive as well as constructive. Nonetheless, without diversity among us, there are no opportunities for positive personal relationships.

Diversity among peoples generally is referred to as cultural rather than social diversity. Cultural differences, however, are differences in values, ideals, and attitudes that are passed from one generation to the next. Thus, cultural diversity tends to define differences among groups of people rather than differences among individuals. Differences among individuals reflect both cultural differences, those associated with the various groups with which one may identify, and individual differences, those characteristics that distinguish the individuals from their groups. Regardless of whether differences are cultural or individual, social diversity is necessary for organizational sustainability.

Social diversity contributes to sustainability in essentially the same ways as do economic diversity and ecological diversity. Differences among individuals and groups are essential for renewing and regenerating human society. As people relate to each other, economically and politically, some of their social diversity inevitably is lost. As they attempt to accommodate each other to improve their economic and political performance, some of their differences are lost. In both cases, social capital is transformed into economic and political capital. The same loss of social capital occurs whenever one culture attempts to accommodate other cultures; they lose some of their diversity. Obviously, economic, political, and even social benefits may be realized from learning to better understand and accommodate each other's cultures. However, if all cultural and individual differences were erased, there would be no further potential benefit from our diversity. An organization that lacks social diversity lacks the ability to renew and regenerate the social capital necessary for long-term sustainability.

Social diversity also contributes to the resilience, resistance, and long-term endurance of an organization. An organization composed of people who all have the same values and tend to think alike on all issues may operate very efficiently; however, it will be highly vulnerable to change in its economic, ecological, or social environment. In a diverse organization, the current environment may favor some individuals, but if the environment changes, other individuals will be at an advantage. Thus, the diverse organization will be better able to cope with the change. A more socially diverse organization may be less efficient under ideal conditions than is the homogeneous organization, but the more diverse organization is less vulnerable to adversity.

Obviously, organizations can become too diverse—economically, ecologically, and socially—just as they can become too standardized or homogeneous. Excessive diversity in managed organizations leads to unnecessary complexity by complicating management decisions while adding neither regenerative capacity nor reducing risks. Beyond some number of enterprises, increasing difficulty in management will offset any potential synergistic gain from greater diversity. For example, it can be shown statistically that an organization with five or six economically independent enterprises—having no correlation of costs, prices, or profits—gains very little economic stability by adding still more enterprises. The specific number of different entities constituting positive diversity is not as important as the extent to which the various entities complement each other in productivity, regenerative capacity, or risk reduction. The important point is that some diversity is necessary for sustainability, but that beyond some point, greater diversity is neither necessary nor sustainable. Through balancing economic, social, and ecological risks and benefits, the natural tendency of the sustainably managed organization is toward neither specialization nor complexity, but instead toward a sustainable level of diversity.

Individuality

Sustainably managed organizations must be individualistic and site-specific, whereas the natural tendency of the industrial organization is toward greater standardization. By eliminating individual functional differences, specialized processes fit together more effectively, thus increasing operational efficiency. Industrialization also seeks to eliminate the uniqueness among organizations producing the same basic products, thus allowing efficient exchange of processes and products among specialized industrial organizations. Standardization in U.S. industry began with Eli Whitney's promotion of interchangeable parts for weapons during the Revolutionary War and continues throughout the U.S. economy today.[17]

In general, the potential for economic gains from industrialization arise from the ability to create greater economic value at a lower economic cost. In economic terms, production may be defined as the creation of utility; that is, production is the process of creating useful goods and services. Economic utility, or usefulness, can be further classified into *form* utility, *place* utility, *time* utility, and *possession* utility.[18] In other words, to know the economic value of anything, one has to know *what* it is (form), *where* it is (place), *when* it is available (time), *who* has it, and *who* wants it (possession). Thus, economic value is created by changing the form (manufacturing or processing), place (transportation), time (inventory or storage), or possession (transfer of ownership) of the good or service in question.

By standardizing the processes involved in manufacturing, transportation, inventory, and transactions, industrial organizations are able to produce and deliver products and services of uniform quality at lower costs. Specifically, by manufacturing large quantities of the same basic product and shipping it in large quantities to large storage facilities to be distributed through large-volume retail outlets, industrial organizations are able to achieve significant economic efficiencies through mass production and distribution. In order to gain these efficiencies, however, industrial managers must either minimize or ignore the most important aspects of economic value that arise from *possession,* or ownership.

Different people value things differently. People do not have the same abilities as producers or the same tastes and preferences as consumers. A given product, at a given time and place, will be valued differently by any two people. Moreover, different people have to expend different amounts of time and energy to produce the same good or service. However, industrial organizations have to treat large groups of people as if they were all essentially the same. They attempt to train people of different aptitudes and abilities to perform the same tasks at the same speed on assembly lines and in offices of industrial organizations. They attempt to standardize the tastes and preferences of consumers through persuasive advertising, while striving to create the illusion of diversity through superficial product differentiation. But industrial organizations cannot meet the unique needs of inherently diverse people without sacrificing the economies of large-scale industrial mass production and distribution.

Conversely, sustainable organizations create value through individualization of processes and products. People within a sustainable organization are encouraged to use their individual aptitudes and abilities and to pursue their passions to the fullest, bounded only by the purposes and principles of their organization. The sustainable organization is made stronger by the diversity of its people. Sustainable organizations honor the sovereignty of their customers; they try to satisfy existing wants and needs rather than persuade or mislead. They customize their products to serve sustainable niche markets, which are the smallest segments of like-minded customers that can be served efficiently.

Sustainable organizations must be site-specific; they must accommodate the geographic niches within nature in which all organizations must operate. All tangible products are produced using material resources extracted from nature. The product–resource linkages, as with environmental impacts, are most obvious for the products of farms, forests, and fisheries. However, any product or process that relies on energy, air, water, or minerals is natural resource–dependent. In addition, all tangible products and processes rely on the natural environment as a sink for disposal of waste.

Industrial organizations gain efficiencies by carrying out the same basic operations and at the same optimum economic scale, regardless of the geographic location. They attempt to modify nature to accommodate their organization rather than modify the organization to accommodate different locations. Virtually all resource depletion problems—including minerals, water, forests, and fisheries—are a consequence of taking too many resources from specific places. Virtually all pollution problems are consequences of dumping too much waste in specific places. No such problems might have occurred if the same levels of resources use and the same levels of waste disposal had been geographically dispersed to fit the regeneration and sink capacities of various places. Sustainable organizations must be managed to fit natural limits of specific places. And even the modern service-based, knowledge-based economies of the world remain critically dependent upon their natural environment.

Sustainable organizations create value by linking people and product with place. Their managers attempt to match unique customers, with specific tastes and preferences, with unique producers, who have the abilities and passion to produce what those customers want, using unique natural resources that are naturally productive and compatible with the products to be produced. Industrial organizations, with their specialization, standardization, and consolidation must dominate or conquer nature, including human nature, to achieve the economies of large-scale production. The concentration of too much of anything in too little space, including too much waste or too many people, inevitably leads to the degradation of naturally diverse ecosystems.

Sustainable organizations, alternatively, work in harmony with nature, including human nature, thereby allowing people to do what they naturally do best, meeting the needs of people who naturally value most the things they do, and in the places where producers can be the most productive and consumers the most happy. Differences in productivity, costs, and value can be tremendous, between working against nature and working with nature for sustainability.

Interdependence

The ultimate economic benefits of industrial management arise from economies of scale, which are achieved through consolidation and centralization of organizational control. The ultimate economic, ecological, and social benefits of sustainable management arise from the natural coherence of harmonious, interdependent relationships—from the synergistic arrangement of parts within an organizational whole.

The reliance of sustainability on interdependent relationships was discussed in detail in previous chapters. To summarize that discussion, *interdependent* relationships are relationships of choice, *dependent* relationships are relationships of necessity, and *independence* implies the absence of relationships. Self-renewal and regeneration are characteristics of living systems, which inherently are holistic in nature and characterized by interdependent relationships among diverse components. Ultimately, the sustainability of any entity—organization, community, or ecosystem—depends on its capacity for renewal and regeneration. Thus, sustainability depends upon interdependence. Interdependent organizations are by nature synergistic; that is, the organizational whole is more than the sum of its component parts. Interdependent organizations also are resistant and resilient; they have the capacity to withstand adversity. Sustainable organizations are interdependent organizations.

Interdependent organizations require leadership rather than management. In an interdependent organization, management is decentralized and dispersed throughout the organization. Each person has a realm of responsibility within which they are empowered to make autonomous decisions. However, each person within the organization is expected to contribute to the overall purpose of the organization by following the fundamental principles of the organization. Thus, they work together in fulfilling the purpose, even though their specific actions are a matter of individual choice rather than of management directive. Each worker is a manager, free to plan, organize, and direct their activities as they see fit, as long as they abide by the principles of the organization.

In order for individuals to maintain synergistic, interdependent relationships, they must have a clear understanding and commitment to their shared purpose within the organization and to the principles by which the organization must function. The leadership of the sustainable organization has the responsibility of interpreting and articulating the organizational purpose. The leadership must ensure that those who share a commitment to the purpose are free to make their own decisions and those who choose not to share a commitment to the purpose, after emphathetic consultation, are encouraged to find more compatible employment elsewhere. A sustainable organization may evolve over time by changing its purpose, but at any point in time, it must have a clearly defined and broadly embraced sense of purpose.

The leadership in a sustainable organization also has the responsibility of articulating and evaluating the principles by which the organization must function. The principles are like the DNA of a living organism—they maintain the identity and integrity of the organization as it continually renews and regenerates its structure. As with genes in living organisms, an organization needs enough principles, but not too many principles. As with the organizational purpose, those who are committed to the principles must be empowered by the leadership to make their own decisions and those who, after consultation, choose not to commit should be encouraged to find other employment.

Although members of the sustainable organization are free to make their own decisions, they must follow a holistic approach to decision making. They must consider the impact of each decision on the organization as a whole—including its economic, ecological, and social dimensions. They must seek out and maintain interdependent relationships. Each member of the organization is responsible for maintaining sufficient diversity within the organization to ensure that the organization is capable of renewal and regeneration and remains resilient and resistant. Each member of the organization is then free to maintain interdependent relationships of choice, not necessity, with others within and outside of the organization.

Managing a sustainable organization is analogous to nurturing life. A sustainable organization is a holistic, diverse, individualistic, interdependent organism. If it is appropriately cared for, it will be naturally productive, resistant to adversity, and self-renewing. And over time, it will evolve to accommodate changes in its economic, social, and ecological environment. Only a living organization is capable of sustainability—of meeting the needs of the present while leaving opportunities for the future.

The Triple Bottom Line

Some business managers adhere to the concept of a *triple bottom line* in managing for sustainability. The triple bottom line came to widespread attention in the late 1990s and has since gained in popularity among businesses of all types.[19] Managing for a triple bottom line suggests managing for balance among the 1) economic, 2) ecological, and 3) social dimensions of organizational performance, rather than maximizing profits or growth. Triple bottom line managers recognize that businesses without social and ecological integrity will not be economically viable over the long run. Such firms eventually will degrade their social and natural environment to an extent that they will lose the ability to sustain their profitability.

In many situations, attention to social and ecological performance can improve profitability, even in the short run. Managers find ways to transform ecological wastes into economic assets and to produce more while using fewer nonrenewable resources.[20] They also find ways to reduce costs and create new markets by developing and maintaining better relationships with their workers, their customers, and others in the communities in which they operate.[21] In general, they improve their efficiency in converting ecological and social capital into economic capital.

However, triple bottom line management has its legitimate skeptics. The critics claim the most significant aspects of the concept are not new and the new aspects of the concept are not workable.[22] The critics correctly assert that corporate organizations have historically made the claim to their stockholders, customers, neighbors, and to society as a whole that they accept social and ethical responsibilities, which go beyond maximizing profits and growth. However, such claims rarely translate into actual performance. Even corporations convicted of financial fraud and environmental pollution have had mission statements reflecting their supposed commitment to social responsibility and ecological integrity. Without naming specific companies, a review of corporate Web sites of the reader's choosing will quickly validate this charge. However, in defense of corporate mission statements, most make clear, if not explicit, that financial returns to stockholders take precedent over all other considerations. The critics admit that if managers could objectively measure social and ecological performance, and if stockholders actually valued such performance, managing for a triple bottom line would be both significant and workable. Lacking adequate measures and stockholder commitments, however, managing for the triple bottom line remains largely a corporate public relations strategy.

Notable exceptions to the rule both verify the potential value of the concept and identify the essentials of effective triple bottom line management. Ray Anderson, of Interface Inc., a large carpet manufacturer, travels the country proclaiming the benefits of triple bottom line management and provides his financial statements as compelling evidence that a large corporation can be profitable as well as socially and ecologically responsible.[23] *Fast Company* magazine hailed Interface as "the most highly evolved big company in the country—a $1.2 billion model for social responsibility and economic growth."[24] Based on the experiences of Interface and other companies, the key to success seems to be a deep personal commitment on the part of corporate management to the concept rather than a desperate corporate management response to growing public pressure and protests.[25]

Sustainable triple bottom line businesses must be willing to make net investments in social and ecological resources, rather than investments that simply improve their economic efficiency. No matter how efficient an organization may be, some social and ecological capital is lost in the process of production, reflecting the inevitable natural tendency toward entropy. Thus, a sustainable firm must be willing not only to eliminate unnecessary wastes, but also to restore the unavoidable depletion and degradation of ecological and social capital.

For individuals, the value of relationships can more than offset personal investments in developing and maintaining social capital. Likewise for individuals, the peace of mind and sense of purpose that results from stewardship can more than offset their personal investment in ecological capital. But, for business firms, the rewards for pursuing a sustainable, triple bottom line are less clear.

For individual proprietorships, partnerships, family corporations, and other closely held corporations, the social and ethical benefits to the owners can more than offset any short-term sacrifices. In addition, most such owners are committed to their firms for the long run, and they know that their investments in social and ecological capital are necessary to sustain the business over time. Of course, some owners of closely held corporations may place no value on social or ecological responsibility, and may insist that the business be managed for a single (economic) bottom line. Some individuals, likewise, place no value on relationships or stewardship. But closely held businesses have the same basic motives for management as individuals have for personal decisions.

Publicly held corporations present a different and more difficult challenge. Once the number of stockholders becomes large, the ownership becomes highly transitory, and the ownership becomes separated from management—as is the case with most large, publicly held corporations—then the single bottom line seems destined to prevail. Most stockholders in large, publicly held corporations, particularly those who invest through mutual funds and pension funds, are interested primarily, if not solely, in profits and growth. Some mutual funds claim to specialize in ecologically and socially responsible companies, but such funds are under pressure to be competitive economically as well.

At some time in the future, triple bottom line corporations may be able to target the sales of their stock to specific investors who share their commitments to social and ecological integrity. However, such investors must be willing to accept lower economic returns whenever net social and ecological investments are necessary to ensure long-term sustainability. Triple bottom line investors also must refuse to sell their stock to single bottom line investors, who inevitably will view triple bottom line companies as undervalued, because they are not fully exploiting their short-term economic potential.

Until then, however, ecological and social responsibility management of large, publicly held corporations will take place only within the context of constitutional commitments and public policies that protect the sustainable organization from competitors who rely on extraction and exploitation to maximize their short-term profits. The manager of a large corporate organization must be provided with an economic milieu within which the corporation can be managed for sustainability.

Endnotes

1. *Microsoft Encarta Encyclopedia 2003*, "Industrial Management." (Redmond, Wash.: Mircrosoft Corp., 1993–2002).

2. Peter F. Drucker, *The Practice of Management* (New York: Harper & Row, 1954).

3. Peter F. Drucker, *The Effective Executive* (New York: HarperBusiness, Harper-Collins Publishing, 1966/1967), 4–5.

4. Alvin Toffler, *Power Shift* (New York: Bantam Books, 1990).

5. Peter M. Senge, *The Fifth Discipline* (New York: Doubleday Publishing Co., 1990), 5–13.

6. Peter F. Drucker, *The New Realities* (New York: Harper and Row Publishers, Inc., 1989).

7. Drucker, *Realities*, 259.

8. Robert B. Reich, *The Work of Nations* (New York: Vintage Books, Random House Publishing, 1992).

9. Dee Hock, *Birth of the Chaordic Age* (San Francisco: Barrett-Koehler Publishers, Inc. 1999), 5–6.

10. Charles Darwin, *The Origin of the Species* (New York: Penguin Putnam, Inc., 1958; original copyright, 1859).

11. Richard Lewontin, *The Triple Helix* (Cambridge, Mass.: Harvard University Press, 1998), 41–68.

12. James Bonar, *Malthus and His Work* (New York: Macmillan Publishing Company, 1885).

13. Hock, *Chaordic Age*.

14. Alan Savory, *Holistic Resource Management* (Covelo, Calif.: Island Press, 1988).

15. Earl O. Heady, *Economics of Agricultural Production and Resource Use* (Upper Saddle River, N.J.: Prentice Hall, 1952).

16. Stuart Kauffman, *At Home in the Universe* (New York Oxford University Press, 1995), 90–91.

17. *World Book, 2002 Standard Edition,* "Eli Whitney."

18. Richard Kohls and David Downey, *Marketing of Agricultural Products*, 4th ed. (New York: Macmillan Publishing Company, 1972), 5.

19. John Elkington, *Cannibals With Forks: The Triple Bottom Line of 21st Century Business* (Stony Creek, Conn.: New Society Publishers, 1998).

20. Paul Hawken, Amory Lovins, and L. Hunter Lovins, *Natural Capitalism* (New York: Little, Brown and Company, 1999).

21. Bob Willard, *The Sustainability Advantage: Seven Business Case Benefits of Triple Bottom Line* (Gabriola Island, British Columbia, New Society Publishers, 2002).

22. Wayne Norman and Chris MacDonald, "Getting to the Bottom of the 'Triple Bottom Line,'" *Business Ethics Quarterly,* April (2004).

23. Ray Anderson, Mid-Course Correction: *Toward a Sustainable Enterprise: The Interface Model* (White River Junction, Vt.: Chelsea Green Publishers, 1998).

24. Charles Fishman, "Sustainable Growth: Interface, Inc.," *Fast Company Magazine,* no. 14 (1998): 136.

25. Willard, *Sustainability Advantage*.

CHAPTER SEVEN

THE THREE ECONOMIES OF SUSTAINABILITY

Economic Philosophy

The term *deep ecology* was first brought to public attention by a Norwegian philosopher, Arne Naess, in 1973. Naess argued that the environmental movement existed at two levels, "shallow" and "deep." The shallow movement was concerned primarily with social welfare issues, such as pollution and depletion of natural resources. The deep movement was concerned with the fundamental philosophical issues of how humans *should* relate to their natural environment. Naess argued that Western philosophy reflects an outdated view of the world, in which humans see themselves as separate from each other and from their natural environment. A deeper understanding, however, reveals that humans are not truly separate or isolated, but instead are integrally interconnected with each other and with the world around them. Humans are "part of the flow of energy, the web of life," he wrote.[1]

The overall economy is an organization. It simply functions at a higher level of organization than does the individual business or nonprofit organization. The economics of sustainability addresses the issue of sustainable development from a *deep* philosophical perspective. Thus, in managing a sustainable economy, the first priority is to transform one's worldview from that of the economic individual in isolation to that of the person in society and in nature. The second priority is to accept the fact that the persons managing the economy are inherently a part of the economy, and, thus, management choices are inevitably personal and subjective. The most important issues affecting economic sustainability concern social values and moral judgments regarding how people *should* relate to each other and to their natural environment. Economists, if they are to be relevant, can no longer disassociate themselves from questions of equity and ethics because they are an integral part of the social and ecological economies they are studying. The fundamental economic issues relate to first principles, things that cannot be proven but that we nonetheless know to be true. The *non-ethic* of neoclassical economics becomes an explicit personal value judgment within the context of the sustainable economy. So at this point, we can drop the pretext of third-person disassociation from the writings in this book. Written discourse on this particular subject is not only less stilted, but also is more realistic when phrased in the personal terms of *we* and *us* rather than *they* and *them*.

Sustainability is a long-term, people-centered concept, and we are the people at its center. The purpose of sustainable development is to maintain a desirable quality of life for people—of current and future generations—but, indeed, for people. Some find fault with this anthropocentric interpretation of sustainability. Some deep ecologists, for example, contend that other forms of life may be just as important as human life in the long-range scheme of things. However, the *deep* in "deep ecology," as explained previously, simply refers to the level of human thinking, not to any particular ecological philosophy.[2]

The economics of sustainability is built upon the premise that our individual well-being is integrally related with the well-being of the entire human society, with all other living species, and with nonliving elements of our natural environment. However, if we humans were not concerned *uniquely* with sustaining the quality of *human* life, there would be no *economic* issue to be addressed. The economy is a human creation, and economics addresses the allocation of scarce resources to meet the needs of humans. So if we weren't particularly concerned about humans, we could simply depopulate the earth of humans to a point at which the sustainability of other species and resources would no longer be in question, or at least would not be threatened by humans.

We humans, like other species, have innate instincts for survival, reproduction, and self-gratification; that's all part of our nature. Thus, we will not reduce our claims on earth's resources for the sole purpose of ensuring the sustainability of other species or of the earth. But the fact that we are concerned *uniquely* with sustaining the human species does not dictate that we are concerned *exclusively* with sustaining the human species. We will protect other species if we perceive it to be in our broader and higher self-interest to do so. Contrary to neoclassical economic thinking, our self-interests are not exclusively individualistic in nature. Our interests as members of our particular societies and of the human race are integrally linked with the integrity of the rest of the biosphere. Thus, our self-interest may be served best through sharing and stewardship, including preservation of other species, rather than through expressing our animalistic urges for immediate self-gratification.

The quality of human life has inseparable individual, interpersonal, and spiritual dimensions, as explained in previous chapters. Thus, the new sustainable economy may be viewed as a whole composed of three inseparable economies—the individual or private economy, the social or public economy, and the ecological or moral economy. *Economy*, as used here, is a reflection of the Greek word for economics, *oikonomia*—which refers to study of resource stewardship for the overall well-being of the household, society, and natural environment—rather than limiting economics to managing scarce resources for the wealth of individuals.[3] Each of the three economies of sustainability are distinct, but are clearly interconnected with and interdependent on the others, as are the individual, interpersonal, and spiritual dimensions of our quality of life.

The Ecological Economy

The ecological economy is the foundation on which rest the other two. All individual economic resources are either ecological or social in origin. All material economic resources—minerals, chemicals, gases, fibers, foods, and so on—are products of the earth. All human economic resources—labor, management, entrepreneurship, creativity, determination, and so on—are products of human society, which also is inherently dependent upon the earth. The sustainability of the individual economy ultimately depends upon the health of the social and ecological economies.

From a "shallow" ecological perspective, the natural ecosystem also contributes to the economic value of goods and services in ways that are not reflected in the marketplace. In the mid-1990s, a group of economists attempted to assess the nonmarket economic value of global ecosystem "services," including the provision of atmospheric gasses, waste assimilation, nutrient flows, and the storage and purification of water. Although such resources have no market value, they can be assigned an alternative or opportunity value by estimating how much it would cost to provide similar services using alternative market-valued means. The group reported their estimated value as a range, from $36 trillion to $58 trillion (1998 dollars).[4] This compares with a gross world product of only $39 trillion in 1998, suggesting that natural ecosystems contributed as much or more in total *economic* value as did all intentional human economic activities. And these non-market economic values include only the productivity from ecological capital that is *not* converted into economic capital, but nonetheless can be measured or estimated in terms of dollars and cents. The group did not attempt to place economic values on the smell of fresh air, the feel of the sun, open spaces, scenic landscapes, or moonlit nights. Some things are truly "priceless."

From a "deeper" ecological perspective, we humans simply cannot exist without the natural resources of the earth,—although many have lost sight of this fact in the highly specialized, industrial economy of today. People cannot live without sunlight, air, water, and soil. Most have at least been reminded of our tenuous dependence on the natural resources of the earth by the industrial pollution of air and water. However, many people became concerned about air and water only when supplies of clean air and water became scarce and thus took on economic value.

Other natural resources are no less essential to our sustainability. Many of these resources have some economic value, but their economic value falls far short of their intrinsic value to humanity. Land, for example, is often valued more as space than as a resource for growing food because, in the United States at least, food is still relatively abundant. Many people never stop to think that humanity is as dependent upon healthy soil as we are upon clean air and water. Virtually all of life arises from the soil—even life that resides in the ocean. Without the mineral and biological resources of the earth, life on this planet would be impossible. Soil is just one among many undervalued yet necessary resources of the ecological economy.

We humans can't absorb enough energy to keep us alive directly from the sun or the earth. Living organisms, mostly plants, convert solar energy, soil, water, and air into energy forms that can be consumed by animals, including humans. We get the energy to fuel our bodies from the energy stored by other living things—plants, animals, and other living things. All energy present on the earth today, including fossil energy, was either stored in the earth at its time of formation or has been captured from the sun and stored since then by living organisms. The only source of new energy is from the sun. The ecological capital of the earth is made up of the existing stocks of available and stored energy and the interconnected web of life by which solar energy can be collected, transformed, and stored.

We humans currently are using fossil energy far faster than we are capturing new energy from the sun. More than 80% of total energy consumption in the United States is from fossil fuels, and nuclear energy accounts for just over 10%.[5] The *renewable* energy usage amounts to less than 10%, and, of that, hydroelectric power accounts for almost half and solar energy accounts for less than 1%. The sun generates about 35,000 times as much energy as humans use. [6] Even with about one-third of total solar energy never reaching the earth, the sun clearly provides sufficient energy to support more life on earth, including more humans, if we can learn to make better use of solar energy, which is the ultimate source of all renewable energy. Instead, we are currently depleting the ecological capital of the earth as we use stored fossil energy and degrade the health and productivity of regenerative living ecosystems.

As indicated in the preceding chapter, we must use the earth as a dump or a *sink* for our wastes, as well as a source of energy to sustain life. There is no "away" where we can throw our wastes, except into the natural environment. And by dumping our waste into the environment, we are degrading or destroying its usefulness to humans.[7] When we pollute air or water, poison the soil with chemicals, or allow the soil to erode, we are destroying ecological capital. Some things we dump into the environment could be reused or recycled, thereby turning wastes into useful resources. However, some waste is unavoidable, because of entropy. Therefore, ecological capital is lost, both through avoidable waste and through the unavoidable tendency toward entropy.

As far as we know, the first and second laws of thermodynamics are inviolable. Thus, in a sustainable economy, the uses of energy and matter, as resources and as sinks, must be equal to or less than the sum of the inflow of solar energy and our reclamation of resources from the natural environment. The sustainability of human life on Earth is related directly to our ability to maintain our stocks of ecological capital. Ultimately, we must reconcile the individual and social economies with the ecological economy, if we are to sustain life, including human life, on Earth.

From a deep ecological perspective, the sustainability of human life on Earth depends upon our willingness and ability to reexamine and redefine our relationships with each other and with the earth. Much of the past work in sustainability has focused on opportunities in the shallow ecological economy, largely accepting the context of existing economic and social relationships as given.[8,9] However, "deep" sustainability deals not only with relationships as they are, but also asks what those relationships *should* be and *must* be to sustain a desirable quality of human life on earth.[10]

The *World Book Encyclopedia* provides three definitions of *ecology*: the branch of biology that deals with the relation of living things to their environment and to each other; the branch of sociology that deals with the relations between human beings and their environment; and the balanced or harmonious relationship of living things to their environment.[11] All three are appropriate and relevant to the subject of deep sustainability. The ecological economy is about the *rightness* of our relationships with the earth and with each other; it is part of the moral and ethical economy.

The Social Economy

The concept of a social economy is less well understood and appreciated than is that of the ecological economy. First, the social economy is not the macro-economy, which is simply an aggregation of all individual economic enterprises. The social economy deals with the interconnectedness of people within society, not just the adding together of individuals. The purpose of the macro-economy is to facilitate the building of a stronger individual, private economy. The purpose of the social economy is to facilitate the building of a stronger society by encouraging positive personal relationships among people.

Social capital is the essence of civilized society.[12] Social capital is reflected in the ability of people to relate to each other; to form families, communities, and nations; to agree on processes of governance and trade; and to define shared principles and values, which are essential for any *civilized* society. "Social capital consists of the stock of active connections among people: the trust, mutual understanding, and shared values and behaviors that bind the members of human networks and communities and make cooperative action possible."[13] Analogous to stocks of fossil energy, our current stocks of social capital have been built up over centuries by past human civilizations, as human societies became more *civilized*. Also analogous to stocks of fossil fuels, there is growing evidence that we are depleting our stocks of social resources at a rate far in excess of our rate of social regenerations, as human societies become less *civil*.[14] As social resources are depleted, societies tend toward incivility, just as surely as the depletion of energy resources causes natural systems to tend toward entropy. Our social resources are at least as important as our ecological resources in supporting and sustaining a desirable quality of human life.

Stocks of social capital are built up through the processes of human *culture*, which is the learning and knowledge that is passed from one generation to the next, as people struggle, successfully or not, to achieve more peaceful, productive, and harmonious relationships. Anything that contributes a higher quality of life through more-positive human relationships builds stocks of social resources. War, crime, confrontation, argument, destructive competition, and other forms of human conflict destroy social capital. Cultures that have lived in peace for centuries can become bitter enemies in the aftermath of simple misunderstandings. Misunderstandings can lead to conflicts, conflicts to confrontations, and confrontations to wars. Accordingly, our ability to live and work together is destroyed, the social capital is depleted, and the quality of life is diminished.

Sometimes, social capital is depleted through deliberate acts of oppression, exploitation, discrimination, injustice, or even indifference. Unfortunately, such acts seem to become commonplace as capitalism tends toward corporatism. A corporatist economy places no value on human relationships, other than those that can be transformed into economic capital for financial gain. Corporations are not real people and thus gain no purely personal value from relationships. Corporations, lacking human compassion, tend to weaken the social fabric of families, communities, and nations as they transform social capital to economic capital in their relentless pursuit of profits and growth.

Stocks of social capital also are depleted through ordinary acts of human incivility, which appear to be an inevitable aspect of any human society. It's been said that 95% of all human conflict is caused by poor communications and the other 5% by clear communications. Misunderstandings among people are inevitable, and, sometimes, people simply do not agree, even when they understand each other perfectly. This unavoidable loss of social capital is analogous to entropy in the ecological world. Thus, social capital must be continually replenished if human relationships are to remain positive and quality of life is to be enhanced over time.

If human civilization is to continue to advance, humanity must learn to conserve and continually rebuild its stocks of social capital. But a sustainable economy must also encourage and support continual social investments by encouraging the formation of new and more-positive personal relationships. Stocks of social capital must be built at rates exceeding their natural rates of depletion, plus rates of any unnecessary exploitation, if human civilization is to advance. This is the fundamental nature of the social economy.

The Individual Economy

The individual or private economy is by far the best understood and most widely appreciated of the three economies. It's the only concept most people associate with the word *economy*. The purpose here is simply to place the private economy within the context of the other two. The role, scope, and functions of the private economy are quite simple and straightforward, at least in concept. The private economy provides the means by which we meet our needs as individuals, and collections of individuals, through our transactions with other people and through our interactions with the natural environment. If we lived totally independent and self-sufficient lives, we would have no need for an economy. But our lives can be made better through specialization and trade and thus we need to relate to other people. Our lives also can be made better through the utilization of natural resources that are beyond our physical grasp; therefore, we need to trade to acquire benefits from those resources to which we would not otherwise have access.

The macro-economy—an aggregation of individual enterprises—is a separate aspect of the private economy. Macroeconomic policy plays a legitimate and important role in the function of the individual economy; however, it does nothing to sustain or support the social or ecological economies. In fact, current macroeconomic policies promote degradation and accelerate depletion of both social and ecological capital, by promoting maximum economic growth.

The relationship of the individual private economy to the other two also is straightforward. The private economy cannot provide ecological and social benefits directly, but first must convert both ecological and social resources into economic resources. Ecological resources are extracted from the natural environment—through mining, logging, or farming—and are converted into marketable raw materials for manufacturing, construction, or processing. Natural resources that were once owned in common, and used for the benefit of all, are converted into private goods for sale to the highest bidder. Without privatization, no incentive would exist for private investment in the resource extraction process, and, thus, nothing would be produced for sale in the private economy.

Social resources are extracted from society through employment, collaboration, or negotiation and are converted into economically valuable human resources that produce goods, provide services, or make deals. Social resources that once supported positive personal relationships among people are converted in labor, joint ventures, and commercial advantages—all commodities for sale to the highest bidder. Without privatization of these social resources, there would be no individual incentive to make deals and or invest in enterprises that employ people, and there would be no jobs in the private economy.

The individual or private economy is an important dimension of any modern society. The conversion of ecological and social resources into economic resources is both necessary and legitimate, if our level of living is to exceed subsistent self-sufficiency and if we are to have sovereignty in our individual decisions. However, we must recognize that when we convert natural resources into economic resources, less ecological capital is left for future extraction. When we take minerals from the earth, cut old-growth forests, or farm ecologically fragile soil, we are disrupting the natural ecosystem in ways that may degrade its ability to remain healthy and productive. When private economic development diminishes or endangers other living species, the ability of nature's ecosystems to assimilate and store solar energy for the future development may be impaired.

Certainly, we realize that humans benefit from resource extraction, but we must recognize also that humans benefit directly from the natural environment—from breathing fresh air; drinking pure water; and simply living in a clean, healthy, and aesthetically pleasing environment. People also benefit from being good stewards of the air, water, and soil; stewardship helps give purpose and meaning to our lives.

Whenever we use the private economy to extract from nature at rates faster than nature can regenerate, we are degrading the productivity of the ecological economy and we ultimately will degrade our overall quality of life.

We must recognize also that when we convert social resources into economic resources, fewer social resources are left to support societies of the future. When we go from voluntarily helping each other to working for each other, we have transformed a personal relationship into a business arrangement. When we start using our personal relationships with other people as business contacts, we have started to transform friends into prospects and social gatherings into business conferences, and, eventually, we begin to compete rather than cooperate. The means by which we relate to each other becomes defined by common business practices, rules, or laws rather than by a sense of caring and compassion. Of course, humans do benefit from their business relationships, but we must realize that humans also benefit from purely social relationships—from belonging, caring, sharing, and loving. When an individual economy extracts social resources at rates faster than it reinvests in building trust, integrity, and civility, it degrades the productivity of its social economy and will ultimately degrade our overall quality of life.

The Hierarchy of Sustainability

An economy is a complex system with many significantly interrelated elements and feedback mechanisms. Neoclassical economists, recognizing the inherent difficulties in dealing with complex systems, chose to focus on a few key economic relationships, and in doing so, created an illusion of manageability. This is a typical reductionist approach to science: to deal with complexity by focusing so narrowly on specific parts of systems that the relationships eventually appear simple. However, other scientific approaches to dealing with complexity are equally valid. Hierarchy theory, for example, offers an alternative to the mechanical, reductionist approaches by focusing on issues of scale, levels of organization, levels of observation, levels of explanation, and the relationships between these levels.[15] The hierarchal approach to scientific inquiry may appear less tidy than the linear logic of reductionism, but it is no less logical or rational. It simply utilizes the logic of creativity, inspiration, and imagination as much as linear thinking. Most importantly, the hierarchal approach to science attempts to deal with complexity as it exists, rather than by creating an artificial simplicity.

A sustainable economy is inherently complex and hierarchal, in that it integrates the individual, social, and ecological economies into a harmonious whole. Individuals are forced to rethink the conventional wisdom of "more is better" and to search for success through harmony and balance among the individual, social, and moral aspects of their lives. If we are already at a point of balance or harmony, anything we do to improve a single dimension of well-being will disturb the balance and will thus make us worse off than before. If our economy is out of balance, we can restore harmony by devoting less time and energy to the dimension that we are overdoing and thus improve our overall well-being by actually doing less.

An element of tension or stress always exists among the economic, social, and moral dimensions of our lives, if for no other reason than that they all demand investments of our limited time and energy. However, tension is not the same as conflict, and stress is not the same as distress. Tension is often necessary to build strength. Similarly, there always will be tension and stress in a sustainable economy, even when the private, public, and moral economies are in harmony. Tensions become conflict and stress becomes distress only when one dimension is made stronger by weakening the others. With positive stress, however, the strengthening of one dimension creates a healthy tension that challenges, encourages, and strengthens the other dimensions as well.

Admittedly, the most difficult challenges in managing a sustainable economy are likely to arise from the integration of the economic, social, and ecological dimensions in order to maintain a positive, dynamic balance or harmony among the three. Some issues clearly relate to the private economy—the costs and benefits accrue almost exclusively to individuals. Other issues are clearly social—the rewards clearly depend on positive personal relationships. Ecological *oikonomia* is a matter of stewardship;—one generation ensures equal opportunities for future generations as a matter of ethical or moral principle. Challenges arise, however, when issues have important economic, social, and ecological dimensions—at the margins or interfaces among the three.

Sustainable economies are hierarchical in a systemic sense, in that the individual or private economy is a subsystem of the social or public economy, which in turn is a subsystem of the moral or ecological economy. In hierarchy theory, *upper-level* systems are the context of, are the constraints on, act more slowly than, have greater integrity and strength than, and are made up of *lower-level* systems.[16] This concept of hierarchy hinges on the distinction between purpose, which comes from above, and possibilities, which come from below. The ecological economy is the context of, the constraint on, acts more slowly than, has greater integrity and strength than, and is made up of the social and individual economies. The ecological economy, being moral and ethical in nature, gives purpose to the social and individual economies. However, the ecological economy also is clearly dependent upon the social and individual economies, which limits its potential and restrict its possibilities. Whether the ecological ecosystem is robust and productive or anemic and barren is largely dependent upon the functioning of the private and public economies.

At first thought, nature might seem to be dominant over society and society dominant over the economy. However, the private economy can either enhance or destroy the civility of society, which in turn can enhance or destroy the health of the natural ecosystem. So the private economy limits the possibilities of the public economy and society limits the possibilities of the natural ecosystem. Thus, an interdependent relationship exists among the three—none can survive independent of the others. Of course, nature might well survive the ravages of both the economy and our current society, but it likely would be a nature incapable of sustaining human society, at least as we know it.

The hierarchy of sustainability arises from the source of organizational principles or rules by which the system as a whole must function. The concept of ecology presumes there are inviolate laws of nature, which define a higher order that gives purpose to humanity and within which all else, including human society, ultimately must function in harmony. An economy is a creation of a human society and its purpose is to serve the needs of that society. And a society inevitably sets, or at least chooses to accept, the rules by which its economy functions. Thus, there is a natural hierarchy among ecosystems, social systems, and economic systems. Violation of this hierarchy principle is neither impossible nor uncommon, but continual or egregious violations, quite simply, are not sustainable.

Laws Versus Principles

The fundamental issue in managing any economy is the allocation of resources among competing ends. Neoclassical economics provides us with a logical means of allocating our scarce resources—including time and money—in acquiring scarce goods and services to maximize our individual material well-being. In contrast, sustainable economics provides us with a logical means of allocating all our resources— including our energy, attention, commitment, and passion, as well as time and money—to sustain a desirable quality of life.

For the individual economy, differences between neoclassical and sustainable economics are mainly matters of perspective. For example, the laws of supply and demand are derived from the fundamental law of neoclassical economics, the law of diminishing marginal returns. Beyond some point, the economic value or utility of consuming an additional or marginal unit of anything will be less than the value or utility realized from consuming the previous unit. As anything becomes less scarce, each unit becomes less valuable. The price, or sacrifice, a consumer is willing to pay declines as the quantity consumed increases. And thus we have the law of demand: The quantity demanded varies inversely with price.

Beyond some point, the economic value of anything resulting from the use of an additional or marginal unit of a production input—land, labor, capital—will be less than the value of production realized from the previous unit. To make anything less scarce, to produce more, its producers must receive a higher value per unit to offset higher marginal costs of inputs. The price, or reward, that the supplier must receive increases as the quantity supplied increases. And thus we have the law of supply: The quantity supplied varies directly with price.

Economists freely admit the difficulty in actually holding other things constant, making it difficult to actually quantify supply, demand, and price relationships. Some early economists worried about the oversimplifications of neoclassical economics. Thorstein Veblen, for example, suggested that higher prices may actually make some things more valuable to some people, and they will buy more, not less, at higher prices.[17] But, most economists seem to accept the economic belief in definite, quantifiable supply, demand, and price relationships as if they were physical laws of human behavior. In reality, economies are complex systems and many things other than price affect both quantities supplied and quantities demanded, including incomes, tastes and preferences, production technologies, prices, and the availability of substitutes. None of these other things remains constant as prices and quantities change. But economists narrow the focus by assuming that the relationships of economic interest can be isolated within the complexity of society and the natural environment.

The inverse relationship between scarcity and value is an essential first principle of economics, but it is a principle of a living system and not a mechanistic law of physics. A principle is a foundational truth, an aspect of pure knowledge, which may or may not be reflected under any specific set of conditions. Principles exist only as abstractions; they can be observed only indirectly, through imperfect examples. Laws, on the other hand, are statements or descriptions of a relationship or sequence of phenomena that invariably occurs under specific conditions.[18] Laws can be validated because the conditions under which they operate can be controlled. Principles can be corroborated, but never completely confirmed, because the conditions under which they operate are always changing, and thus, cannot be controlled.

The economic first principle linking value and scarcity seems to operate in the social and ecological economics, as well as in the individual economy. As social beings, humans value relationships. Scarcity in relationships might be thought of as increasing isolation. The greater the isolation, the more scarce are relationships. A person who has a close-knit family and many good friends is considered a fortunate person. Solitary confinement, at the other extreme, is considered to be among the harshest of human punishments. In general, more good relationships seem to be preferred to fewer.

A negative correlation between the number of relationships and the value of a marginal or additional relationship might also be hypothesized. Having one good friend, rather than none, may make a tremendous difference in quality of life, as might having three rather than two. But the value of having fifty friends rather than forty-nine, while positive, may be much less than the marginal value of the first one or two. Of course, relationships are not necessarily positive. We might prefer to have a few less enemies, even if it meant fewer relationships. This is analogous to being asked to consume more of something that we don't like; we don't prefer more of it, but instead, avoid it. In both cases, however, having some of something, even something we don't prefer, may still be better than having nothing.

In general, as we add positive relationships, at some point the value of each marginal relationship tends to diminish, hence the principle of diminishing value of relationships. Obviously, the cost and value of relationships cannot be expressed as neat, linear, monotonic, or even continuous mathematical functions. The value of human relationships may be inherently difficult to quantify, but in principle we know it exists and is important.

Relationships also have marginal costs, as well as marginal value. And as with the law of supply, the costs of an additional relationship might be expected to rise as the total number of relationships rise—at least over some relevant range. Relationships require time and attention to develop and maintain, in addition to any sharing of material possessions among friends. As more time and attention are taken away from pursuing economic or personal interests, the value of the sacrifice becomes greater. As we have less money or less time, the value of each dollar or minute increases. Thus, the marginal opportunity cost of relationships rises as we develop more relationships.

The same principles also seem to hold true for ecological relationships. As ethical and moral beings, most humans value stewardship, which means doing something for others, even if there is no expectation of an individual material benefit in return. Stewardship helps give purpose and meaning to life; its only reward is greater peace of mind. People benefit from taking care of the natural ecological environment because it is a *right* and *good* thing to do.

In the case of ecosystems, ecological integrity might be thought of as abundance, and thus ecological impairment might be analogous to scarcity. As the integrity of an ecosystem becomes increasingly impaired, the risk of permanent damage or its eventual death increases. The more impaired the ecosystem, the greater will be the benefit of a marginal increment of environmental stewardship. As an ecosystem approaches optimum health, it becomes increasingly capable of repairing incremental damage, adapting to the threat, and eventually self-renewal. The marginal benefits of ecological stewardship decline as an ecosystem becomes less impaired. As with relationships, the marginal value of ecological stewardship cannot be expressed as some linear, monotonic, or continuous mathematical function. Ecosystems are living systems. The processes of life, health, and death do not follow some precisely predictable pattern.

Environmental stewardship has costs as well as benefits. It requires money, time, effort, attention, and commitment that could be devoted to some other economic or social activity. As explained, the marginal economic and social sacrifices become greater as more money, time, and attention are devoted to stewardship. Therefore the marginal opportunity cost of stewardship rises as more resources are devoted to maintaining higher levels of ecosystem integrity. Although the linkages between scarcity and marginal values and costs of ecological stewardship may not be quantifiable, we know they exist.

Substitutes, Complements, and Balance

At this point, the economist may be tempted to calculate economic equilibria for individual, social, and ecological economies, by equating their diminishing marginal benefits with increasing marginal costs. However, this would be possible only if the three were independent or separable, which they clearly are not. We cannot simply assume that our individual quality of life will be unaffected by our social and moral quality of life, when our common sense tells us the three are but separate aspects of the same whole. Obviously, all three compete for the same scarce resources—money, time, effort, attention, and commitment. Again the neoclassical economist may be tempted to derive a conceptual economic equilibrium by allocating these scarce resources among the individual, social, and ecological economies to simultaneously equalize the ratios of marginal benefits to marginal costs.

However, the equal marginal approach to deriving equilibria assumes that marginal costs and marginal benefits are continuous, linear, monotonic relationships, and in this case, they are not. This traditional economic approach also assumes that the cost–benefit relationships are static, or stable; however, all three economies of sustainability are clearly dynamic in nature. But perhaps most important, equating ratios of marginal costs and benefits would result in an optimum balance only if the individual, social, and ecological benefits were substitutes, meaning that more of one can make up for less of another.

Although they may appear to be substitutes in a very narrow time frame, with respect to issues of sustainability and quality of life, they are more accurately viewed as complements rather than substitutes. Herman Daly, a noted ecological economist, points out the very limited extent to which natural capital, manmade capital, and human capital are substitutable, arguing that these three forms of private economic capital instead are more generally *complements*.[19] The limited degree of substitutability and the high degree of complementarity are even clearer in the case of relationships among private, social, and ecological capital.

Once a position of balance and harmony is achieved, more of one without more of the others only serves to create imbalance and disharmony, and detracts from overall quality of life. The three dimensions, individual, social, and ethical, are inevitably interconnected. Obviously, if we spend more money, time, attention, and the like on one dimension, we have less to devote to the others and we consequently disturb the balance. But even if we gain individual benefits without investing more money, time, or energy—by receiving some gift, winning the lottery, or becoming more self-centered—the change will inevitably affect our social relationships and our sense of ethical or moral well-being. We will probably then need to spend more of our scarce resources on relationships and stewardship in order to restore balance and harmony. Likewise, even if we expend additional money, time, or energy in gaining more social or ethical benefits, we will have changed the balance. We will then need to spend more of our scarce resources on individual benefits to restore the balance. Such is the logical process of maintaining some sense of dynamic equilibrium among the complementary dimensions of quality of life.

The objective of this chapter is not to develop a new theory of optimization for the three economies of sustainability but instead to illustrate that existing principles of economics are both relevant and useful in allocating resources for sustainability. However, the fundamental principles of economics must be viewed as living principles rather than mechanistic laws. Minimums, maximums, and optimums must be viewed as dynamic approximations, rather than as precise fixed values, and must be derived through insight and judgment, rather than through mathematical modeling. Values based on conventional economic scarcity can be measured in dollars and cents. But in evaluating social scarcity, every person is of equal worth, and in matters of morality, including environmental ethics, scarcity relates to truth and rightness, rather than to either dollars or votes. The first principles of economics provide a sound foundation for a new economics of sustainability, but economists must be willing to recreate much of the rest of neoclassical economic theory.

Endnotes

1. W. Devall and G. Sessions, *Deep Ecology, Living As If Nature Mattered* (Salt Lake City, Utah: Peregrine Smith Books, 1985), 63–77.

2. Alan Drengson, "An Ecophilosophy Approach, the Deep Ecology Movement, and Diverse Ecosophies," *The Trumpeter: Journal of Ecosophy,* 14, no. 3 (1997): 110–111.

3. H. S. Daly and J. B. Cobb, *For the Common Good: Redirecting the Economy Toward Community, the Environment and Sustainable Future* (Boston: Beacon, 1989).

4. R. Costanza, R. d'Arge, R. de Grott, S. Farber, M. Grasso, B. Hannon. K. Limburg, N. Naeem, R. O'Neill, and R. Paruelo, "The Value of the World's Ecosystem Services and Natural Capital," *Nature,* no. 387 (1997): 253–260.

5. U.S. Department of Energy, Energy Information Administration, "Energy Overview," *Annual Energy Review, 2003,* http://www.eia.doe.gov/emeu/aer/overview.html (accessed October, 2004).

6. Peter Winteringham, *Energy Use and the Environment* (Ann Arbor, Mich.: Lewis Publishers, 1992).

7. Peter Benchley and Harry N. Abrams, *Ocean Planet: Writings and Images of the Sea* (Washington, D.C.: Times Mirror Magazines and Smithsonian Institution, 1995).

8. Paul Hawken, *The Ecology of Commerce* (New York: HarperBusiness, HarperCollins Publishing, 1993).

9. Paul Hawkens, Amory Lovins, L. Hunter Lovins, *Natural Capitalism* (Boston: Back Bay Books, Little, Brown, and Company, 1999):

10. Drengson, *Ecoposhy.*

11. *World Book, 2002 Standard Edition,* "Ecology." (Chicago: World Book, Inc. 2001).

12. James S. Coleman, "Social Capital in the Creation of Human Capital," *American Journal of Sociology Supplement,* 94 (1988): 95–120.

13. D. Cohen and L. Prusak, *In Good Company: How Social Capital Makes Organizations Work* (Boston: Harvard Business School Press, 2001).

14. Robert Putnam, "Bowling Alone: America's Declining Social Capital," *Journal of Democracy,* 6, no. 1 (1995): 65–78.

15. Valerie Ahl and T. F. H. Allen, *Hierarchy Theory: A vision, Vocabulary and Epistemology,* (New York: Columbia University Press, 1996), 29–30.

16. T. F. H. Allen and T. B. Starr, *Hierarchy: Perspectives for Ecological Complexity* (Chicago: University Chicago Press, 1982).

17. Thorstein Veblen, *The Theory of the Leisure Class: An Economic Study of Institutions* (New York: Macmillan Publishing, 1902), 68–101.

18. *World Book,* "principles and laws."

19. Herman E. Daly, "From Empty-World Economics to Full-World Economics: A Historical Turning Point in Economic Development," in *The Future of World Forests: Their Use and Conservation,* eds. Kilaparti Ramakrishna and George M. Woodwell (New Haven, Conn.: Yale University Press, 1993).

CHAPTER EIGHT

MANAGING THE MORAL ECONOMY

Society, Ecology, and Morality

The moral economy provides the cultural context within which the private and public economies must function. Without moral guidance and restraint, there can be no assurance that either the private or the public economy will serve the long-term interest of society. The moral economy is rooted in the concept of *deep* ecology, in the philosophical *rightness* of our physical and social relationships. Management of the sustainable economy begins with the moral and ethical questions of how we *should* relate to each other and *should* relate to our natural environment. The answers to these questions cannot be determined and dictated by those in positions of power and authority. A sustainable economy is a knowledge-based organization; it must be managed by leading, nurturing, and empowering rather than ordering, directing, and controlling. Thus, the social and ethical values held by the people of a society must provide the moral context within which their economy functions. And although they might prefer to remain aloof from ethics and morality, economists can no longer escape the fact that they are a part of the economy—affecting and affected by the object of their study.

The moral economy guides and constrains the public and private economies by providing the fundamental principles by which they must function. As discussed previously, first principles exist by nature and thus are beyond the discretion of society or humanity. However, an economy is a human creation—created by people to serve the needs of people. Thus, people must agree upon the principles by which they want their economy to be organized and to function. Although chosen by humans, these principles are no less critical to the functioning of an economy than are first principles to the functioning of natural systems. The public and private economies cannot be managed for the benefit of a society unless there is a clear sense of what is right and good for that society. The principles of the moral economy provide the common sense of rightness of relationships that is necessary to manage an economy sustainably.

The Purpose of Government

The principles of the moral economy are encoded in a society's culture, customs, constitution, and laws. The moral economy provides the means by which a society defines the principles by which it chooses to be organized and to function. In the United States, the moral economy embodies the principles of equity and justice, which must guide a sustainable public economy, and such principles as honesty, fairness, compassion, responsibility, and respect, which must guide a sustainable private economy.[1] Any society must define its guiding principles through a process of moral consensus.

Culture reflects a society's basic patterns of thought and behavior, which are shaped by customs and experiences and are passed down from one generation to the next. Thus, the culture and customs of any society can be affected or managed only by the people themselves. When deemed necessary, however, customs and culture can be articulated and encoded into constitutions and laws, requiring all within the society to comply with the dominant norms and values of that society. As indicated previously, a constitution reflects the moral consensus regarding the principles by which it is to be governed.

Constitutions and laws transform moral and ethical rights and wrongs into legal rights and wrongs—both reflecting current cultural values of a society and helping to shape its culture of the future. Thus, constitutions and laws represent the principal means by which the moral economy can be managed—by leading, nurturing, and empowering people to build the legal foundation for a sustainable economy. And government provides the means by which people can manage their moral economy through their choices of constitutions and laws.

Governments, at least all forms of self-government, have two basic functions. First, governments define the consensus of the governed, and, second, governments serve the public interests of the governed. Consensus reflects the *common sense* of the governed regarding what is to be considered right and good, and thus, acceptable within the society. Public interests reflect what is considered to be for the *common good*, and thus what must be done together, in common, rather than separately. Thus, the fundamental purpose of any government is to allow people to use their common sense to pursue their sense of the common good.

Two Philosophies of Government

Current threats to ecological, social, and economic sustainability are in no small part a reflection of growing skepticism regarding the legitimate role of government. Most Americans seem willing to accept, if not embrace, the view that government should be limited in role and scope to the protection of private property rights. This willingness is reflected by the current dominance of a free enterprise ideology of government in the United States. Although most people still voice support of social programs, such as Social Security and Medicare, many have no understanding of how such programs can be justified in any sense other than the protection of self-interests: They have paid into these programs and have a right to receive something in return. The privatization of public services, including Social Security and Medicare, is seen as a means of giving taxpayers a higher return on their individual investments. The emphasis is on individual self-interests, with little apparent appreciation of government as a means of working together for the common good.

This free enterprise philosophy of government, typically labeled as *conservative* or *neoconservative*, is articulated most clearly, if not always most rationally, by popular writers and commentators such as Rush Limbaugh,[2] Bill O'Reilly,[3] Cal Thomas,[4] and Ann Coulter.[5] Such voices have found legitimacy through political leaders such as Ronald Reagan, Margaret Thatcher and, more recently, George W. Bush. These people represent the growing number of modern-day advocates of the historical *enterprise belief system,* which was discussed in Chapter 4. These popular advocates of the free enterprise philosophy of government find firm ideological support in neoclassical economics, particularly in the philosophies of Hayek[6] and Friedman[7] and others of the Chicago school of economics.[8]

Free enterprise ideologues tend to view a democracy as analogous to a free market economy. Their unspoken assumption is that no societal well-being exists apart from that which is realized by individuals. Equity is interpreted as every person having an opportunity to do as well as he or she can under the circumstances. Justice means that every person is rewarded in relation to his or her productivity. If everyone has an opportunity to acquire private property and is equitably rewarded according to their productivity, all are assumed to have the maximum incentive to become productive individuals and, consequently, to contribute as much as possible to building a strong, productive economy and society.

Under this ideology, national defense is but a means of protecting private property against the threat of invasion by other nations or, more recently, a means of facilitating and protecting private U.S. investments in other nations. Those who have little private property are protected only because it would be impractical to exclude them during times of war. Criminal laws likewise are designed primarily to protect one person's property from being stolen by another. The protection of life and health are prerequisites for benefiting from the ownership of property and therefore must be protected in order to protect the *value* of property. Although the life and health of those without property are protected, they are not always protected equally well. For the most part, it's simply easier to protect everyone than to determine who is worthy of what level of protection, based on his or her current and potential future productivity and value of property.

Civil laws are supported because such laws clearly are designed to protect property rather than people. To bring a civil case, one must have suffered some loss that can be measured in terms of private economic value. In civil court, those without property, and no potential to acquire it, can have no claim because they have nothing of value to lose. Enterprise advocates oppose civil laws that seem to go beyond a narrow interpretation of property. For example, court judgments providing large awards for pain and suffering are opposed by those who view the protection of private property as the only legitimate role of civil courts. Limits on corporate liability are considered necessary for a strong economy, and trial lawyers are considered drags on the economy and, thus, enemies of society.

Public education is supported by enterprise advocates as a means of ensuring that everyone has an opportunity to realize their potential to become productive citizens—meaning citizens capable of creating and acquiring property. Public health programs are similarly justified as a means of protecting the productivity of a nation's human resources. Public transportation and communications systems also are viewed as facilitating work, thus enhancing individual productivity and the creation of private wealth.

Direct government involvement in providing public services has been supported by free enterprise advocates only if the job was too large or otherwise could not be carried out effectively by private enterprise. Increasingly, few tasks, including the waging of war, are considered too large or beyond the scope of large publicly held corporations. Neoconservatives seem to believe that government is inherently corrupt, inefficient, and wasteful. Thus, anything that must involve government spending can be done most efficiently through privatization—through government contracts with private corporations. Public education, health care, incarceration, and even Social Security are seen as prime candidates for privatization.

Advocates of a free enterprise philosophy of government generally oppose ownership or control of property by the government and believe that decisions concerning the use of land should be left to the marketplace. They typically oppose laws designed to protect workers, consumers, and the natural environment from economic exploitation. Many even oppose enforcement of existing antitrust laws as being inherently restrictive of the free market economy and, thus, too costly to investors and consumers. To reiterate, those who bring an enterprise belief system to the role and scope of government believe the primary function of government is to ensure that all have a right to acquire and accumulate private property.

The alternative philosophy of government is that of government as the defender of equity and justice. Defenders of this philosophy are the modern-day advocates of the *democratic belief system,* as discussed in Chapter 4. They view the whole of a society as something more than the sum of its individual members; to them, relationships among people matter. Equity means that all are created equal with certain inalienable rights, and justice means that everyone must receive equally those things to which they have equal rights. Equity and justice are seen as essential principles in maintaining positive relationships among people within society. Government is considered both a necessary and desirable means of ensuring equity and justice and of protecting the common good.

Defenders of the democratic belief system do not advocate government ownership of all property or even most property; they are not socialists or communists. They believe that private property rights are both necessary and desirable in those cases in which interests are clearly individual, rather than social, in nature. They believe that free markets are the best means of allocating most, but not all, resources. They believe many values of a society accrue to the people in common, not just to individuals, and that many costs of a society must be borne by people in common, not just by individuals. Government is the legitimate means of pursuing the common good through an equitable and just society.

Under this democratic ideology of government, all people within a society are deemed to have an equal right to be protected from both foreign and domestic threats. The primary responsibility of national defense and domestic criminal law enforcement is to protect people, not property, and all people are to be protected equally. Property is protected also, but without regard to who owns it or how much of it they own. Protection of life and health are considered rights of all, regardless of their wealth or their potential ability to contribute to the economy. Even though it would be far more cost effective not to protect the life or health of those who are less productive, all are to be treated equally.

Civil laws are supported because such laws are meant to ensure that all are treated fairly. The ability to be secure in possessing and trading private property is important to the economy, but no more important than is the right to be treated fairly, regardless of one's wealth or position in society. Punitive court judgments serve as punishment for past offenses and deterrents to future violations of the principles of fairness and honesty in civil relationships.

Public education is supported by the democratic belief system because an educated society is considered essential to self-determination, which is a cornerstone of all democratic forms of government. Public health programs are justified by the benefits that accrue to society in common when its members feel cared for and are healthy. Government subsidies for transportation and communications systems are means of ensuring the basic freedoms of speech and of mobility.

In all cases in which public services are linked to basic rights, direct government involvement is deemed not only desirable but also essential. Private providers of public services inevitably are lured by economic incentives to provide more services to those who can be served less expensively and less service to those who are more costly to serve. Even in cases in which privatization increases the efficiency of public services, it inevitably does so by decreasing the equality of service, yet equity is the primary justification for providing services publicly.

Social Security and Medicare cannot be privatized without losing the assurance that all old people will have at least the necessities of life, including basic health care. Public schools should be taught by local teachers and under the direction of local administrators because the preparation of local citizens for citizenship is a responsibility of local citizens, not corporate investors. Prisons should be operated as public institutions, not private human storage facilities, because society must confront the consequences of failed relationships if it is to be motivated to address their causes. When wars are waged, they must be waged by citizen soldiers, not contract warriors, because, in a democracy, wars should never be waged unless citizens are willing to bear the burden—equally.

Democratic governments are never economically efficient because they must provide *public* goods and services equally to all. Large government agencies are subject to the same types of bureaucratic inefficiencies as are large corporate organizations; both tend to thrive through political and economic power more than through organizational efficiency. But an effective government agency in a democratic society must give priority to equality over efficiency, whereas an effective business enterprise gives priority to efficiency over equality. Thus, the privatization of public services is not a logical approach to improving the efficiency of government in matters requiring equity and justice.

This democratic philosophy of government, typically labeled as a liberal, or neoliberal, has few highly visible, articulate proponents. Neoconservatives have effectively linked liberalism with socialism and even communism, in their efforts to remove democratic constraints on their free enterprise beliefs. The most well known political liberals probably are Ted Kennedy, Bill Clinton, and now, Hillary Clinton, although all three have been forced to advocate corporatist economic policies in order to maintain their political support. The principles of the democratic belief systems are articulated with far greater purity and clarity by social activists such as Ralph Nader[9] and

Robert F. Kennedy Jr.,[10] although such voices have been marginalized politically. The most articulate popular proponents of liberalism include Al Franken,[11] Michael Moore,[12] and Jim Hightower,[13] although all three have found it necessary to wrap their political philosophies in humor. Proponents of the democratic belief system have few advocates among the most prominent economists of today. However, many noted earlier twentieth-century economists, such as Keynes[14] and Galbraith,[15] supported a proactive role of government in promoting the general welfare or well-being of society.

Advocates of the democratic belief system typically support public ownership of property for specific public purposes and public involvement in land use planning. They generally support laws intended to protect workers, consumers, and the natural environment and antitrust laws to maintain competition. People are assumed to have a basic right to a clean environment and a safe workplace, and to fairness in the marketplace, regardless of the impact on corporate profits. To reiterate, to those who bring a democratic belief system to the role and scope of government, the primary function of government is to ensure that all receive equally those things to which they have equal rights.

Constitutional Sustainability: The U.S. Example

Effective government is an absolute necessity in managing a sustainable economy. Economists cannot simply leave issues involving government to the political scientists or the politicians and assume that the ecological and social context of the private economy will be compatible with economic sustainability. Management of the moral and public economies is no less critical to the sustainability of the private economy than is management of the private economy to the sustainability of the public and moral economies. With respect to issues of sustainability, the three economies are essential elements of the same whole, and they must be managed as such.

Even if one can only see government as a *necessary evil*, it is nonetheless necessary. As Thomas Paine wrote in his essay *Common Sense*, "Society is produced by our wants, and government by our wickedness; the former promotes our happiness positively by uniting our affections, the latter negatively by restraining our vices." He concludes that government is "rendered necessary by the inability of moral virtue to govern the world."[16] Apparently, people inherently lack the moral virtue to ensure the inalienable rights of others without the authority of government to interpret and enforce their moral consensus. At a time in the United States when our preoccupation with economic self-interest increasingly restricts government to protecting private property interests, there is a need to reexamine the fundamental purpose and principles of our government.

The initial purpose for the government of the United States is clearly articulated in the preamble to the U.S. Constitution.

> We the People of the United States, in Order to form a more perfect Union, establish Justice, insure domestic Tranquility, provide for the common defense, promote the general Welfare, and secure the Blessings of Liberty to ourselves and our Posterity, do ordain and establish this Constitution for the United States of America.[17]

No later amendment to the Constitution has altered this clearly stated purpose in any way. Thus, the fundamental purposes of the U.S. government remain to establish justice, to maintain peace and order, to provide national defense, to promote the general welfare, and to ensure freedom and liberty, both now and in the future.

An earlier statement of purpose for forming governments in general was included in the Declaration of Independence.

> We hold these truths to be self-evident, that all men are created equal, that they are endowed by their Creator with certain unalienable Rights, that among these are Life, Liberty and the pursuit of Happiness.—That to secure these rights, Governments are instituted among Men, deriving their just powers from the consent of the governed.[18]

Thus, the philosophical foundation for the purposes later stated in the U.S. Constitution was a clear understanding that governments are necessary to ensure the inalienable rights of the governed to life, liberty, and the pursuit of happiness. When taken together, the Declaration of Independence and the preamble to the U.S. Constitution clearly support the democratic belief system as the guiding philosophy for the government of the United States. Ensuring domestic tranquility, providing for the common defense, and even securing the blessings of liberty might be consistent with government as the protector of private property, as indicated previously. However, it's something of a mental stretch to argue that the purposes of establishing justice, promoting the general welfare, and, certainly, securing liberty for posterity either validate or justify a limited, passive role for government as the protector of private property rights. Indeed, all of the stated purposes for the U.S. government are clearly consistent with the democratic belief system as justification for a proactive government, committed to defending equity and justice for all.

In addition, the Declaration of Independence clearly articulates that the Founding Fathers considered the protection of inalienable rights to be the fundamental purpose of any government. "To secure these rights, governments are instituted among men," they wrote. It was not a matter of the signers of the Declaration of Independence not being aware of the importance of private property rights. In fact, Thomas Jefferson is said to have been strongly influenced by John Locke's book *Two Treatises of Government*.[19,20] Locke also believed that people by nature had certain rights and duties; his list included life, liberty, and *estate*, the latter meaning ownership of property. However, Jefferson and the signers of the Declaration of Independence chose "pursuit of happiness" as the third inalienable right, instead of adopting Locke's ownership of private property. In addition, in the late 1700s, happiness was still widely interpreted as the natural product of righteous relationships, as being social and spiritual as well as material in nature. Whereas the pursuit of happiness might well have included the right of estate, it most certainly included the right to live in an equitable and just society.

The purposes of the U.S. government, as expressed in these historical documents, are clearly consistent with the moral context necessary for a sustainable economy. Just as clearly, a government that is limited in its role and scope to protecting private property rights cannot provide the necessary moral context for sustainability. The enterprise belief system is consistent with a sustainable private economy, but only if the private economy—that is, free enterprise—functions within the context of a moral economy rooted in a democratic belief system. Thus, in spite of any preferences of economists to avoid issues of ethics and morality, the economics of sustainability must embrace the private, public, and moral economies.

The principles by which the U.S. economy is to function also are expressed in the U.S. Constitution. The first four articles of the Constitution define the structural principles of government. Article I defines the legislative structure, beginning with the statement, "All legislative Powers herein granted shall be vested in a Congress of the United States, which shall consist of a Senate and House of Representatives."

Article II defines the administrative structure, beginning with "The executive Power shall be vested in a President of the United States of America." Article III defines the judicial structure; "The judicial Power of the United States shall be vested in one supreme Court, and in such inferior Courts as the Congress may from time to time ordain and establish." Article IV defines the nature of the relationships among states within the union. And Article V defines the process by which the Constitution is to be amended, which will be discussed in detail later in this chapter. The last two articles resolve issues deemed necessary in colonial times to facilitate the initial formation of the union.

The Bill of Rights, which comprises the first ten amendments to the Constitution, was added in 1791 to address specific concerns expressed by various states during the constitutional ratification process. These concerns—regarding the freedoms of religion, of speech, and of the press; the right to bear arms and to privacy, and numerous rights of those accused of crime; and the rights of individuals and states to powers not ceded to the national government—are all addressed in the Bill of Rights. The basic purpose of the Bill of Rights is to protect individuals and states from potential political exploitation by a strong central government. These basic rights, along with others included in later amendments, define the functional or operational principles of the U.S. government.

Early U.S. citizens were particularly concerned about the potential abuse of government power, as their revolution against Great Britain had been fueled by their desire to free themselves from such abuse. Even today, valid reasons exist for a continuing vigilance against the potentially abusive power of *big government*. However, a government with too little power may be no less a threat to the sustainability of a society than is a government with too much power. A government that is too weak to protect its people and its natural resources from economic exploitation is no less a threat to sustainability than is a government that is so strong that people cannot protect themselves from political exploitation.

A Bill of Rights for Sustainability

If the U.S. Constitution were to be written today, by the true scholars of today, it probably would include specific articles or amendments to protect individuals from economic exploitation. At the time the U.S.

Constitution was written, however, there was no reason to believe that the people needed such protection, at least not by government.

Adam Smith's *Wealth of Nations* had been written a couple of decades earlier and was widely read among literate Americans, including the Founding Fathers. People of that time quite logically would have trusted the *invisible hand* of the free market economy to transform individual greed into societal good. In a free market economy, people were thought to be incapable of any economic vice against which their neighbors might need protection by government, no matter how vigorously they pursued their self-interests. The pursuit of happiness and the promotion of general welfare would have seemed assured by the new government's advocacy of free markets.

People of that time had no reason to believe that government needed to protect the natural environment in order to promote the general welfare of people or to ensure the liberty of posterity. Nature seemed more than capable of enduring any damage mere humans might inflict upon it. After forests were cleared, fields were plowed, and soils were depleted by cultivation, the land would be abandoned, the forests would grow back, and nature would restore fertility to the soil. The United States seemed to have far more land that the colonists would ever be able to clear and cultivate. If anything, they probably thought that government should encourage exploitation of the land.

However, nothing in today's society indicates that the happiness and general welfare of the people can be further promoted without constitutional assurances that both the people and the land shall be protected from further economic exploitation. The liberty of future generations to pursue their happiness, as we have been able to pursue ours, is clearly being placed at risk by a largely unrestrained, exploitative economy.

Management of the moral economy for sustainability will require the establishment of a moral consensus concerning the protection of the people, and of their posterity, from the consequences of economic exploitation. Perhaps these rights can be written into a set of laws and regulations designed to both constrain and guide the public and private economies toward sustainability. However, each such law and each regulation will be subject to constitutional challenge, as most such laws will seem to infringe in some way on individual private property rights. Accordingly, the more certain and more logical approach to ensuring sustainability would seem to be to encode the principles of sustainability into the U.S. Constitution, to develop the Bill of Rights for Sustainability.

Obviously, amending the Constitution is a long and arduous process, requiring much thought and many lengthy discussions of principles as well as particulars. However, something of the nature of the following statement of basic human rights might serve as a starting point for such thought and discussion.

Bill of Rights for Sustainability

These basic human rights shall not be denied or restrained, unless the exercise of these rights by one person denies or restrains the rights of another. Even in these cases, rights cannot be denied or restrained without due process of law, except in self-defense of one person's rights against an imminent, unlawful threat of another.

These rights are to be made available to all, to the extent that they are available to any within the society being governed. The current generation has a responsibility to ensure these rights for future generations, to the extent that they are available to those of the current generation. These rights may not be bought, sold, or otherwise obtained or given away for any reason.

The Right to Life: Every human being has the basic right to live and to grow—physically, mentally, and spiritually.

- Political: The right to protect and defend oneself against any threat to life or against any physical restraint to one's personal health and development

- *Economic: The right to have adequate food, clothing, shelter, education, and health care needed for survival and full physical, mental, and spiritual development, including the right to live in a safe and healthful natural environment*

The Right of Individual Thought and Expression: Every human being has a basic right to think their own thoughts and to express those thoughts to others.

- Political: The right to protect and defend oneself against the immediate repression of thought and expression—including speech, writing, publishing, education, or other means of sharing information—and the right to practice the religion of one's choice

- *Economic: The right to obtain accurate and unbiased information, to connect and commune with nature, and to protect against attempts by others to manipulate or subversively influence one's thoughts for economic purposes*

The Right of Individual Action: Every human being has a basic right to independent action and freedom of movement.

- Political: The right to protect and defend oneself against any restraint of action or movement or any invasion of the privacy of one's person, thoughts, or actions
- *Economic: The right to pursue economic and aesthetic opportunities of one's choosing, including access to wild and scenic places, and to be protected against all oppressive, exploitive, or coercive economic actions of others*

The Right of Interaction: Every human has the basic right to interact with other human beings.

- Political: The right to communicate; meet; congregate; form civil unions; have or not have children; organize for social, religious, or political purposes; and to formulate and conduct the processes of self-government
- *Economic: The right of individuals to collaborate, organize, and pursue joint economic activities, but only to the extent that such organizations and associations clearly contribute to the social and ecological well-being of society—meaning that economic extractions from society and nature cannot exceed reinvestments in society and nature*

The U.S. Constitution currently includes the political rights associated with the above list of basic human rights, but it does not include any of the rights of people to be protected from economic exploitation. Thus, the task of writing such rights into the Constitution would seem quite formidable. In the United States, the tendency has been to change the Constitution only rarely, and even then, only one amendment at a time. However, a sustainable economy must be built upon a moral commitment to do far more than just *tinker* with the laws here and there. Management of the moral economy for sustainability will require a commitment to fundamental change.

The Moral Consensus for Sustainability

Under true constitutional government, the constitution must be a creation of the people governed, not a document created by the government. As Thomas Paine put it, "A constitution is a thing *antecedent* to a government, and a government is only the creature of a constitution.

The constitution of a country is not the act of government, but of the people constituting a government."[21] Since it is a creation of the people, all those within a constitutionally governed society must agree to abide by their constitution, regardless of whether they might have preferred something a bit different. Thus, a constitution must be created and adopted through a process of consensus—not by a simple majority vote.

Changes in the Constitution also must be made only with the consent or consensus of the governed. The U.S. Constitution was adopted with unanimous consent of all states in the Union at the time. And the U.S. Constitution can be amended only by a series of *supermajority* votes at both federal and state levels, constituting a process of national consensus, even if falling short of unanimous agreement.

The drafters of the Constitution clearly meant it to be a living document, capable of changing to meet the changing needs of the times. In the words of Thomas Jefferson, "I am not an advocate for frequent changes in laws and constitutions, but laws and institutions must go hand in hand with the progress of the human mind. As that becomes more developed, more enlightened, as new discoveries are made, new truths discovered and manners and opinions change, with the change of circumstances, institutions must advance also to keep pace with the times."[22]

And Thomas Paine wrote, "It is perhaps impossible to establish any thing that combines principles with opinions and practice, which the progress of circumstances, through length of years, will not in some measure derange, or render inconsistent. . . . The rights of man are the rights of all generations of men, and cannot be monopolized by any. . . . The best constitution that could now be devised, consistent with the conditions of the present moment, may be far short of that excellence which a few years may afford."[23]

Article V of the U.S. Constitution states, "The Congress, whenever two thirds of both Houses shall deem it necessary, shall propose Amendments to this Constitution, or, on the Application of the Legislatures of two thirds of the several States, shall call a Convention for proposing Amendments, which, in either Case, shall be valid to all Intents and Purposes, as Part of this Constitution, when ratified by the Legislatures of three fourths of the several States, or by Conventions in three fourths thereof, as the one or the other Mode of Ratification may be proposed by the Congress."

Clearly, the Constitution was designed to facilitate the process of constitutional change. Jefferson and Paine could not have foreseen today's social and ecological consequences of their country's later pre-occupation with the pursuit of materialistic, individual, economic self-interests. Yet, they clearly anticipated that such "derangements and inconsistencies" might arise. And to limit their accumulation and prevent revolution, Jefferson suggested that Americans must at times stop and remove the yoke of their "barbarous ancestors" by amending, or rewriting, the Constitution.

It is not easy to create a national consensus for constitutional change; it was not meant to be easy but was thought nonetheless necessary. A potential national consensus does seem to be emerging with respect to protecting the natural environment. However, many environmentalists have a shallow commitment to reducing pollution, rather than a deep commitment to ecological sustainability. For example, nearly all Americans claim they value a clean environment, but only a minority seems willing to make the smallest of economic sacrifices to ensure it. Protection of the environment has obvious private and public benefits, but the kind of environmental stewardship necessary for sustainability is an ethical and moral commitment—a deep commitment. Protection from the negative effects of pollution on health and quality of life can be supported as a matter of protecting one's person or one's private property from being damaged by another. Protecting natural resources held in common for the edification and enjoyment of the public can be supported as a matter of managing public goods and services. But the protection of natural resources for the benefit of future generations is an act of true stewardship—taking care of something for the sole benefit of someone else. Stewardship is a deep moral commitment.

Even if there were an American consensus supporting a true stewardship ethic, it is doubtful that U.S. citizens would support a constitutional amendment committing the nation to the stewardship of nature for the sake of nature. Within U.S. culture, stewardship is considered a personal value, to be expressed by people individually, at their own discretion. Constitutions generally lack effectiveness in forcing people to behave ethically and morally, even if they are mostly inclined to do so. The amendments establishing and repealing the prohibition of alcohol consumption in the United States serve as prime examples of this fact. Constitutions are most effective when used to protect the rights of people, to protect people from exploitation. Thus, in managing the moral economy for sustainability, it may prove more productive to express sustainability in terms of the fundamental rights, rather than as prohibitions.

The constitutional amendments needed to create a moral context for sustainability might be as simple as the two following statements, patterned after Article IV of the Bill of Rights in the U.S. Constitution.

- The rights of the people to be secure in their persons, possessions, living environment, and in their access to productive natural resources shall not be compromised for economic purposes.
- The rights of the people of future generations to economic and political opportunities equal to those of the present shall not be compromised for economic purposes.

The specific interpretations of such amendments would evolve over time from the inevitable series of legal challenges in the courts to the constitutionality of various instances of alleged economic exploitation. Hopefully, this process would result in the evolution of a set of economic rights, to complement the current political bill of rights, as suggested earlier in this chapter. However, it might prove far easier to achieve a national consensus supporting the right of all people, of both current and future generations, to be protected from economic exploitation than to secure an initial consensus supporting a specific set of economic rights.

Although the initial reaction to this approach to managing the moral economy may be skepticism, a growing movement within U.S. society provides reason for hope, if not optimism, for the future. Environmentalism, which emerged in the United States less than 50 years ago, has grown into a major social and political movement, in spite of strong opposition from advocates of the enterprise belief system. Even though much of the movement remains shallow, it could be deepened as a result of an increased public understanding of the current threats to sustainability. The civil rights movement, which also emerged during the 1960s, might find new strength in taking up the cause of environmental justice as well as social justice. A book published in 2000, *The Cultural Creatives*, provides evidence that the numbers of adult Americans identifying with environmentalism, civil rights, and other movements logically related to the broader sustainability movement had grown from virtually zero to more than 50 million, accounting for almost 30% of the adult population.[24] The sustainability movement still represents the values of a minority, certainly not a public consensus, but its growth reflects an impressive movement of society toward a new consensus and possibly a new U.S. culture.

Lacking a moral consensus, however, the immediate agenda for managing the moral economy obviously must emphasize the development of regulations and laws designed to protect and encourage ecological and social sustainability. Unfortunately, current political trends in the United States seem to point in the opposite direction—toward greater economic exploitation. However, the environmental and social justice movements will not go away. They represent legitimate public concerns about important issues, and they will continue to resurface until they are adequately addressed. The sustainability movement seems to be growing in direct proportion to a growing awareness of threats to ecological and social equity and justice.

Thus, the political will already exists at least to blunt the economic exploitation of people and nature through vigorous enforcement of existing laws and through creative new legislative and regulatory initiatives. All that is lacking is a means of bringing the different movements together in pursuit of the common cause. The challenge in the long run is to deepen the environmental and social justice movements until a consensus of Americans embrace the ethics and morality of sustainability. Economists with an understanding of the three dimensions of sustainability have an important role to play in this process.

Most economists likely will be inclined to reject the call to become involved in helping to manage the moral economy, just as most other academics resist involvement in ethical and moral issues of society. However, economists should remember that it's only within the last century that economics has abandoned its earlier commitment to the pursuit of happiness and the first principles of self-interests in relationships and rightness. Nothing today suggests that economics and economists are incapable of returning to the principles of classical economics. Nor is it clear that the recent dominance of neoclassical economic thinking has contributed more to societal well-being than it has contributed to ecological and social exploitation. Classical economists were concerned about the social well-being of people and about the natural order of things. Twenty-first-century economists might contribute most to their profession by returning to such concerns, by returning to the fundamental principles of their discipline.

Eventually, there must be a global consensus that protecting the natural ecosystem and civil society are fundamental human responsibilities because those of future generations also have inalienable rights to a clean, productive environment and a civil global society. This will represent a major philosophic step forward for humanity—a major milestone in the transition to a more sustainable human society. This will perhaps require the development of an international charter or global constitution committing all nations of the world to the protection of basic human rights, including the right to be protected from economic exploitation and equal rights for current and future generations.

Charters and constitutions are not the essence of the moral economy; they are but tools for managing the moral economy. National charters and constitutions will not be changed until people within global societies find the courage to express their true moral and ethical principles in their everyday lives. A sustainable economy must be built upon a solid moral and ethical foundation. Economists cannot ethically continue to deny their moral responsibility to help build that foundation.

Endnotes

1. Institute for Global Ethics, "Mission Statement," Institute for Global Ethics, http://www.globalethics.org (accessed February, 2005).

2. Rush H. Limbaugh III, *The Way Things Ought To Be* (New York: Pocket Books, Simon and Schuster, 1992).

3. Bill O'Reilly, *The O'Reilly Factor* (New York: Broadway Books, Random House, 2000).

4. Cal Thomas, *Blinded by Might* (Grand Rapids, Mich.: Zondervan Publishing Co., 1999).

5. Ann Coulter, *Slander: Liberal Lies About the American Right* (New York: Three Rivers Press, Random House, 2002).

6. Friedrich Hayek, The Pure Theory of Capital (London: Routledge and Kegan Paul, 1941; Chicago: University of Chicago Press, 1975).

7. Milton Friedman and Rose Friedman, *Free to Choose* (New York: Avon Books, 1979).

8. The History of Economic Thought Website, "Chicago School philosophy," The New School, http://cepa.newschool.edu/het/schools/chicago.htm (accessed February, 2005).

9. Ralph Nader, *The Good Fight: Declare Your Independence and Close the Democracy Gap* (New York: Regan Books, HarperCollins, Harper Publishing Co., 2004).

10. Robert F. Kennedy Jr., *Crimes Against Nature: How George W. Bush and His Corporate Pals Are Plundering the Country and Hijacking Our Democracy* (New York: HarperCollins Books, Harper Publishing Co., 2004).

11. Al Franken, *Lies and the Lying Liars Who Tell Them: A Fair and Balanced Look at the Right* (New York: Dutton Books, 2003).

12. Michael Moore, *Dude, Where's My Country?* (New York: Warner Books, 2003).

13. Jim Hightower, *Thieves in High Places: They've Stolen Our Country and It's Time to Take It Back* (New York: Viking Books, Penguin Group, Inc., 2003).

14. John Maynard Keynes, The General Theory of Employment, Interest, and Money (Boston: Mariner Books, Houghton Mifflin, 1998; original copyright, 1936).

15. John Kenneth Galbraith, *The Affluent Society* (Boston: Houghton Mifflin, 1958).

16. Thomas Paine, *Common Sense* (Mineola, N.Y.: Dover Publications, Inc., 1997; original copyright, 1776).

17. U.S. Government Printing Office Web Site, "Constitution of the United States," U.S. Government Printing Office, http://www.gpoaccess.gov/coredocs.html (accessed February, 2005).

18. Government Printing Office, "United States Declaration of Independence."

19. *World Book, 2002 Standard Edition,* "John Locke."(Chicago: World Book, Inc., 2001).

20. John Locke, *Two Treatises of Government* (Cambridge, England: Cambridge University Press, 1970; original copyright, 1690).

21. Thomas Paine, "Rights of Man," in *The Life and Major Works of Thomas Paine,* ed. Philip S. Foner (New York: The Citadel Press, 1936), 278.

22. This paraphrase appears on Panel Four of the Jefferson Memorial in Washington, D.C. Please see http://www.monticello.org/reports/quotes/memorial.html (accessed May, 2005). The complete quotation can be found in Thomas Jefferson, "Reform of the Virginia Constitution, Letter to Samuel Kercheval, July 12, 1816," in *Thomas Jefferson Writings* (New York Library of America Edition, Penguin Putnam, Inc., 1984), 1401.

23. Paine, "Rights of Man," *Life and Works,* 396.

24. Paul Ray and Sherry Anderson, *The Cultural Creatives: How 50 Million People Are Changing the World* (New York: Three Rivers Press, 2000).

CHAPTER NINE

MANAGING THE PUBLIC ECONOMY

The Common Good

Managing the public economy is a matter of helping people, as a society, to pursue their *common good*. The term *common* can be defined as "that which belongs equally to all."[1] Thus, the pursuit of the common good means the pursuit of good for society as a whole, not just as a collection of individuals, but as owners in common of things in which they have shared interests.

As indicated previously, in neoclassical economics, there is no recognition of the common good, of values that accrue to society as a whole rather than to its individual members. Neoclassical economics deals only with the *collective good*, with costs and benefits that accrue to individuals—and with the neoclassical society being nothing more than a collection of individuals. However, the whole of a society is far more than the simple sum of its individual parts. The sustainable public economy must include individual costs and benefits, but it also must include costs and benefits that arise from the quality of personal relationships among people. The values arising from personal relationships are shared values. Shared values disappear when interests are divided among individuals, and, thus, shared values must be managed in common for the common good. And as explained in the preceding chapter, government is a primary means by which people manage common resources for the common good.

In neoclassical economics, government involvement in the economy is viewed from the perspective of the enterprise belief system of government. Government intervention is justified only in instances of market failure or market imperfections, in which markets cannot reasonably be expected to allocate economic resources with acceptable efficiency.[2] In neoclassical economics, there is no recognition of the inherent inability of markets to serve the *common good*, only an admission of potential failures of the markets to serve the *collective good*.

In sustainable economics, the public economy is viewed from the perspective of the democratic belief system, a belief that people have certain inalienable rights, which they all share equally, in common. And the fundamental purpose of government is to guarantee those rights. Consistent with these beliefs, managing the public economy for sustainability involves three distinct but related functions. The first is to provide public goods and services—to ensure that all receive those things to which all have equal rights. The second is to protect people from exploitation—to ensure the basic civil rights of all people. The third is to protect natural resources from exploitation—to ensure the basic ecological rights of future generations. The first can be thought of as providing *common goods*, the second as protecting the *common good*, and the third as preserving the *commons' good*.[3]

Providing Common Goods

In neoclassical economics, all public goods are defined as having two closely related characteristics: nonrival in consumption and nonexcludable from consumption.[4] Some public goods have both characteristics, whereas others have only one or the other. *Nonrival in consumption* means that one person can consume as much as he or she wants of something without diminishing the amount available for anyone else, as in the case of breathing fresh air or being protected by a national defense system. Such goods or services are not scarce because everyone can have all they want.

Nonexcludable from consumption means that once something is produced, there is no reasonable means of excluding anyone from benefiting, as in the case of national parks or national defense. Such goods or services cannot be made scarce because, once produced, their supplies cannot be controlled or be limited to specific individuals. Markets are incapable of allocating resources to provide such goods or services because they are not scarce and therefore have no market value.

Instances in which goods and services have obvious value to individuals but have no market value are called *market failures*. The neoclassical role of the government in such cases is to allocate resources so as to provide such things by equating marginal social costs and marginal social benefits, using market-based criteria to allocate non-market goods and services. But marginal social costs and benefits, as used by economists, are collective values and not common values. The neoclassical assumption is that societal well-being can be maximized by maximizing the sum of individual benefits, even if some of these benefits have no market value. Government allocation of resources is simply viewed as an imperfect substitute for markets in those cases in which markets fail. There is still no recognition of the common social value of personal relationships that arise among people within an equitable and just society.

Alternatively, in a sustainable economy, public goods and services are defined as those to which all have equal rights. Such rights must be defined by the consensus of the people governed, as explained in the preceding chapter. The set of economic rights from Chapter 8 can be used to illustrate the basic nature of public goods and services in a sustainable economy. All people are to be afforded an equal "right to have adequate food, clothing, shelter, education, and health care needed for survival and full physical, mental, and spiritual development, including the right to live in a safe and healthful natural environment." This statement defines a specific set of public goods and services that must be provided equally to all within an equitable and just society. The specific rights are clear from the statement; they include food, clothing, shelter, education, health care, and a clean environment. However, a major challenge in managing a sustainable public economy is determining *how much* of each public good and service is necessary to ensure that all have equal access to those things to which they have equal rights.

Again, sustainability does not suggest socialism or communism; it does not imply that all have an equal right to everything, or that all must be allocated an equal *total* amount of those things to which they have equal rights to *some* amount. For example, to state that all people have a right to *adequate* food, clothing, or shelter does not imply that all have a right to equal total amounts of food, clothing, and shelter. A majority of Americans, for example, have access to far more food, clothing, and shelter than actually needed to *ensure survival and full physical, mental, and spiritual development*. The relevant question in providing public services is to decide how much of each is *adequate* and then to ensure that all have access to at least that much. This leaves the private economy to allocate resources toward the production of food, clothing, and shelter in excess of the ensured amounts, either through free markets or through collective purchases, as will be discussed in the following chapter.

Some levels of food, clothing, and shelter are currently provided as public goods, available to all, in the United States and in most developed countries of the world. However, these provisions, for the most part, are justified as matters of economic investment in productivity or as public charity, rather than as a matter of ensuring equity and justice. By defining levels of these necessities to which all have rights, a clear distinction could be drawn between the role of government in providing for common needs and the role of the private economy in providing for individual wants or desires, as well as individual needs. Both are legitimate functions of a sustainable economy.

Questions of public education present challenges and opportunities similar to those for food, clothing, and shelter. It seems obvious that some level of education for all people is essential to an equitable, just, and civil society, as well as a stronger economy. Thus, some level of education should be provided as a common good or service that is afforded to all, not simply because education enhances the productivity of human resources, but because it is a basic right. It seems equally obvious that people do not have a right to any amount of education that they might choose to pursue. In addition, no society could afford to keep everyone in school for as long as they might choose to attend; someone has to work to pay taxes to support public schools. By defining the level of education to which all have a right, the role of public education in meeting the needs of society can be distinguished clearly from the role of private education in providing whatever level of education people desire and can individually or collectively afford.

The United States's commitment to public health care is less clear than its commitment to public education. However, the two issues are quite similar in concept. For the most part, Americans accept access to some minimal health care as a basic right, in that no one is to be denied care during a medical emergency. In addition, the federal Medicare and Medicaid programs provide minimum health care for the old and the poor. However, many Americans are left without access to affordable basic health care. The strongest argument against universal public health care seems to be that such a program would simply be too costly. The underlying assumption of this argument is that everyone would be provided equal access to essentially all approved medical practices and procedures. However, it seems more logical to accept the proposition that some level of public health care is a basic right, as in the case of public education. Beyond that level, people could choose to pay individually or purchase health insurance collectively to cover additional medical procedures and practices, according to their preferences and their individual ability to pay.

The fundamental difference between health care and the other public services is that no one would likely die from a lack of additional education or a lack of food, clothing, or shelter—at least beyond some minimal survival level. However, as suggested in Chapter 8, "basic human rights shall not be denied or restrained, unless the exercise of these rights by one person denies or restrains the rights of another." Thus, one person's *quantity* of life does not necessarily take precedence over other persons' *quality* of life. For example, it makes no sense to deny the right of basic health care to millions of children simply because the economy will not support providing every possible life-extending medical technology to thousands of older people. In addition, legitimate questions exist regarding whether society as a whole would actually benefit from providing everyone with every available medical benefit, many of which would ultimately prove futile, particularly near the natural end of life. It seems reasonable that society might actually be better off providing everyone with basic health care, treating readily curable illnesses, allowing the wealthy to pay for refinements of expensive treatments and the research into potential miracle cures for the future, and allowing the rest of us, when our natural time comes, to die with dignity. Universal access to basic health care, but not to all possible health care, could provide a cornerstone for a socially sustainable economy.

If *everyone* were ensured adequate levels of those things to which they have inherent rights, little or no need would exist for additional special programs for the young, the old, or the disabled. People would then be free to pursue their individual and collective interests in the private economy, knowing that adequate common goods were being provided to ensure the common good. Obviously, needs and opportunities would still exist for individuals to contribute privately to individual and organized charitable causes of their choosing. However, their shared public responsibility for an equitable and just society would have been met.

Defining the appropriate levels of public goods and services may not be an easy task, but it would provide a clearly defined objective in formulating public policies. In some cases, rights will be absolute and therefore may not be compromised for anything short of the denial of other basic rights. In other cases, in which rights are not absolute, the level of public good or service provided must be weighed against a society's ability to pay the associated public costs. Again, the moral, public, and private economies must be managed as three dimensions of the same whole, not as separate economies.

Challenges in managing the public economy are certainly not limited to defining the appropriate levels of public services. The administration of public services would also be daunting—that is, to ensure that all receive equally the things they are deemed to deserve equally. However, as stated previously, the task cannot simply be turned over to the private sector. The distribution of public goods and services cannot be privatized because private organizations will always have economic incentives to provide services unequally. Public goods can be produced under government contracts without encountering conflicting motives; however, common goods and services must be distributed by public organizations and public employees who are committed to serving the common good, with equity and justice for all.

Protecting the Common Good

In neoclassical economics, the role of government in protecting the common good is generally limited to issues involving externalities and access to information. National defense and law enforcement typically are treated as public goods, as nonrival or nonexcludable goods or services. With respect to externalities, protecting one person's well-being or property from costs imposed by another person's actions is simply a means of forcing each person to consider the full economic costs of their decisions.[5] Asking a person to share in the costs of those things from which they receive benefits is simply a matter of linking benefits with costs. In neoclassical economics, if externalities are effectively internalized, the allocation of resources will be the same as if they were allocated by markets; marginal social benefits will equal marginal social costs.[6] The existence of external costs and benefits is considered to be just another type of market failure.

The role of the government in providing information is justified by neoclassical economists as a means of ensuring against the misallocation of economic resources. In order for markets to work efficiently, consumers and producers must have full and accurate information concerning the quality, availability, and price of products and inputs.[7] Producers do not always have an economic incentive to supply such information, and, for an individual consumer, it may not be practical to pay the full cost of acquiring such information. By providing such information, the government within the neoclassical economy attempts to ensure the efficient allocation of economic resources, to prevent market failure.

By contrast, in the sustainable economy, all people must be afforded an equal right to be protected from economic exploitation. The level of such protection cannot be determined by equating marginal social costs and benefits, but must instead be provided as a matter of equity and justice for all. In the set of economic rights, the right of all people to equal protection against costs imposed by others is expressed as the "right to live in a safe and healthful natural environment . . . and be protected against all oppressive, exploitive, or coercive economic actions of others. The right of all people to a clean environment is not something that can be bought, sold, or even priced; it is an equal right of all regardless of their economic means or political influence. People may act individually or collectively, through the private economy, to acquire environmental amenities in addition to those to which all have a basic right. But the right of all people to a safe and healthful natural environment cannot be compromised in a sustainable society.

In the sustainable economy, all people must be afforded an equal "right to obtain accurate and unbiased information . . . and to be protected against attempts by others to manipulate or subversively influence one's thoughts." Economic efficiency requires that people have accurate information, but social equity requires that people not be systematically misled by those with greater access to more-complete information. Economic efficiency requires consumer sovereignty, but social equity requires freedom from mental manipulation by those with a better understanding of basic human frailties. The right of all people to be protected from exploitation by those who have more market power, or more political influence, or simply more-complete or more-accurate information is not something to be bargained for; it is an equal right of all regardless of one's economic or social status.

In a sustainable economy, trade policy provides a prime example of the necessary involvement of government in protecting the common good. Trade relations between individuals, communities, regions, states, and nations are all relevant issues in formulating the trade policies of a sustainable economy. Governments in most developed nations of the world have largely abandoned any previous role in regulating trade among communities, regions, and states, focusing instead on preventing all such restraints to trade.

The goal of U.S. international trade policy, for example, is to remove all government restraints on trade among nations and to thereby achieve a single global free market. This goal is stated as "to expand access for American exporters to overseas markets, and to ensure that commercial competitors and partners abroad observe fair trade practices."[8] To achieve these goals, the United States pushed for the establishment of the World Trade Organization (WTO).[9] The U.S. trade negotiators work to reduce or remove restraints on trade through both multilateral negotiations, as in the WTO, and bilateral negotiations, as in the North American Free Trade Agreement (NAFTA).[10] Their stated goal is to negotiate with "individual nations and regional groups" to make trade "more free and fair."[11] Their explicit assumption is that all nations will benefit from freer trade.

However, as explained in Chapter 1, the classical economic theory of free trade does not reflect the reality of global free trade today. The elimination of all constraints and barriers to trade probably would increase the level of economic activity and profitability, but there is no assurance that freer trade would be mutually beneficial to all traders or would enhance the overall quality of life of global society. In fact, there are logical reasons to believe that current U.S. trade proposals would lead to even further exploitation of people and natural resources, both in the United States and around the world. Economic sustainability requires a fundamentally different approach to trade policy.

In a sustainable economy, all trade policies should be based on the premise that every economic entity has both a right and a responsibility to protect itself from economic exploitation. Thus, every *nation*, through its government, has both a right and a responsibility to protect its natural resources and its people from exploitation by outside economic interests. In reality, beneficial free trade can occur only among sovereign entities that are willing and able to protect themselves from exploitation. Because some economic entities are weak and others are strong, society, through government, must make it possible for the weak to protect themselves from the strong. Thus, the first priority of trade policy should be the protection of the common good.

Current efforts to globalize markets have critically important implications for economic sustainability. Sustainable economies must function in harmony with natural ecosystems. Boundaries in natural ecosystems, as explained in Chapter 3, define the diversity of landscapes, life forms, and resources needed to support healthy, natural, and sustainable production processes. Fencerows, forest edges, streams, and ridges define unique watersheds, ecosystems, and bioregions within which nature can sustain different types of human enterprises. The removal of economic boundaries among geographic entities eventually leads to the destruction of natural boundaries, as spatial constraints on industrial development are removed. Lacking governmental restraints, industrial developers remove fencerows, clear forests, divert streams, and level the ridges to facilitate standardization and homogenization of industrial production processes. The natural boundaries needed for sustainability are removed to achieve greater economic efficiency. Globalization of markets ultimately leads to the loss of ecological sustainability.

Sustainable economies also must function in harmony with human communities—including towns, cities, and nations. Social and cultural boundaries define those communities—towns, states, and nations. Humanity is inherently diverse, and diversity among people is necessary for interdependent relationships—relationships of choice among distinct sovereign individuals. Although we have our humanity in common, each person is unique, and we need unique human communities within which to express our uniqueness. The globalization of markets eventually will remove social and cultural boundaries in order to achieve a homogenous global industrial economy. The natural boundaries needed to sustain social responsibility will be removed in order to achieve greater economic efficiency. The globalization of markets will in due course lead to the loss of social sustainability.

Economically sustainable systems must facilitate harmonious relationships among people and between people and their natural environment. The inherent diversity of nature and of humanity must be reflected in the diversity of the economy. Although potential gains from specialization are real, such gains are based on the premise that people and resources have unique contributions to make to the economy. In addition, competitive capitalism is based on the premise that individual entrepreneurs make individual decisions and accept individual responsibility for their actions. If globalization is allowed to destroy the boundaries that define the diversity of nature and of people, it ultimately will also destroy both the efficiency and sustainability of the economy. The globalization of markets ultimately will lead to the loss of economic sustainability.

One of the most serious challenges confronting humanity today is maintaining the healthy, semipermeable ecological, social, and economic boundaries needed to sustain a desirable quality of human life. The answer will not be found in isolation or self-sufficiency. Ecological, social, and economic relationships among people, communities, states, and nations are essential to sustainability. Nor will the answer be found in the dissolution of all boundaries. Ecological, social, and economic identities are essential for sustainability. The key is to find harmony and balance between vulnerability and security in community, state, and national relationships, just as in positive personal relationships.

People must learn to make common sense choices concerning what they allow to move across ecological, social, and economic boundaries and what they choose to keep inside those boundaries. Government trade policy is the means by which people make such choices. This concept seems to be reasonably well understood for trade among individuals. Government involvement is generally accepted as legitimate in preventing fraud and other deceptive, coercive, or exploitive trade practices involving individuals. The same principles that justify such involvement are equally relevant for trade among all *communities* of people, including cities, states, and nations. In a sustainable economy, people must demand the right and accept the responsibility to decide how relationships within boundaries need to be different from relationships across boundaries in order to sustain a desirable quality of life. Mutually beneficial free trade can occur only across selective boundaries. People must work together, through government, to protect their common good.

To protect the global common good, the World Trade Organization could possibly be redirected to ensure that every nation of the world has the right and accepts the responsibility to protect its people and its resources. This organization, which was established to remove boundaries, can be redirected to ensure that boundaries remain permeable—but only to the extent necessary to ensure the ecological, social, and economic integrity of every nation. A redirected WTO could ensure that nations neither close their borders to beneficial trade with the rest of the world nor open their borders to economic exploitation by the rest of the world.

On broader issues, perhaps the United Nations could be redesigned and redirected to become not only the arbitrator of political and ecological relationships among countries, but arbitrators of economic relationships as well. Perhaps all international trade and economic development organizations, such as the World Trade Organization, International Monetary Fund,[12] and World Bank,[13] could be brought under the auspices of the United Nations to ensure harmony and balance among the ecological, social, and economic development initiatives of the world community.

In an increasingly interconnected world, some means must be found for defining acceptable and unacceptable relationships among nations, even it means restructuring or replacing the United Nations. An international *rule of law* must be established to replace the international *rule of might*. Each nation should be ensured of the sovereignty it needs to maintain its ecological, cultural, and economic identity and integrity, but each must be willing to engage in a process of international consensus concerning how it will relate to the others. A global consensus must arise out of this process concerning the responsibility of each nation to develop its resources in ways that ensure the ecological, social, and economic sustainability of the global community. In matters of sustainability, the actions of all nations are interrelated, and thus their common good must be considered in defining the nature of relationships among nations.

The role of government in protecting people from economic exploitation is definitely not limited to international trade policies and regulations. However, economic exploitation is invariably associated with market transactions, employment conditions, contractual arrangements, or other forms of economic relationships between people or other economic entities, including all types of *communities* of people. And anytime these relationships involve *communities* of people, the government has a responsibility to protect the common good.

Preserving the Commons' Good

All natural resources were once common property—equally accessible to all. Historically, the concept of private real property emerged in England sometime in the thirteenth century.[14] Some four centuries later, John Locke declared that "the natural world is the common property of all men, but that any individual could appropriate some bit of it for himself by mixing his labor with the natural resources"—his classic justification for private property rights. However, in this same treatise Locke also introduced the so-called Lockean proviso, in which he stated that the right to take goods from the natural commons is limited by the condition that "there was still enough, and as good left; and more than the yet unprovided could use."[15] Even Locke recognized that society could not allow people to take whatever they wanted from the commons, thus ignoring their innate responsibility for respecting the common good.

In neoclassical economics, however, natural resources do not fit the definition of common goods. Land, for example, is neither nonrival *in* use nor nonexcludable *from* use. If one person uses land, rivals are not left with as much good land as they could use. Once the private property rights of a piece of land have been purchased, others can be excluded from using the land. Economists treat land as a common good only if land is owned in common, as in the case of government ownership of state and national parks, wildlife preserves, and wilderness areas. Even then, economists frequently recommend restricting access to public lands through user fees as a means of improving the efficiency of land management. They seek to allocate the use of public land as if it were private land. There is little recognition of an equal right of access of all to the natural commons.

Economists frequently refer to the story of the *tragedy of the commons* in arguing against common ownership or control of property.[16] "The tragedy of the commons develops in this way. Picture a pasture open to all. It is to be expected that each herdsman will try to keep as many cattle as possible on the commons. . . . As a rational being, each herdsman seeks to maximize his gain. Explicitly or implicitly, more or less consciously, he asks, 'What is the utility *to me* of adding one more animal to my herd?'"[17] So each herdsman sharing the commons logically decides to increase the size of his herd. "Therein is the tragedy. Each man is locked into a system that compels him to increase his herd without limit—in a world that is limited. Ruin is the destination toward which all men rush, each pursuing his own best interest in a society that believes in the freedom of the commons." [18]

However, such tragedies of the commons occur only when land held in common is used by individuals for their short-term, individual benefit, with no consideration given to preserving the good of the commons for the long-term common good. The tragedy of the commons is a consequence of the neoclassical economic assumption that people pursue *only* their narrow individual self-interests, which is not the basic nature of people. People are perfectly capable of preserving the good of the commons, once they recognize that their broader and higher self-interests are best served by caring for others and by caring for the earth for others' benefit, in addition to caring for themselves.

Preserving the good of the commons or the commons' good is a matter of stewardship, of taking care of something for the material benefit of someone else. Stewardship is not an irrational, illogical human motive, but instead has been a strongly held human value across many cultures, over many generations. Stewardship is a moral virtue. However, as Thomas Paine suggested, government involvement in stewardship is "rendered necessary by the inability of moral virtue to govern the world."[19]

The stewardship role of government in the public economy is that of ensuring intergenerational equity. In the set of economic rights suggested in Chapter 8, the stewardship ethic is reflected in the responsibility of the current generation to "ensure these rights for future generations, to the extent that they are available to those of the current generation." The responsibility for ecological preservation or the commons' good are made more explicit in the "right to pursue economic and aesthetic opportunities of one's choosing, including access to wild and scenic places . . . to connect and commune with nature" and in the requirement that "economic extractions from society and nature cannot exceed reinvestments in society and nature." Regardless of how such rights are defined, economic sustainability depends upon a willingness of the people in common, through government, to guarantee the rights of future generations to the ecological resources needed to meet their needs. To ensure intergenerational equity, the good of the commons must be preserved.

In neoclassical economics, land use policy typically focuses on protecting landowners from economic externalities because land is considered to have no natural common goods attributes. Internalizing the externalities of land use ensures that one person's land use decisions do not adversely affect the economic well-being of his or her neighbors. Restrictions on private property rights, such as planning, zoning, and other forms of restrictive covenants, typically are justified as means of minimizing economic externalities. In neoclassical economics, land use policy is still a matter of maximizing individual economic interests.

Conversely, in a sustainable economy, public land use policy is a matter of ensuring the rights of those of the future. As John Locke suggested, the right to take land from the commons must be limited by the condition that there will be enough good land left for those of the future. Markets will not ensure that people of future generations have adequate resources to meet their needs because markets over-value the present relative to the future, as discussed in Chapter 4. People of future generations cannot buy land to set aside for their use, nor can they vote for public policies that will preserve and protect the land they will need in their times. Thus, people of future generations must depend on people of current generations to choose public policies that will ensure their basic right to enough good land to meet their needs.

The right to land essentially is a right to life. People are still as dependent upon the earth, and the living things of the earth, as they were when all people were hunters and gathers; the dependence is just less clear and less well understood. All of life is supported by the nonrenewable and renewable resources of the earth, as it always has been and always will be. Nonrenewable resources are finite and must be allocated equitably across generations by means of public policy, as explained in Chapter 4. However, the finite stocks of nonrenewable resources eventually will be depleted, no matter how equitably they are distributed over time. Thus, people of some future generations will be even more dependent upon the renewable resources of the earth than we are today. Consequently, the earth's renewable resources are inherently a part of the commons and must be preserved for the common good.

In a sustainable economy, land ownership rights must be treated as land *use* rights, not as absolute private property rights. Free enterprise advocates may declare such a principle to be a violation of existing private property rights. However, a "taking" of private property exists only if the government takes ownership of private land or restricts its use in ways that make the land essentially worthless for private use.[20] Most "takings" arguments arise from disagreements concerning the amount by which land values have been diminished by additional restrictions on its use. However, a right must have first existed before it can be taken away. In the case of preserving the regenerative capacity of land, no landowner has ever had the moral right to deprive those of future generations of their right to productive land. As Thomas Paine suggested, no former generation has even had a right to give away the basic rights of the current or future generations—"from such principles, and such ignorance, Good Lord deliver the world."[21] Thus, no compensation is required for taking away economic land use rights that had no moral right to exist in the first place. In addition, the authority of governments to restrict land use already has been deemed constitutional in the United States, as reflected in private property currently zoned for specific uses or covered by restrictive covenants. In a sustainable economy, this same authority would simply need to be used to preserve the regenerative capacity of land.

In a sustainable economy, no private property owner would be allowed to use his or her property in any way that reduced its natural regenerative capacity or otherwise to infringe upon the rights of future generations to the benefits of its renewable resources. The productive capacity of good agricultural land, for example, could not legally be destroyed through industrial or urban development, simply because of its locational value. Similarly, areas best suited for the generation of energy from wind or water, or for direct solar energy collection, could not be diverted to incompatible private recreational or residential uses. Landowners could be rewarded economically through the private marketplace for enhancing the productive capacity or the aesthetic value of their property, but they would not have a right to diminish its commons' value.

Economists can simply return to the classics to find appropriate principles to be used in formulating sustainable land use policies. Thomas Paine, in his paper "Agrarian Justice," pointed out that all land was initially held in common. He then argued that the previous removal of land from the commons deprived those of later generations of their common birthright—the right of access to land.[22] Initially, land could only be removed from the commons if there was as much and as good land left for any others who chose to claim it, following the "Lockean proviso." Consequently, land taken from the commons had no market value; by definition, it could not have been scarce. Thus, its use could not be allocated by markets. Its market value arose only from "improvements" to the land brought about through the application of labor. These "improvements" to land eventually led to the pricing of land, as if it were just another marketable commodity. Today, the locational value of land probably has far greater negative consequences than do land "improvements," but the problem of market allocation of land persists.

Economist Henry George in his 1879 book, *Progress and Poverty*, proposed that the "unimproved" value of land be taxed away to prevent the pricing of land itself as a market commodity.[23] This was meant to encourage the "improvement" of land through application of labor. However, a more logical approach today might be to devise a policy for capturing any increases in land values attributable to the rezoning of land to allow higher-market-valued uses, with the tax proceeds being used to compensate those whose land is rezoned to lower-valued uses. Changes in zoning typically are associated with the changing locational value of land rather than any improvements to the land made by the owner. Thus, rezoning land to allow higher-valued uses is essentially a public grant, and rezoning to lower-valued uses is a publicly assessed penalty to the landowner. Because landowners did nothing to deserve either the grant or the penalty, it seems only logical that grants should be taxed away for use as compensation for penalties. Such a policy would remove any economic incentive for landowners to rezone land to either higher- or lower-valued uses and would allow communities as a whole to make logical long-term land use decisions with far less outside pressures from landowners. A similar capturing of capital gains in land values attributable to growing population demands would remove speculative incentives for landownership and would generate public funds to sustain and enhance the productivity and regenerative capacity of land.

Regardless of the policies chosen, sustainability will require that land use decisions be made by means that achieve harmony among the long-term economic, social, and ethical values of a society. Buying and selling the right to *misuse* land is no more defensible than is buying and selling the right to misuse another person. The natural regenerative capacity of land is a fundamental resource upon which all life ultimately depends. It cannot be allowed to belong to anyone individually or to any generation of individuals—just as people cannot be allowed to belong to other people. The regenerative capacity of the land, the commons' good, must be preserved for the benefit of all people of all generations—for the common good.

Land use decisions must be made by the people in common, through the institution of government, not just to minimize externalities, but also to protect the commons' good. Market allocation of land use, justified by neoclassical economics, has actually diminished the value of the commons, as people have been encouraged to pursue their individual material self-interests. In a sustainable economy, people must accept the responsibility for making land use decisions, in common, through government, to preserve the commons' good.

Endnotes

1. *World Book, 2002 Standard Edition,* "common." (Chicago: World Book, Inc., 2001).

2. Bernard Salanie, *Macroeconomics of Market Failure* (Cambridge, Mass.: MIT Press, 2000).

3. John Hart, "Water: A Sacramental Commons," unpublished paper, workshop sponsored by National Catholic Rural Life Council, Washington, D.C., February 8, 2003.

4. Karl E. Case and Ray C. Fair, *Principles of Economics* (Englewood Cliffs, N.J.: Prentice-Hall Inc., 2nd ed., 1992), 459.

5. Tyler Cowen, *The Theory of Market Failure: A Critical Evaluation* (Somerset, N.J.: Transaction Publications, 1988).

6. Case and Fair, *Principles,* 446–449.

7. Case and Fair, *Principles,* 465.

8. U.S. Department of State, *Trade Policies and Programs,* U.S. Department of State, http://www.state.gov/e/eb/tpp/ (accessed October, 2005).

9. World Trade Organization, "Welcome to WTO Website," WTO, http://www.wto.org/ (accessed February, 2005).

10. NAFTA Secretariat, 2004, "Welcome Page," http://www.nafta-sec-alena.org/DefaultSite/index_e.aspx (accessed February, 2005).

11. WTO.

12. International Monetary Fund, "IMF—International Monetary Fund Home Page, http://www.imf.org/ (accessed February, 2005).

13. The World Bank Group, "The World Bank Group homepage," The World Bank Group, http://www.worldbank.org/ (accessed February, 2005).

14. Jonathan Hughes and Louis P. Cain, *American Economic History* (San Francisco: Benjamin-Cummings Publishing Company, 2002).

15. *Wikipedia, the Free Encyclopedia,* "John Locke," http://en.wikipedia.org/wiki/John_Locke (accessed October, 2005).

16. W. F. Lloyd, *Two Lectures on the Checks to Population* (Oxford, England: Oxford University Press, 1833).

17. Garrett Hardin, "The Tragedy of the Commons," *Science,* 162 (1968): 1243–1248.

18. Hardin, *Science.*

19. Thomas Paine, *Common Sense* (Mineola, N.Y.: Dover Publications Inc., 1997; original copyright, 1776).

20. Lawrence Blume, Daniel L. Rubinfeld, and Perry Shapiro, "The Taking of Land: When Should Compensation Be Paid?" *Quarterly Journal of Economics,* 99, no. 1 (1984): 71–92.

21. Thomas Paine, "Rights of Man," in *The Life and Major Works of Thomas Paine,* ed. Philip S. Foner (New York: The Citadel Press, 1936), 325.

22. Paine, "Agrarian Justice," *Life and Works.*

23. Henry George, *Progress and Poverty* (New York: Random House, 1879).

CHAPTER TEN

MANAGING THE PRIVATE ECONOMY

The Scope of the Private Economy

The sustainable private economy must be managed in accordance with the hierarchy of sustainability; the private economy is a subset of the social economy, which in turn is a part of the ecological economy. Managing the private economy for sustainability begins with questions about the rightness of relationships and ends with questions about appropriate boundaries. Within such boundaries, private markets can be left free to function so as to serve the individual and collective interests of the people within society. Thus, the legitimate scope of the private economy is defined by the hierarchy of sustainability.

As indicated previously, human priorities are commonly defined by the "hierarchy of needs," as defined by Abraham Maslow.[1] Maslow identified several levels of human needs, suggesting that lower levels must be satisfied before the higher levels can be met. He identified bodily drives, such as hunger and thirst, as the lowest, or most basic, levels of individual needs. The next-higher levels included needs for security and love, which can be met through relationships with others. Maslow defined the highest human need as self-actualization, or the fulfillment of one's unique potential or purpose in life.

Following a similar hierarchy, neoclassical economics places the highest priority on individual material needs, which are acquired by following one's basic physical drives or urges. This proposition accounts for the seductiveness of Adam Smith's conception of a free

177

market economy, in which the butcher, the brewer, and the baker could best meet the needs of society by pursuing their "self-love" and their "own advantage," with no concern for the "necessities" of others.[2] People could benefit society most effectively by simply pursuing their basic drives and urges as self-seeking individuals.

Neoclassical economists view most relationships as being purely instrumental, a means of acquiring something of benefit to oneself. Economically rational people become altruistic, as in showing concern for the unmet needs of others, only after their own needs and wants have been met. For example, economists typically assume that poor people simply cannot afford to be concerned about the economic well-being of their neighbors. Ethical issues, such as ecological stewardship are assumed to be of concern only to those who are affluent, those who have already fulfilled most of their individual and social needs and desires. For example, we are told that poor nations simply can't afford to take care of their environment. To neoclassical economists, the satisfaction of individual needs and wants comes first, social relationships come next, and stewardship and other such ethical concerns are viewed as luxuries of the leisure classes.

The hierarchy of human needs arises from a hierarchy of *humanness*. At the most basic level, humans are like other living things; we seek to survive, to thrive, and to reproduce—as naturally self-seeking individuals. At the next-higher levels, humans share traits with many other animals, such as forming social relationships with others of our own kind and forming relationships of usefulness and convenience with other species. At the highest levels, the levels of self-actualization and self-knowledge of purpose and meaning, we are uniquely human. As far as we know, no other living species is capable of our self-knowledge of rightness or goodness.

The motivations of our actions at each of these levels, likewise, reflect different levels of *humanness*. At the lowest levels, we are driven by our basic urges and animalistic instincts, such as hunger, greed, and lust. At the next-higher levels, we are driven by our emotions and thoughtfulness—valuing love, civility, equity, and justice—as we seek satisfaction through our relationships with others. Finally, at the highest levels, our actions are motivated by wisdom and common sense, as we seek to achieve *rightness* in our relationships with others and with the earth. The most basic levels can be thought of as *primal*, the next higher levels as *thoughtful*, and the highest levels as *philosophical* or even *spiritual*. As far as we know, only humans have a capacity for philosophy or spirituality.

In the hierarchy of economic sustainability, however, individual, social, and ecological integrity are all considered equally essential aspects of an inseparable whole. The hierarchy of sustainability is a *nested* hierarchy, which focuses on different levels of organization, observation, explanation, and relationships. As explained in Chapter 7, higher levels of organization provide context for, contain, and constrain the lower levels. Higher levels act more slowly and have greater integrity and strength than do lower levels of organization.[3,4] Thus, the hierarchy of sustainability reverses the economic hierarchy of needs. The moral economy is the highest; the public economy is next; then the private economy follows. Consequently, managing the sustainable economy requires a reversal of the priorities suggested by neoclassical economics.

Management of the sustainable economy begins with common sense and collective wisdom, which guide our thoughts and emotions in establishing the public or social boundaries within which we may pursue our private urges for self-gratification. Neoclassical economics is about the present, the individual, the here and now, whereas sustainability spans from the individual, here and now, to the whole of humanity, everywhere and immortal. The individual exists within one generation; humanity spans all generations. Thus, common sense and wisdom must constrain our thoughts and emotions, which in turn must constrain our drives and urges. And the scope of the private economy in meeting individual needs and wants must be bounded by the higher-level priorities of the public economy in serving the common good, which in turn, is bounded by a moral consensus of the rightness of relationships. Only within these boundaries can the private economy function sustainably, and only within these boundaries can the private economy contribute to human happiness and a desirable quality of life.

The Role of the Private Economy

The fundamental role of the private economy is to provide goods and services for the benefit of individuals. Private goods and services account for the vast majority of all goods and services produced in the United States, as is the case for most developed nations of the world.

The U.S. gross domestic product (GDP) reflects an attempt to measure the total value of all goods and services produced in the nation during a given time period.[5] In 2003, for instance, governmental consumption expenditures and investments accounted for about $2.1 trillion, or about 18%, of the $11-trillion U.S. GDP.[6] Government transfer payments, primarily Social Security and Medicare, added another $1.3 trillion, or roughly 7%, to total government outlays, which do not show up in the GDP. This left about 75% of all economic activity in the United States accounted for by the private sector of the economy.

If government costs of providing true public goods and services were separated from government costs of facilitating and subsidizing the private economy, the public sector contribution to the GDP would appear even smaller and the private sector of the economy would appear even larger. Large portions of total government expenditures and transfer payments contribute little if anything to the common good. For example, many current government expenditures either subsidize private businesses or represent collective purchases, which may contribute to the *collective* good but do nothing for the *common* good. National defense accounts for about one-third of total federal government expenditures. However, current levels of U.S. military spending reflect the current economic and political power of the military industrial complex as much as or more than the legitimate defense needs of the nation.

A significant amount of current U.S. government spending represents *corporate welfare* rather than *social welfare,* under some misguided assumption that the primary role of government is to create private sector employment. According to a 1996 *Boston Globe* series on corporate welfare, "The $150 billion for corporate subsidies and tax benefits eclipses the annual budget deficit of $130 billion. It's more than the $145 billion paid out annually for the core programs of the social welfare state: Aid to Families with Dependent Children (AFDC), student aid, housing, food and nutrition, and all direct public assistance (excluding Social Security and medical care)."[7]

The government certainly has a legitimate role in *facilitating* private sector employment, investment, and various types of market transactions by providing the legal, financial, institutional, and physical infrastructure necessary for an efficient, complex economy. Government is the only logical means of ensuring the integrity of the national currency and banking system, protecting private property rights, facilitating the enforcement of contracts, and creating the legal structure within which private transactions can take place. The government also has a legitimate role in formulating and implementing macroeconomic policy; creating a more stable economic environment; and thus facilitating private employment, saving, and investing. But the government has no moral responsibility to *subsidize* corporations or individual businesses in order to create private employment or other purely private benefits for individuals.

Subsidization of private enterprise is a purely discretional function of government that promotes individual or collective interests, but it does not promote the common good. In addition, government subsidization of private investment often leads to the exploitation of both natural and human resources, diminishing the overall well-being of society. The jobs created by government subsidies may benefit individuals in the short run but may degrade the well-being of society in the long run.

In a sustainable economy, the accounting cost of the public economy should include only those government activities that serve the common good—those things to which all have equal rights. The discretionary use of government funds to serve individual and collective interests should be charged to the private sector of the economy. The legitimate role of the private economy includes all of those things that can be done best by people as individuals and collections of individuals, and therefore need not be done by or for society as a whole.

Managing for Competitiveness

The highest priority in managing a capitalistic, private economy must an unwavering commitment to maintain competition. If the competitiveness of a capitalistic economy is lost, no other aspect of the economy will be able to function effectively or sustainably. When governments fail to maintain competition, capitalism inevitably degenerates into corporatism, as explained in Chapter 1. Under corporatism, the private sector no longer serves the good of individuals, the public sector no longer serves the good of society, and nations lose their common sense of rightness of relationships. In the historic words of Karl Marx, under unbridled capitalism, the "bourgeoisie," today's corporate aristocracy, "has resolved personal worth into exchange value, and in place of the numberless indefensible chartered freedoms, has set up that single, unconscionable freedom—free trade. In one word, for exploitation, veiled as religious and political illusions, it has substituted naked, shameless, direct, brutal exploitation."[8] Lacking the moral courage and political conviction to maintain the competitiveness of free markets, a capitalistic economy inevitably becomes exploitive and extractive and thereby accelerates the natural tendency toward entropy, just as Marx suggested. Thus, a sustainable economy depends upon people finding the courage and conviction to defend, or if necessary, to reclaim the competitiveness of their private economy.

Historically, the people of the United States have defied Marx by showing remarkable moral and political courage in constraining the private economy, at least when it has been most necessary to do so. Following the U.S. Civil War, the consolidation of businesses producing basic commodities, such as sugar, kerosene, meats, and rubber goods, set the stage for John D. Rockefeller in late 1882 to form his first corporate trust, Standard Oil.[9] Rockefeller exerted market power over the petroleum industry—manipulating supply and influencing prices and profits in ways that were clearly contradictory to Adam Smith's concept of free markets.

Soon large corporations not only dominated the U.S. economy but controlled much of the American political process as well. Politicians and elections were clearly influenced through bribes, lobbying, and corporate financing of campaigns. Upton Sinclair's book, *The Jungle*, published in 1906, provides vivid insights into the nature of early-twentieth century industrialism.[10] Sinclair focused on the powerful beef trusts' inhumane and unethical treatment of both animals and people, but he also illuminated the pervasive corrupting influence of the powerful corporations on U.S. politics and government in general.

However, the people rebelled against the growing monopoly power of corporations. A strong Progressive political movement emerged, demanding political and economic reforms. At the urging of Teddy Roosevelt, Congress passed a number of new laws designed to help enforce antitrust laws already on the books, such as the Sherman Antitrust Act of 1890. During Roosevelt's two administrations, the Justice Department brought more than 40 antitrust actions against the corporate trusts and won several important judgments, one of which resulted in the split up of Rockefeller's Standard Oil Company Trust.[11]

The Progressive Era in U.S. politics, begun during the late 1800s, continued through the Woodrow Wilson administration following World War I. During this period, the Civil Service replaced political patronage, thereby crippling the powerful political machines. Primary elections were instituted to select candidates for offices, replacing corporate deals in smoke-filled rooms. And labor unions were exempted from antitrust legislation to provide a countervailing power against corporations in negotiations for wages and working conditions. The monopoly power of corporations was restrained, if not controlled, and at least a degree of market competitiveness was restored.

Although revolutionary at the time, the reforms instituted during the Progressive Era have been slowly whittled away. Neoclassical capitalism, being cancerous by nature, systematically seeks to disable or destroy all external restraints to its growth. American industrialists, from Henry Ford to Bill Gates, have worked diligently to remove all restraints to the growth of their corporations, perhaps sincerely believing that corporate growth somehow promotes societal good. One by one, the most important constraints imposed on corporations in the early 1900s have been weakened or removed. Labor unions no longer represent an effective countervailing force to corporate power. Corporate money and economic influence again dominate most political campaigns. Particularly during the last two decades, antitrust laws have been virtually ignored as corporate mergers have proceeded on an unprecedented scale. In addition, today's corporations are multinational in scope, exceeding the span of control of any single nation, and often exceeding the size of many national economies. Widespread alliances and joint ventures, virtually untouched by antitrust regulators, add still further to both the horizontal and vertical span of control of the multinational corporate giants.[12]

Many people have been led to believe that markets are too complicated to understand without some formal economic education. However, the most powerful economics concepts are the most simple and are evident to all who seek to understand. Market performance is one of those concepts. Widespread public understanding of market performance could lay the foundation for another Progressive movement.

Through the mid-1900s, industrial organization—focusing on corporate structure, conduct, and performance—was a subject of great interest to economists. They referred to the number and size of firms in an industry as market *structure*. Market *conduct* referred to the presence or absence of collusion among firms, including price fixing and market sharing arrangements. Market *performance* was reflected in prices and in the output level of an industry.[13] The basic assumption was that industries with a large number of small firms would produce a larger quantity of products at lower prices and thus would perform better than industries with just a few large firms. Furthermore, industries comprising few firms that did not conspire to raise prices would also produce more at lower prices than would industries in which firms collude in setting prices.

Over time, however, economists began to focus more directly on market performance, reasoning that if markets performed well, there was little cause for concern about their structure or conduct. The focus of market performance eventually shifted from the study of industrial organization to the study of game theory.[14] And the study of market efficiency shifted to assessing the accuracy with which capital markets reflect all available information.[15]

The term *workable competition* became popular among economists to describe situations in which government intervention to restore competition in an industry would not improve societal benefits.[16] In such cases, economists felt that a few large firms might perform more efficiently, in terms of quantity and price, than would a large number of small firms. Some economists also added product innovation to their criteria for workable competition because monopolies theoretically suppress innovation in order to maximize profits from their current technologies. So large corporate firms fighting for increased market share, through strategic pricing and constant innovation, were viewed as competitive performers, even as they moved their respective industries farther away from the conditions of classical economic competitiveness. However, the performance of markets in the long run is still as dependent on the conditions of pure or perfect competition as they were in the days of Adam Smith.

Market performance cannot be measured solely in terms of quantity, price, and innovation. Market performance can be thought of as market efficiency, and markets exhibit two distinctly different types of efficiency—efficiency of operation and efficiency of resource allocation.[17] *Operational efficiency* is a reflection of the technical efficiency of production and can be measured in terms of output and price. Industries with lower overall production costs can produce larger quantities of output at lower prices and thus are said to be more efficient. In industries exhibiting economies of scale, a few large operations would have lower cost of producing than would a large number of small operations. Hence, an industry dominated by a small number of large corporations may appear to be very economically efficient, if each firm in vying for an increasing market share keeps industry profit margins temporarily low.

Allocation efficiency, however, must be measured in terms of whether resources are being used effectively to give consumers an assortment of goods and services, at the appropriate *relative* quantities and prices, to best meet their individual wants and needs. Adam Smith's claim that competitive markets were capable of meeting the needs of society was primarily about the efficiency of resource allocation, not about the efficiency of operation. In addition, the premise that market economies are more effective than are centrally planned economies in meeting the needs of society depends upon the allocative efficiency of markets and the related assumptions of highly competitive markets, if not purely competitive markets.

The resource-allocating ability of markets is derived from the basic laws of supply and demand, which were explained at some length in Chapter 7. In summary, quantities demanded and quantities supplied tend to move in opposite directions in response to changes in market price. As prices go *down,* the quantities demanded *increase,* but the quantities supplied *decline.* As prices go *up,* the quantities demanded *decline,* but the quantities supplied *increase.* Changes in prices ensure that the quantity demanded always equals the quantity supplied; the markets always clear, without residual surpluses or deficits.

Markets also determine wage rates for labor, interest rates for capital, rental rates for land and other real estate, and salaries for managers. The demand for inputs or factors of production is derived directly from prices at the consumer level. Higher prices for a given product increase profitability, strengthen demand, and increase the prices for the things used to produce it. Falling product prices reduce profits, weaken demand, and reduce the prices for the affected factors of production.

The supply of production inputs responds to prices in the same way as the supply of consumer products. If wage rates fall in a given industry, workers move to better-paying jobs elsewhere. As producers in a growing industry attempt to expand production, they need more capital, they bid up interest rates, and capital flows in from other uses to finance their expansion. Thus, productive resources—land, labor, capital, and management—are shifted from one use to another as changing prices make them more or less valuable in producing different goods and services. They are shifted from less-valued to more-valued economic uses.

This is the process by which scarce resources are allocated among alternative uses in meeting the needs and wants of consumers. Individual consumers seek to maximize their utility or satisfaction and business firms seek to maximize their profits. As each pursues individual self-interest, they are guided, as if by an *invisible hand*, to allocate scarce resources so as to maximize the collective economic welfare of society. However, it should be evident for all to see that the efficiency of the allocative process depends on the extent to which actual market conditions conform to the conditions of pure competition.

Excessive profits, anywhere in the system, distort price signals and lead to misallocation of productive resources in relation to consumers' preferences. Competition among a large number of independent sellers eliminates these excessive profits. Barriers to entry and exit keep new producers from increasing production to accommodate greater demand of some items while encouraging existing producers of other items to continue producing more of things that consumers now value less. Competitive markets must be easy to enter or exit. Misleading advertising leads consumers to purchase things that do not meet their needs, leaving no market incentives to produce the things that would better meet their needs. Competitive markets require unbiased, accurate information. And finally, persuasive advertising is designed to create wants rather than to satisfy needs, and thus may reduce, rather than increase, consumer well-being. Competitive markets depend upon sovereign consumers, with tastes and preferences free of persuasive or coercive influences. In the absence of these conditions of competition, markets are incapable of efficient resource allocation.

No objective means are available for measuring allocative efficiency in terms of market performance. Price and output measure operational efficiency, and product innovation does not ensure economic progress. The absence of excessive profits in today's economy is more likely to be a reflection of competition among firms trying to gain monopoly control, than a reflection of competition among firms that are powerless to raise prices or increase profits. The only way to measure allocative efficiency is to evaluate the competitiveness of markets. The more an industry deviates from the classic conditions of perfect competition, the less the likelihood that it is meeting the real needs and wants of society.

Operations efficiency is a legitimate concern in assessing the overall efficiency of markets. However, the fact that an industry provides a lot of "cheap stuff" is no assurance that it is providing the "right stuff" to meet the true wants and needs of people. The primary responsibility of government in managing the private economy is to ensure the competitiveness of markets.

The government has the power to restore competitiveness to U.S. markets, but the corporations will not willingly relinquish their positions of influence either in the marketplace or in politics. Congress clearly has the power to strengthen antitrust laws, as they did in the early 1900s. The President has the power to enforce existing antitrust laws more vigorously without any legislative action. And the Supreme Court has the power to reinterpret the economic and political "personhood" of corporations, as it has never made a *formal* ruling on this matter.[18] But any success in government efforts to restore competitiveness to markets must be supported by an understanding among the American people of the importance of doing so. The government must derive its powers to restore competitiveness from the consent of the governed.

Providing Collective Goods and Services

Another legitimate function of the private economy is the provision of collective goods and services. The characteristics of being *nonrival in consumption* and *nonexcludable from consumption* accurately define collective goods but fail to address whether such goods and services contribute to the civility, equity, or justice of a society. Thus, the neoclassical definition of *common* goods more accurately applies to *collective* goods. Most common goods and services—such as military protection, public transportation, and public education—are logically acquired collectively, through taxing and government spending, rather than individually. However, such things are common goods only to the extent they are considered basic rights, shared equally by all.

Neoclassical economics tends to treat all collectively purchased goods alike, regardless of whether they have common goods characteristics. Thus, economists seek means of privatizing all collective purchases, by making them *exclusive* in consumption and *rival* in consumption, without regard to their common goods characteristics. When pressures to cut government expenditures arise, the pressure tends to fall disproportionately on common goods, rather than collective goods. Individuals benefit directly from collective goods, whereas they benefit from common goods through their common membership in society. By failing to distinguish between the two, many people fail to comprehend that many collective goods are discretionary but all common goods are necessary, and thus choose the discretionary over the necessary.

Collective purchases of goods and services may be justified for a number of legitimate reasons. First, government procurement may be the least-cost means of securing goods and services whenever significant savings can be realized through large-scale purchases. Most common goods and services also fit this criterion. For example, it wouldn't make much sense for people to use vouchers or tax credits to buy their own tank or missile, to build little pieces of highways, or to hire a teacher for a few hours to educate their children. Therefore, governments purchase such things in large quantities for the benefit of all.

However, people choose to buy many things collectively that are not inherently common in nature, such as electrical power for appliances and air conditioning, interstate highways and freeways to move traffic more quickly, electronic and satellite telecommunications systems, water and sewer lines for industrial development. Such things may make life more comfortable or convenient, but they are not things to which people have basic rights. Economists say that such things present a "drop in the bucket" problem, in that the amount each person could afford to contribute individually to acquire them would be too small to justify any level of individual investment. Or they may present a "free rider" problem—meaning that, after such things are purchased, individuals cannot easily exclude those who did not share in the costs from receiving the benefits.[19] Thus, all people can be granted equal access to government goods and services, not because they have a right to them, but simply because it's impractical to exclude those who didn't pay taxes or to limit access for those who paid less. In many cases, collective purchases could be and are made through private for-profit or nonprofit organizations. However, in cases in which the individual interests are not clear and direct and the number of potential benefactors is large, it's just more convenient and practical to make collective purchases through government.

A common justification for collective purchases in the past was to prevent "natural monopolies."[20] Examples of natural monopolies include electrical power lines, telephone and telegraph lines, railroads and highways, and sewer and water lines. Natural monopolies often include enterprises for which the costs of building the infrastructure needed to deliver the product were very high in relation to the total market, making competition among several suppliers impractical. For example, it is impractical to run three or four power lines or phone lines to every house, to build two or three parallel railroad beds, or to run a half-dozen different water or sewer lines around town.

Obviously, the company that built the first one of any of these things would have a natural monopoly, because no one else could afford to build another with the promise of only half of the market. Or the new company would have to count on eventually driving the old one out of business in order to survive and, thus, become the new monopoly.

Historically, government would intervene in natural monopoly situations. Government would build the necessary infrastructure and provide the service, or they would grant a private company the exclusive right to provide the service. Government would then regulate the quality and price of the service. Because the company granted the right would have a monopoly position in the market, there would be no competition to ensure quality of service or a competitive price.

However, because the focus of economic attention has shifted from ensuring market competitiveness to the assessment of operational and technical market performance, preventing natural monopolies is no longer seen as an automatic justification for government intervention. Today, privatization seems to be considered a viable option for virtually all public goods and services and is being actively explored in many areas, including electrical power, space travel, and even national defense.

Collective goods and services represent a logical and legitimate function of government in the management of the private economy. People have the right to make decisions collectively, through government, for their collective good. And people should be free to devote as much or as little of their income as they choose to discretionary collective purchases rather than private purchases. But voluntary collective purchases should not be confused with common or public purchases. Paying for common goods is an obligation of all individuals so that they contribute some part of their income and wealth toward maintaining the integrity of the social and political structure within which they are able to acquire and accumulate income and wealth. Collective goods may be privatized, but common goods may not. And to protect the common good, the competitiveness of markets cannot be compromised by privatizing natural monopolies.

Paying for the Public Economy

A primary responsibility in managing the private economy is to ensure that individual contributions to the public good are assessed and are shared as fairly and equitably as possible. Everything governments do must be supported by either taxing or borrowing. Because borrowing requires interest payment, in addition to eventual equity repayment, borrowing eventually leads to increased taxing. So all government spending eventually must be matched by government taxing. And all taxes that support the public economy are assessed to and paid by the private economy.

In specific terms, "a tax is an involuntary fee or, more precisely, 'unrequited payment,' paid by individuals or businesses" to support the functions of their government.[21] In a representative democracy, elected representatives generally decide which functions the government will perform, and at the same time, should decide how much and what kinds of taxes must be paid to support those functions. Most people would agree that systems of taxation chosen by their government should be simple, straightforward, and sensible. In paying for the public economy, questions that must be answered include who should be taxed and how much they should pay for each specific type of public goods or services.

Tax collections generally should be linked as closely as is practical with the public goods and services for which the taxes are to be used, so that taxpayers will know what they are receiving in return for their taxes. This principle should be easy to follow in cases of collective purchases. For example, electrical power, communications systems, and highways could be supported by taxes on those who benefit most directly from the service—as is generally the case today. However, the costs of ensuring and protecting the fundamental rights of all, the cost of serving the common good, should be shared broadly across the whole economy.

National defense, law enforcement, and basic public education are among the most clearly defined common goods and services. Accordingly, it might be reasonable to support the costs of such services through a value-added tax, which is a tax on final output levied in relation to increases in value of goods and services as they change hands in the course of production.[22] Each business involved in a production process deducts their costs—including employee wages and salaries, interest on borrowed money, and rent for production facilities—from the value of their sales of products and pay a percentage tax on the difference. The value of output at one level of production would represent cost at the next level of production. The net result would be a tax on the total value of production, with a business involved in the value creation process paying taxes in proportion to the value they added to, and the returns they received from, the total production process.

A similar tax might be levied on services, including such things as brokerage fees, consulting fees, and legal fees, as well as tangible products. Total collections from value-added or gross margin taxes would then represent a percentage of the contribution of the business sector to total national value of production, or the gross domestic product, the broadest measure of national economic activity. All taxes on businesses, including corporations, partnerships, and individual proprietorships, could be assessed as value-added taxes. The broadest, most-inclusive functions of government should be funded through the broadest, most-inclusive form of taxes.

Personal income taxes could be reserved to support those public goods and services that are most easily addressed through a redistribution of income to meet the necessities of life, such as adequate food, clothing, and shelter for needy children and those who are elderly, disabled, or otherwise unable to earn a socially acceptable income. Clearly, Americans might benefit from rethinking the whole issue concerning why and how income is taxed. Politicians argue endlessly over the appropriate tax rates for the poor relative to the rich. Those who believe all that society owes anyone is an opportunity to acquire private property tend to favor flat tax rates—taxing the wealthy and the poor alike. Those who believe in ensuring equity and justice generally are more willing to share their wealth with others.

A more logical approach to income taxes might be to provide everyone with a tax credit sufficient to ensure some socially acceptable standard of living, and then assess everyone the same *marginal* tax rate for each dollar he or she earns, without further exemptions or deductions. If a person failed to earn enough income to owe more taxes than the amount of the tax credit, the government would pay them the difference, ensuring them a living income, as in Milton Friedman's negative income tax proposal.[23] For those with large incomes, the tax credit would be incidental. The amount of the tax credit and the marginal tax rate could be adjusted to ensure that adequate tax revenues are collected to pay for the credits. Such a tax program could replace all other income assistance programs, including Social Security and Medicare.

For the sake of illustration, suppose that a 33% *marginal* tax rate would pay the cost of all tax credits and would raise as much money as the government needs to collect from income taxes, including current

Social Security and Medicare taxes. The total employee–employer contribution to Social Security and Medicare is currently more than 15%, so the marginal federal income tax rate would be less than 18%. The necessary tax rate would be relatively easy to calculate, once the amount of money the government would need from income taxes is determined, or at least easier to calculate than future federal revenue under existing tax laws.

Under this scenario, everyone would pay 33%, one-third, of everything he or she earned to the government as income taxes. All deductions and exemptions would be eliminated—all income would be taxable income. Furthermore, assume that the government credits each working adult $9,000 to ensure that no one lives in poverty, regardless of how much they are able to earn in the job market. The credit could be adjusted for different sizes of families, and obviously would need to be higher for those who are physically or mentally unable to work. Even at minimum wage of $5.00 an hour, a person could earn more than $10,000 per year in addition to their income supplement. Everyone would have an incentive to work—and would be expected to work, if able.

Under this proposal, a single person wouldn't owe the government anything until their income exceeded $27,000 per year (one-third of $27,000 equals $9,000, which would just offset their credit). At any lower income, the government would pay them the difference between the $9,000 credit and 33% of their earnings. At an $18,000 income, for example, a person would owe $6,000 in taxes (one-third of $18,000). But with their tax credit of $9,000, they would receive $3,000 ($9,000 minus $6,000) from the government, raising their total income to $21,000.

Money for tax credits would be raised from positive taxes on those earning more than $27,000 per year. For example, a taxpayer earning $60,000 per year would owe $11,000 in income taxes (one-third of $60,000, or $20,000, minus $9,000), and a person with a $1,000,000 income would owe $321,000 ($330,000 minus $9,000).

Such an outcome is quite reasonable, although a large percentage of all taxpayers would pay no net income taxes at all and instead would receive an income supplement. The personal income of the wealthiest segment of the U.S. population, the upper 20%, amounts to around half of the total national personal income.[24] These people would be paying net taxes (after adjusting for their credit) equal to about 20% of their total household income, which averaged over $82,000 in the year 2000.[25] Half of total income would be taxed at more than 20%. For those with the highest levels of income, the $9,000 tax credit would be insignificant in relation to the taxes owed, and their effective tax rate would near 33%. In fact, the marginal tax rate might be considerably less than 33%, if deductions and exemptions were eliminated and all current individual and corporate tax loopholes were closed. Regardless of whether this or some other alternative system is chosen, few would argue that the current income tax system in the United States is simple, straightforward, or sensible. Income tax reform should be a high priority in managing the private U.S. economy.

Governments at the national, state, and local levels have different roles and functions. Some public goods and services should be made available to everyone in the nation, some legitimately can be left up to the states, and others are fundamentally local matters. Most of the fundamental rights discussed previously are rights to be shared equally by everyone in the nation. Public goods and services that need to be equally accessible to everyone in the nation should be supported by federal taxes and administered by the federal government. The states should not be forced to pay for national public goods and services through mandates from the federal level.

However, individual states and cities might choose to provide some higher level of public service than is guaranteed to all at the federal level, and those supplements, likewise, should be supported by state and local taxes. Nothing that can be done fairly and effectively at the local level should be done at the state level, and nothing that can be done fairly and effectively at the state level should be done at the federal level. This is a basic philosophy of government. It follows that discretionary collective purchases made at the state and local levels should be paid for from tax revenues collected at the state and local levels, that is, at the same level as those receiving the services.

Neoconservative politicians are fond of saying, "It's the people's money; they have a right to spend it any way they choose, so it shouldn't be taxed away by government." But people aren't wasting their money when they decide to buy things they need and want collectively rather than individually. And people aren't wasting their money when they decide to spend it to ensure that all receive those things to which they have inalienable rights. Instead, people have a right and a responsibility to use the institution of government to help build a more equitable, just, and sustainable society. The future of humanity depends on the willingness of people to spend some of their money together in pursuit of the common good. The effective management of the public economy can ensure that the money people choose to spend collectively is spent wisely.

Managing Within the Private Economy

In a sustainable economy, most economic decisions will still be made privately, by individuals pursuing their self-interests. This chapter has focused on maintaining the competitiveness of private markets, acquiring collective goods and services, and paying for the public economy, because management within the private economy should remain mainly a matter of individual choice. The government has a legitimate role in facilitating private decisions, by providing the legal, financial, and physical infrastructure needed to allow private product markets and resource markets to function efficiently. The government also has a legitimate role in maintaining a stable economic environment for investment and employment, through macroeconomic policies. Current economic theories and policies related to these roles of government are quite compatible with a sustainable economy and need only be adjusted and redirected to accommodate the social and ecological requirements of sustainability. For example, the purpose of macroeconomic policy must shift from maximum economic growth to sustainable economic development. In addition, government regulations must create an economic environment within which individual organizations can function with ecological and social integrity.

In the sustainable economy, however, individual decisions will be guided by the pursuit of happiness or quality of life, rather than the maximization of profit or wealth. Consumers in pursuing their enlightened self-interest will choose products priced to reflect their full ecological, social, and economic costs of production, rather than choose products priced lower because the social and environmental costs have been externalized. They will choose to pay the full costs of production rather than support social and ecological exploitation. Profits will be shared vertically, among resource providers, producers, manufacturers, distributors, and consumers. Those operating at each stage of production will then be able to contribute to the integrity and regenerative capacity of the entire production process. Business organizations will voluntarily limit their size and span of control, so that they can effectively care for the natural environments and the social communities in which they operate; they will manage for the triple bottom line.

Current economic principles related to business management will continue to be appropriate and useful, but only in managing the individual economic dimension of the organization. The social and ethical aspects of performance will operate according to different sets of principles, as discussed in Chapter 6. The economic, social, and ecological dimensions of the organization will be managed holistically, to ensure long-term sustainability, by contributing to the happiness and quality of life of customers, workers, suppliers, neighbors, and society. These choices will be made privately and freely, without threat or coercion, because they will have found to be a better way to do business, a better way to work, and a better way to live.

Endnotes

1. *World Book, 2002 Standard Edition,* "Maslow." (Chicago: World Book, Inc., 2001).

2. Adam Smith, *Wealth of Nations* (Amherst, Mass.: Prometheus Books Great Mind Series, 1991; original copyright, 1776), 20.

3. Valerie Ahl and T. F. H. Allen, *Hierarchy Theory: A Vision, Vocabulary and Epistemology* (New York: Columbia University Press, 1996), 29–30.

4. T. F. H. Allen and T. B. Starr, *Hierarchy: Perspectives for Ecological Complexity* (Chicago: University Chicago Press, 1982).

5. *World Book,* "Domestic Product."

6. U.S. Department of Commerce, Bureau of Economic Analysis, *Frequently Requested Tables: National Economic Accounts, 2004,* http://www.bea.gov/bea/dn/nipaweb/ SelectTable.asp?Popular=Y (accessed October, 2004).

7. Charles M. Sennott, "The $150 Billion 'Welfare' Recipients: U.S. Corporations," *The Boston Globe,* July 7, 1996.

8. Karl Marx and Friedrich Engels, *The Communist Manifesto* (New York: Pocket Books, Simon and Schuster, 1964; original copyright 1848), 62.

9. *Microsoft Encarta Encyclopedia, 2003,* "Industrial Revolution." (Redmond. Wash.: Microsoft Corp., 1993–2002).

10. Upton Sinclair, *The Jungle* (New York: Bantam Books, 1981; original copyright, 1906).

11. *World Book,* "Theodore Roosevelt, Trust Busting."

12. Mary K. Hendrickson and William D. Heffernan, "Opening Spaces through Relocalization: Locating Potential Resistance in the Weaknesses of the Global Food System," *Sociolgia Ruralis,* 42, no. 4 (2002): 347–369.

13. Oz Shy, *Industrial Organization: Theory and Application* (Cambridge, Mass.: The MIT Press, 1995).

14. Jean Tirole, *The Theory of Industrial Organization* (Cambridge, Mass.: The MIT Press, 1988).

15. Eugene Fama, "Efficient Capital Markets II." *Journal of Finance*, (1991): 1575–1617.

16. *Free Dictionary.com*, "Workable Competition," Farlex, http://encyclopedia.thefreedictionary.com (accessed October, 2004).

17. *Economics with a Touch*, "Operational Efficiency, Technical Efficiency, AmosWeb of Whimsy http://www.amosweb.com (accessed October, 2004).

18. *Wikipedia, the Free Encyclopedia*, "History of Corporate Personhood," http://en.wikipedia.org/ wiki/Corporate_personhood (accessed October, 2004).

19. Karl E. Case and Ray C. Fair, *Principles of Economics* (Englewood Cliffs, N.J.: Prentice-Hall Inc., 2nd ed., 1992), 460.

20. *Wikipedia*, "Natural Monopoly," http://en.wikipedia.org/wiki /Natural_monopoly (accessed October, 2004).

21. *Wikipedia*, "Taxation," http://en.wikipedia.org/wiki/Taxation (accessed October, 2004).

22. *Encarta*, "Value Added Tax."

23. Milton Friedman, *Capitalism and Freedom* (Chicago: University of Chicago Press, 2002, original copyright, 1962).

24. U.S. Census Bureau, "Income Inequality." U.S. Census Bureau, http://www.census.gov/hhes/income/incineq/p60asc (accessed October, 2004).

25. *Look Smart*, "2000 Data in a Post-Sept. 11 World: Income and poverty reports based on 2000 figures may seem outdated, but still have important uses over the long term." 2000 http://www.findarticles.comp/articles/mi_m0GDE/is_20_21/ai_80848021/pg_2 (accessed October, 2004).

CHAPTER ELEVEN

A CLOSING COMMENTARY ON SUSTAINABLE CAPITALISM

Karl Marx was wrong. He believed that a workers' revolution was the only means to stopping the relentless extraction and exploitation of an uncontrollable capitalistic economy. He also believed in the possibility of a utopian communistic society, in which each person would contribute according to his or her ability and each would be provided for in relation to his or her needs. Marx could not conceive of a moral and just society in which people would find the political courage to defend their inherent rights and freedoms against capitalistic exploitation. He could not conceive of a society sufficiently enlightened to value righteousness and relationships as highly as individual material self-interests. Marx could not envision an economy that could equitably meet the needs of the present while leaving equal or better opportunities for those of the future.

However, Marx also was right. He was right in believing that unbridled capitalism would continue its uncontrolled growth until it had extracted resources from every nook and cranny of the earth and had exploited people in every community everywhere on the globe. He was right in believing that capitalism would seek to destroy personal relationships among people, within families and communities, and would seek to remove all economic boundaries among nations in its relentless pursuit of greater wealth. He was right in believing that unrestrained capitalism would lead to global economic domination by an elite class of capitalists; he just didn't anticipate that the capitalists would be corporations rather than individuals. Marx also was right in

197

believing that the seductiveness of laissez-faire economics would tempt people to abandon their "chartered freedoms" for the worship of free markets.

Adam Smith also was wrong. He believed that the individual left unrestrained in the pursuit of their self-interest, their "self-love," as he called it, would lead to the greatest benefit for society as a whole. He believed that the investor who thought only of his or her self-interests would be guided, as if by an *invisible hand*, to serve the best interests of his or her nation. Smith couldn't conceive of a society in which people would sacrifice their moral and social integrity for the sake of individual sensory pleasures. He couldn't conceive of a time when trade would be carried out by transnational corporations, with no citizenship, no nationality, and no sense of connection with any particular country or place. Smith could not envision a society that would abandon the things necessary for a desirable quality of life in the pursuit of ever-greater financial wealth.

However, Smith was also right. Smith was right in believing in potential economic benefits from specialization and he was right also in anticipating its ultimate social costs. He was right in believing that purely competitive markets are the most effective means conceivable of allocating scarce resources to meet the needs and wants of individuals and of collections of individuals. He was right in believing that free trade among informed, sovereign individuals, who are free to trade or not trade, leads to improvement of the individual economic well-being of all. Smith also was right in believing that the protectionist policies of preindustrial guilds and mercantilist traders had become wasteful and exploitive; he just didn't realize that unrestrained capitalism eventually would suffer a similar fate.

Neither Marx nor Smith understood the physical and social ecology of economic sustainability, having achieved their prominence during the Industrial Era. They had no way of anticipating the risks of applying mechanistic principles to living things. They failed to appreciate that an economy is a living system, created by people, to be nurtured by people, for the benefit of people.

An economy uses the resources of nature for the benefit of people. Like all living systems, an economy is inherently dynamic, continually remaking and regenerating itself. Economies apparently also go through life cycles of birth, growth, maturity, reproduction, decline, and death. But the mechanistic science that drove industrialization in the days of Marx and Smith assigned no importance to such things.

In Smith's day, the preindustrial economies were beyond maturity, growing old and burdensome to society. The preindustrial eras of guilds and mercantilism apparently served some unmet needs of the people at the times of their emergence; otherwise, they would have not grown to their positions of prominence. Laissez-faire capitalism also addressed some important unmet need of society at the time of its emergence; otherwise, it would not have grown to prominence. But, when Smith wrote *Wealth of Nations* in 1776, it was time for the old economic thinking to pass away and to make room for new capitalistic economies.

For many decades, capitalism appeared to be a strong, healthy, and highly productive system of economics. However, somewhere during its growth to maturity, capitalism became cancerous; it lost its natural internal social and moral controls, and it now resists all external efforts to restrain its relentless growth. It now seems destined to continue growing until it depletes or destroys the global physical and social ecosystems that now feed its unquenchable thirst for ever-greater power and wealth. Marx was among the first to detect this fundamental flaw, or susceptibility, in the genetic makeup of capitalism, but Marx's communistic solution proved not to be a realistic cure. Total rejection of capitalism is not the solution because we can't kill the cancer without risking the life of the host. But neither will we find a cure by rejecting the proper diagnosis—even if it was first made by a communist. Ultimately, we must accept the fact that an unbridled capitalistic economy quite simply is not sustainable.

We cannot internalize the externalities of a cancerous growth as a means of restoring health to its host. Instead, we must reestablish the internal mechanisms that naturally control growth and reproduction so that economic growth no longer depends upon externalizing costs to or internalizing benefits from the social and natural environment. The cancerous cells of the old capitalistic economy must be replaced by healthy cells, with internal mechanisms for controlling growth and reproduction. In the case of cancer, the host cannot choose between cells that promote rapid growth and cells that promote good health, regardless of growth. In the case of capitalism, however, society has a choice. We can choose the rapid growth of unbridled capitalism, or we can choose the healthy growth of sustainable capitalism; but we can't have both. We can cure the cancer of capitalism, but only by restoring and sustaining the ecological and social health of the economy. Cures are achieved first by acknowledging the cause and then by correcting it.

Living organisms cannot revert to their youth, or to some earlier stage of life, as a means of restoring health and vigor. Similarly, the sustainability of capitalism cannot be restored simply by reverting to the days of classical economics. However, the same basic principles of health are relevant at all stages of life, and the basic principles of capitalism are relevant to all stages of economic evolution. Adam Smith didn't reject the *principles* of guilds or mercantilism; he simply pointed out that the principles were being used in abusive and exploitive ways. Likewise, we need not reject the principles of capitalism, mercantilism, or even guilds, simply because they have been used in abusive and exploitive ways in the past. Adam Smith did not create the principles of the division of labor or trade; he simply put them into a new context and used them in ways that seemed more appropriate for his times. Likewise, the principles of classical capitalism need not be recreated, but instead, must be put into a new context and used in ways appropriate for these times.

Neoclassical economics has misused the principles of capitalism to support extractive and exploitive approaches to economic development. The legitimate principle of private property rights has been used to deny an equally legitimate principle of common property rights. The principle of individually held values has been used to deny the legitimacy of commonly held values. The principle of free market allocation of resources has been used to defend the monolithic, monopolistic power of transnational corporations that now dominate both markets and politics. The principle of free trade has been used to degrade the semipermeability of healthy, selective boundaries that define communities and nations. Removal of economic boundaries leads to the destruction of social and cultural boundaries, thus accelerating the natural tendency of all exploitive systems toward entropy. And the principles of financial wealth and economic growth have been used to replace the principles of happiness and quality of life. The principles of classical economics are not invalid or irrelevant; they are simply being misused.

To achieve a sustainable capitalistic economy, the principles of economics and sustainability must be used in ways that reflect harmony and balance. Private property rights must be balanced with common property rights in managing for sustainability. A more enlightened self-interest—an individual, social, and moral self-interest—must balance individual and common values in meeting the needs of the present while leaving opportunities for the future. Free markets must be used as a means of allocating resources to meet individual wants and needs, but only in harmony and balance with the necessity of regenerating social and ecological capital. Free trade must take place across semipermeable boundaries, which allow specialization and gains from trade, while protecting resources and people from exploitation. Economic growth must take place in balance and harmony with social equity and moral justice in the pursuit of happiness and a desirable, sustainable quality of life.

The economic principles that supported preindustrial guilds and mercantilists' trade policies are still valid for use in allowing communities, states, regions, and nations to choose economic development that is consistent with their unique ecological and cultural niches. But such principles cannot be used to close boundaries to mutually beneficial trade or to isolate communities from opportunities for positive social or cultural evolution. The principles of classical economics can be used to support economic growth, but those principles cannot be used to justify economic exploitation. Sustainability is rarely achieved by choosing either *this or that*, but instead requires *some of this and some of that* to maintain balance and harmony. In a discipline accustomed to maximizing and minimizing as means of achieving optimums, the economics of sustainability has not been readily embraced by economists.

Society need not wait for economists to change. The United States has all of the institutions and means in place to move toward an economics of sustainability. We have a constitution, and a means of amending it, which we can use to reflect a moral consensus to ensure the fundamental rights of all people, both for ourselves and for all posterity. We have a government that derives its power from the consent of the people, which we can use to ensure the common good of all people, of this and of all future generations. We have the infrastructure for a free market economy, and the means of restoring competition and internalizing the controls that markets need to function effectively. And finally, we have people with the innate common sense needed to understand that their individual self-interests are served best by making conscious, purposeful decisions to care for each other and care for the earth as they care for themselves. All we need to do is to use these things wisely.

The change from an exploitive capitalism to a sustainable capitalism must begin with a change in worldview. Neoclassical capitalism has evolved from a mechanistic worldview, a reductionist philosophy of science, and an industrial paradigm of development. Such ways of thinking seemed appropriate in a largely empty world, where humans were few in number and natural resources were abundant. However, such ways of thinking are no longer appropriate in a rapidly filling world, where the human population is exploding and natural resources are being rapidly degraded and depleted. Sustainable capitalism begins with an ecological worldview, which recognizes that the world is made up of both living and nonliving things. Sustainable capitalism requires a *holistic* approach to science, and a *deep* approach to ecology, which value both the importance and the rightness of relationships among all living things, including humans, and between the living and nonliving elements of the biosphere. Sustainable capitalism requires a self-renewing, regenerative paradigm of development. But the transition to a sustainable form of capitalism begins with a change in worldview.

A sustainable economy is still a capitalistic economy, in that it provides a means of increasing the wealth of society. However, the economics of sustainability explicitly recognizes the value of the commonwealth, of people in society, and the ecological wealth, of an abundant earth, as well as the financial wealth of individuals. All economic financial capital is extracted from social and ecological capital. Thus, the sustainability of any financial economy depends upon the sustainability of its sources of social and ecological capital, and sustainable capitalism requires continual regeneration and reinvestment in ecological and social capital in order to sustain its financial capital. Sustainable capitalism is about maintaining the ability to generate wealth and well-being—individually, socially, and ecologically.

Perhaps the most important and most difficult task in bringing sustainability to our capitalistic economy will be the task of internalizing the controls necessary for sustainable economic growth. Sustainability cannot be achieved if we view the moral and social controls, enforced through government, as just another form of external constraint on the private economy and on our individual well-being. The governed must understand that government is but the means by which we can choose to restrain our basic drives and urges to exploit each other and to exploit the earth for our individual gratification. The governed must understand that our lives are made better when we choose to restrain our physical urges and drives, not just individually, but also collectively; otherwise, some minority of any society will always choose destructive ways of living, in defiance of any social and moral consensus regarding appropriate behavior. Most people do not view laws against robbery and murder as constraints on their behavior; instead, they are grateful for laws restraining others from criminal behavior. Laws simply cannot be enforced when the majority of the people view them as constraints rather than voluntary controls. Laws against robbery and murder represent internal controls, not external constraints. People must view their constitutions, laws, and regulations that protect them from social and ecological exploitation as internal controls, not external constraints, if a capitalistic economy is to be sustainable.

Thus, sustainability requires recognition on the part of the people that the moral, social, and individual economies are but three dimensions of an inseparable whole—that all three are essential for a desirable quality of life. The moral and social economies provide the internal mechanisms necessary to sustain the healthy and regenerative capacity of the individual economy. An understanding of the holism of sustainability must begin in the individual, with a common sense understanding that our quality of life is not just a matter of individual self-interests, but depends upon the quality of our relationships with other people and the rightness of our relationship with the earth. Our common sense tells us we are physical, mental, and spiritual beings, not just pleasure-seeking, pain-avoiding organisms. To achieve sustainability, we must reflect this self-knowledge as we participate in all types of relationships in our families, communities, and nations. As individuals strive for right relationships within families and friendships, as families strive for right relationships with other families in communities, and as communities strive for right relationships with other communities within nations, and as nations strive for right relationships among nations in a global society, we will move toward sustainable economies and a sustainable global society.

Sustainable capitalism begins in the hearts and minds of people. It begins with a common sense understanding of the fundamental first principles that define an enlightened concept of self-interest. It begins with a return to the pursuit of a more desirable quality of life, instead of the pursuit of financial wealth. It begins with an understanding that a desirable quality of life depends upon the rightness of our relationships with each other and with the earth. Sustainable capitalism begins with our willingness to return to the pursuit of happiness.

INDEX

ABOUT THE AUTHOR

Dr. John Ikerd spent the first half of his 30-year academic career as a traditional free-market, neoclassical economist. During his career, he served on the faculties of four major state universities: North Carolina State University, Oklahoma State University, University of Georgia, and University of Missouri. Growing concerns over the lack of ecological, social, and economic sustainability of American agriculture during the 1980s led to broader concerns, over the lack of sustainability for American Society in general. As an economist, Dr. Ikerd eventually came to understand that the growing threats to ecological and social sustainability are rooted in the neoclassical paradigm of econimc development, which is inherently extractive and exploitive and, thus, is not sustainable. Dr. Ikerd has spent the second half of his academic career and much of his time since retirement on developing and testing the concepts and principles of an alternative development paradigm— the economics of sustainability— which are elucidated in this book.

 Also from Kumarian Press...

Civil Society and Global Development

A Civil Republic: Beyond Capitalism and Nationalism
Severyn T. Bruyn

Capitalism and Justice: Envisioning Social and Economic Fairness
John Ibister

Creating a Better World: Interpreting Global Civil Society
Edited by Rupert Taylor

Unequal Freedoms: The Global Market as an Ethical System
John McMurtry

When Corporations Rule the World
David C. Korten

New Kumarian Titles of Similar Interest

Building Democratic Institutions: Governance Reform in Developing Countries
G. Shabbir Cheema

Reducing Poverty, Building Peace
Coralie Bryant and Christina Kappaz

Working for Change: Making a Career in International Public Service
Derick W. Brinkerhoff and Jennifer M. Brinkerhoff

Visit Kumarian Press at **www.kpbooks.com** or
call **toll-free 800.289.2664** for a complete catalog.

 *Kumarian Press, located in Bloomfield, Connecticut, is a
forward-looking, scholarly press that promotes active international
engagement and an awareness of global connectedness.*